The Politics of Energy

This book brings together leading scholars on the politics of energy, examining the natural resources and developing technologies that are essential to its production and the various public and private factors affecting its use, along with the ecological consequences of both. Section One examines the looming challenges posed by continuing dependence upon oil as a primary energy source, including "peak oil" scenarios and the social and political consequences of resource extraction upon the developing world. Section Two considers proposals to dramatically increase nuclear power production as a means to reduce carbon emissions, with both the risks and potential of this "nuclear option" carefully weighed. Although many tout renewable energy sources for their environmental benefits, Section Three calls attention to several potential problems with large-scale renewable energy development and the dilemmas that they have caused for would-be supporters of such efforts. Finally, Section Four weighs the prospects for developing sustainable energy systems on the ground, including conservation measures that reduce energy demand and system-wide energy policy efforts. Together, these essays demonstrate the importance of sound energy policy along with the numerous obstacles to developing and implementing it.

This book was originally published as a special issue of *Environmental Politics*.

Steve Vanderheiden is Associate Professor of Political Science and Environmental Studies at the University of Colorado at Boulder, USA.

The Politics of Energy
Challenges for a Sustainable Future

Edited by
Steve Vanderheiden

LONDON AND NEW YORK

First published 2012
by Routledge
2 Park Square, Milton Park, Abingdon, Oxfordshire OX14 4RN

Simultaneously published in the USA and Canada
by Routledge
711 Third Avenue, New York, NY 10017

First issued in paperback 2014

Routledge is an imprint of the Taylor and Francis Group, an informa business

© 2012 Taylor & Francis

This book is a reproduction of *Environmental Politics*, vol. 20, issue 5. The Publisher requests to those authors who may be citing this book to state, also, the bibliographical details of the special issue on which the book was based.

All rights reserved. No part of this book may be reprinted or reproduced or utilised in any form or by any electronic, mechanical, or other means, now known or hereafter invented, including photocopying and recording, or in any information storage or retrieval system, without permission in writing from the publishers.

Trademark notice: Product or corporate names may be trademarks or registered trademarks, and are used only for identification and explanation without intent to infringe.

British Library Cataloguing in Publication Data
A catalogue record for this book is available from the British Library

ISBN13: 978-0-415-52307-3 (hbk)
ISBN13: 978-0-415-75488-0 (pbk)

Typeset in Times New Roman
by Taylor & Francis Books

Publisher's Note
The publisher would like to make readers aware that the chapters in this book may be referred to as articles as they are identical to the articles published in the special issue. The publisher accepts responsibility for any inconsistencies that may have arisen in the course of preparing this volume for print.

Contents

Notes on contributors   vii

1. The politics of energy: an introduction
   Steve Vanderheiden   1

2. Poor little rich countries: another look at the 'resource curse'
   Sudhir Chella Rajan   11

3. Energy and human ecology: a critical security approach
   Shane Mulligan   27

4. Confronting risks: regulatory responsibility and nuclear energy
   Steve Vanderheiden   44

5. *Déjà vu* all over again: climate change and the prospects for a nuclear power renaissance
   Robert Duffy   62

6. 'Hasta la vista, baby!' The Solar Grand Plan, environmentalism, and social constructions of the Mojave Desert
   Christian Hunold and Steven Leitner   81

7. A middle range theorization of energy politics: the struggle for energy efficient appliances
   Rachael L. Shwom   99

8. Regional integration to support full renewable power deployment for Europe by 2050
   Anthony Patt, Nadejda Komendantova, Antonella Battaglini and Johan Lilliestam   121

9. Climate deadlocks: the environmental politics of energy systems
   Karena Shaw   137

Index   159

Notes on contributors

Robert Duffy is Professor and Chair of the Political Science Department at Colorado State University, USA. His publications include *Nuclear Politics in America: A History and Theory of Government Regulation* (University Press of Kansas, 1997), and *The Green Agenda in American Politics: New Strategies for the Twenty-First Century* (University Press of Kansas, 2003).

Christian Hunold is Associate Professor of Political Science at Drexel University, Philadelphia, USA, where he teaches environmental politics and public policy, and co-directs the Drexel Engineering Cities Initiative. His publications include (with K. Travaline) 'Urban Agriculture and Ecological Citizenship in Philadelphia', *Local Environment*, 15(6) 2010 and (with J. S. Dryzek and C. Hendriks) 'Turning Up the Heat: Partisanship in Deliberative Innovation', *Political Studies* 55(2) 2007.

Shane Mulligan is a Consultant in Community Renewable Energy and Co-operative Development for Radicle Consulting, in Kitchener, Ontario, Canada. His recent publications include 'Energy, Environment, and Security: Critical Links in a Post-Peak World', *Global Environmental Politics* 10(4) 2010, and 'Reassessing the Crisis: Ecology and Liberal International Relations', *Alternatives: Global, Local, Political* 35(2) 2010.

Anthony Patt is a Senior Research Scholar at the International Institute for Applied Systems Analysis (IIASA) in Laxenburg, Austria. A lead author and Review Editor for the Intergovernmental Panel on Climate Change, his recent publications include 'Estimating least-developed countries' vulnerability to climate-related extreme events over the next 50 years', *Proceedings of the National Academy of Sciences* 107 (4) 2010.

Nadejda Komendantova is a Research Scholar at IIASA.

Johan Lilliestam is a Research Assistant at IIASA.

Antonella Battaglini is a Senior Scientist at the Potsdam Institute for Climate Impact Research (PIK).

NOTES ON CONTRIBUTORS

Sudhir Chella Rajan is a Professor in Sustainable Development and Political Theory in the Department of Humanities and Social Sciences, Indian Institute of Technology, Madras, Chennai, India. His recent publications include 'The Ethical Implications of Sea-level Rise Due to Climate Change', *Ethics and International Affairs* 24(2), 2010 (co-authored with Sujatha Byravan) and *How We Can Save the Planet: Preventing Global Climate Catastrophe* (St. Martin's Press, 2008) (co-authored with Mayer Hillman and Tina Fawcett).

Karena Shaw is Associate Professor in the School of Environmental Studies and member of the Institute for Integrated Energy Systems at the University of Victoria, Canada. Her publications include *A Political Space: Reading the Global Through Clayoquot Sound* (University of Minnesota Press, 2003) (co-edited with Warren Magnusson), and *Political Theory and Indigeneity: Sovereignty and the Limits of the Political* (Routledge, 2008).

Rachael L. Shwom is an Assistant Professor of Climate and Society in the Department of Human Ecology and member of the Rutgers Energy Institute at Rutgers University, USA. Her publications include 'Strengthening Sociological Perspectives on Organizations and Environment', *Organization and Environment* 22(3) 2009, and 'Understanding Changing Public Opinion on Climate Change' (co-authored with S. Marquett-Pyatt, T. Dietz, R. Dunlap, A. McCright, S. Kaplowitz, and S. Zahrar), in *Environment: Science and Policy for Sustainable Development* 53(4) 2011.

Steve Vanderheiden is Associate Professor of Political Science and Environmental Studies at the University of Colorado at Boulder, USA and Professorial Fellow with the Centre for Applied Philosophy and Public Ethics (CAPPE) at Charles Sturt University, Australia. His publications include *Atmospheric Justice: A Political Theory of Climate Change* (Oxford University Press, 2008), and 'Globalizing Responsibility for Climate Change', *Ethics & International Affairs* 25(1) 2011.

The politics of energy: an introduction
Steve Vanderheiden

Just minutes after the magnitude 9.0 earthquake struck off Japan's northeast coast on the afternoon of 11 March 2011, waves from the 14-meter tsunami that it triggered crashed over the seawalls built to protect the six reactors at Fukushima Daiichi nuclear plant. Designed to withstand tsunami waves less than half that height, the seawalls were powerless to protect against the flooding that would ensue, cutting off electricity to the plant as power lines were downed by the earthquake and backup generators that had been stored below ground were rendered useless by the flood. Over the next several days, workers scrambled feverishly to cool overheating fuel rods in four of the reactors, then to restore power so that cooling systems could be brought back online, and authorities ordered a precautionary evacuation of those within a 20 km radius of the plant. Despite these efforts to avert a crisis, three of the plant's reactors experienced partial or full meltdown, rating a Level 7 'Major Accident' on the International Nuclear Events Scale (the most serious category of event, and the second in history) contaminating the site with plutonium and radioactive isotopes and releasing airborne radiation that would reach the United States at measurable levels a week later, and spreading renewed worries about nuclear power further and more quickly.

This, the world's second-worst nuclear accident (after Chernobyl), prompted concerns about the safety of nuclear plants elsewhere, leading state authorities to conduct emergency safety inventories of existing facilities, and casting a pall over plans to construct new ones. Switzerland and Germany both announced plans to completely cease nuclear energy production by 2034 and 2022, and Italian voters in June resoundingly rejected an ill-timed government proposal to revive the country's nuclear program. Although several political leaders defended the industry's safety record and the sector's role in their country's low-carbon future – most notably US President Obama, who reaffirmed his administration's support for the industry in the weeks following the accident – public opinion has once again turned against nuclear power, as it did following earlier accidents, with market capital options for financing planned expansions of nuclear capacity in the United States and elsewhere evaporating, throwing the industry's future into jeopardy. Even before Fukushima, the prospects of a revival of nuclear energy were already dubious. Whether or not the worldwide reaction to events at Fukushima will precipitate a long-term decline in support for nuclear energy – as Robert Duffy's contribution to this volume suggests it will – those galvanizing events forcefully remind those charting the world's energy future of an unfortunate fact of which few needed reminding. In a carbon-constrained future, and with forecasters predicting rapidly-growing demand for energy over the next half century, virtually all options for accommodating that demand look like bad ones, even if some appear to be worse than others. If anything turns public opinion in favor of revived nuclear programs, it is likely to be 'lesser evil' comparisons with other bad options.

The US Energy Information Administration estimates that world energy consumption will increase by 1.4% per year, and 49% by 2035 (2010, p. 1), driven largely by rapidly increasing demand from non-OECD countries, especially China. Even with substantial growth in renewable sources of energy and steady growth in nuclear power, and with continued growth in electrical generation from natural gas, the US Energy Information Administration forecasts continued reliance upon coal and oil as satisfying the bulk of that demand, with each contributing more than twice what combined renewables will be able to supply by 2035. When set against the forecasts of climate science, which call for cuts in greenhouse gas emissions in excess of 50% from 1990 levels over that same period if dangerous climate change is to be averted, meeting expected future energy demand while also preventing potentially catastrophic environmental change will be challenging. The phase-out of fossil fuels, or at least the development and widespread deployment of sequestration technologies designed to capture carbon emissions from coal and oil and capable of extending the viability of such fuels in a carbon-constrained future, raises challenges of its own (and, as we shall see in several upcoming articles, serious doubts), as does meeting those growing needs through some combination of rapidly expanded renewable energy sources and aggressive conservation efforts. Given this interrelated set of energy policy challenges, it is hardly surprising that the Obama White House, which has taken the threat of climate change more seriously than its predecessor but has yet to deliver effective climate policies in support of its concerns, has continued to insist that nuclear energy must remain 'in the mix' for the United States and the world into the foreseeable future, despite the industry's already-tenuous support compounded by the public relations disaster that accompanied the environmental and economic disaster at Fukushima.

Were it possible to set aside political obstacles, and to design a carbon-constrained global energy system capable of meeting the world's projected future needs on the basis of available technologies, human and natural resources, and sincere concern about the failure to do so, or to design such systems through the idealized processes that Charles Lindblom (1959) terms 'rational-comprehensive' policy-making, significant challenges would remain. Economic and technological obstacles must still be surmounted before clean and renewable energy can be made widely available, and existing infrastructure must be maintained while new plants, facilities, and grids are brought online. However, these obstacles are relatively tractable in comparison with the political challenges that are the subjects of this volume. While Jacobsen and Delucchi (2009) demonstrate the technical and economic possibility of meeting global energy needs in 2030 with a significant expansion of wind, water-based, and solar power, eliminating the need for fossil fuels as well as nuclear energy in supplying future electrical generation and transport fuels, the magnitude of the changes they outline reveals the daunting political obstacles to their plan's realization. Aside from problems related to the early decommissioning of existing coal, oil, and natural gas plants, they propose bringing online 3.8 million large wind turbines and 89,000 large-scale photovoltaic and concentrated solar power plants worldwide over the next two decades, at a cost of approximately $100 trillion, excluding necessary upgrades to transmission infrastructure (Jacobsen and Delucchi 2009, p. 64). As they note, such an ambitious plan would probably encounter technical obstacles such as shortages in the rare earth minerals needed for photovoltaic cells or storage batteries, but far and away its biggest obstacle is political will. More accurately, political rather than technical or technological challenges now pose the most difficult problems in the pursuit of a sustainable future, and only through a more thorough understanding and appreciation of the nature of these issues can a viable way forward be identified. This volume aims to contribute toward that aim.

The eight contributions to this volume investigate a variety of case studies and engage several related aspects of the politics of developing sustainable energy systems, but cannot by themselves offer a comprehensive picture of the policy or political landscape. Nonetheless, they together offer suggestive insights into the challenges and possibilities associated with developing energy systems for a sustainable future. No examination of the politics of energy can ignore the multifaceted problems associated with the world's continued reliance upon fossil fuels. As primary sources of greenhouse gases, especially the carbon dioxide released upon their combustion, coal-based and oil-based energy are leading contributors to anthropogenic climate change as well as a host of other forms of environmental degradation resulting from their extraction, refinement, and combustion. Given their status as non-renewable and 'dirty' energy sources, these fuels are often and aptly identified as anathema to future 'clean' and sustainable energy systems. But fossil fuels are cheap and relatively easily deployed sources of energy, largely due to market failures that fail to take account of their social and environmental externalities, giving them a significant market advantage over their renewable rivals. Coal is relatively abundant and remains the cheapest fuel for electrical generation, despite its well known association with destructive mining practices and its profligate carbon footprint. In the absence of a concerted effort to replace its electrical generating capacity with more sustainable alternatives, or to control its effects on global climate through massive public investment in nascent and unproven carbon capture and storage technologies, coal poses an environmental and economic problem to be solved while also creating social and political obstacles to such solutions – as oil also does in the nearer term future, with its long-term pernicious effect constrained by its more limited supply.

If, as climate science suggests, the development of a sustainable energy system requires a dramatic reduction in the use of fossil fuels, the politics of this transition to a low-carbon economy must focus upon the harm associated with current reliance upon coal and oil and the various obstacles to speeding up the conversion to other fuels. Analyses of those obstacles could be institutional, examining the role of interested industry parties in maintaining high levels of fossil fuel use, or behavioral, examining the norms and attitudes that frustrate efforts to induce consumers to voluntarily switch to more sustainable energy sources or adequately support policy efforts to require this transition. Some of these are considered in this volume through studies of efforts to move away from fossil fuels. The social and environmental costs of oil and coal are widely known, and their dissemination has played a central role in efforts to move away from them. Aside from their role in climate change, in which fossil fuel combustion contributes 80–85% of anthropogenic carbon dioxide emissions (with land-use changes accounting for the remainder), the combustion of coal and oil has rightly been impugned for contributing to air and water pollution and their associated harm to human health and environmental integrity, their extraction linked to such galvanizing ecological impacts as mountaintop removal and catastrophic oil spills, and their international sale and transport to the finance of bad state and non-state actors as well as the social and economic costs of conflict and military intervention in oil-exporting regions. Critics point to such impacts in calculating the 'social cost' of coal and oil (for example, Tamminen 2006), noting that the majority of such costs are externalities imposed upon the most vulnerable, and that the inclusion of such costs in the price of coal and oil would significantly reduce if not negate the market advantage that fossil fuels currently enjoy over cleaner renewable sources of energy.

Such critical perspectives often underscore state policy efforts to regulate fossil fuels, whether through pollution control standards or market-based measures like carbon taxes or emissions trading schemes that price carbon. The critical claim that reliance upon fossil fuels contributes to a variety of harmful impacts often appears alongside discourses of ecological modernization that identify sources of opportunity in carbon pricing schemes, as with the 2011 debate over Australia's adoption of a carbon tax, with climate change often the leading motivating consideration. The political resilience of the coal and oil industries to such calls for increasing regulation partly explains the proliferation of analyses of harmful impacts of their continued role in energy production. Two other emerging critical discourses about the costs of fossil fuels appear in this issue, both specifically concerning international markets in mineral resources like coal and oil. Both suggest that the politics of energy can be usefully linked to other issue areas – of development and security, respectively – in order to build the case for accelerating the global transition away from fossil fuels, but both also sound important cautionary notes about the critical perspectives under scrutiny.

Sudhir Chella Rajan examines the so-called 'resource curse', in which natural resource wealth evidently sometimes serves as an obstacle to, rather than an instrument of, political development, as such wealth has in several cases fuelled corruption and violence rather than bringing about the social and political progress that development scholars have conventionally associated with the exploitation of national resource wealth. Using case studies of oil development in Mexico, Venezuela, and Angola, Rajan challenges prevailing accounts of the curse that attribute it to the effect of macroeconomic forces upon domestic political institutions, in which resource wealth crowds out development efforts by exposing resource-dependent economies to volatility in international markets and concentrating wealth within a privileged elite rather than employing it on behalf of development efforts. While accepting that conventional explanations provide part of the causal story, Rajan points also to the effect of neoliberal political economy and the legacy of colonialism, arguing that rent-seeking 'extraversion' accounts for the misuse of resource wealth in these three cases. In the context of energy politics, the domestic social and political consequences of oil extraction and export are often ignored in favor of consideration of its environmental effects, or the way that resource wealth can finance or otherwise drive violent conflict. Less well appreciated, and certainly less prominent in policy debates about the effects of fossil fuel dependence on the developing world, is this link between international oil flows and impaired development. Going beyond the sustainable development discourse that links imperatives of environmental sustainability and human development, Rajan's study suggests a further link between the profligate demand for imported oil in affluent developed countries and the frustrated efforts at development in poor ones, reinforcing the importance of sustainable energy policy in the former by considering the consequences of its absence on vulnerable peoples in the latter.

Shane Mulligan considers whether 'peak oil' scenarios might justify the securitization of oil supplies, and if so what advantages and disadvantages this might confer upon efforts to forge more sustainable domestic energy strategies. Drawing on Critical Security Studies, Mulligan considers whether the 'energy descent' that would accompany post-peak oil prices and availability so long as the developed world continues to rely heavily upon oil for its energy needs, with oil scarcity's ripple effect across economic sectors and throughout oil-dependent societies, fits well within existing security discourses, which seek to identify imminent threats to freedom, perilous forms of uncertainty, and risks of death. As he notes, the acceptance by policy-makers of oil dependence and national security comes with discursive benefits as well as costs. Because security issues command the highest priority, mobilizing emergency powers if necessary, successfully securitizing oil dependence could potentially create momentum for weaning developed countries from their insatiable thirst for both domestic and imported oil, bolstering policy imperatives for sustainable energy with much more powerful and visceral security imperatives. Moreover, it concerns the role of oil in domestic energy portfolios rather than merely dependence upon imported oil. Post-9/11 campaigns attempted to link decreasingly salient sustainable energy issues with ascendant concerns about national security. Hence, it can only be addressed by diminishing reliance upon oil as an energy source, not through intensified development of domestic oil resources, as some 'energy security' and 'energy independence' campaigns have suggested. As Mulligan notes, however, 'securitization carries consequences', and he aptly cautions those considering invoking security discourses on behalf of the transition to low-carbon or sustainable energy sources to keep those in mind.

Concerns about security are not, however, limited to the socioeconomic insecurity of dependence upon imported oil. Indeed, nuclear energy is often suggested as an antidote to the kinds of security concerns that Mulligan discusses, as well as for the climate benefits inherent in a zero-carbon energy source that is capable of being deployed on a wide scale, but carries with it several unique security concerns related to the insidious potential to convert its fuel into weapons-grade plutonium. Steve Vanderheiden examines these and other risks associated with proposed expansions of nuclear energy capacity, which defy straightforward comparison with the risks associated with the climatic changes that conversion from coal-based to nuclear power could help to avoid. He argues that the ubiquity of risk should not obscure the ethical imperatives to minimize it, and to consider also the social justice aspects of its distribution across vulnerable peoples. While it may not be possible to definitively say whether or not the increased risks of expanded nuclear energy programs are warranted by the resulting declines in climate-related risk, despite analyses from decision theory that suggest otherwise, this need not be the problem that those positing a false dichotomy between these two alternatives suggest. Since the future impacts of both complicate the democratic resolution of these competing forms of risk, he suggests that it would be mistaken to view the tradeoff between the likely, moderate, and widely distributed risks of unmitigated climate change and the unlikely but concentrated and severe risks of nuclear accidents as posing a genuine dilemma, as some now advocating expansion of nuclear energy capacity maintain. Rather, he argues that that these two putatively competing forms of risk should draw our attention to the social justice aspects of imposing risks upon vulnerable others, whether through nuclear power or climate change, and motivate consideration of alternatives that diffuse the false choice between these two bad choices, including energy conservation efforts and development of less risky renewables.

Robert Duffy also considers various risks associated with expanded nuclear energy programs in the context of the decarbonizing imperatives of climate policy and as measures for securing energy independence, asking whether the 'nuclear renaissance' that some have recommended is politically plausible, particularly in the United States. While the March 2011 events in Japan may have drawn heightened public attention to the risks associated with nuclear power, and while worries about similar accidents have led Germany and Switzerland to announce plans to phase out nuclear energy production altogether, Fukushima merely added an additional obstacle in renewed concerns about accidents to an already-poor prospect for the industry's expansion in the United States, given the existing difficulties based in waste disposal issues, ongoing licensing, siting, and safety concerns, and the economics of start-up facilities given various uncertainties regarding state support for the industry and a history of cost overruns. Despite their clear climate benefits, their potential for advancing a prominent energy security imperative, new reactor designs, and promised new economic and regulatory support, Duffy concludes that the promises of expanded reliance upon nuclear energy in the United States cannot overcome such obstacles. Absent significant state subsidies of the industry, Duffy argues, nuclear energy cannot compete with fossil fuel-based energy sources. With such a subsidy, on the other hand, it must compete with renewable energy sources that are not accompanied by comparable risks or adverse public opinion. While nuclear energy may enjoy advantages over renewables in energy politics, given its organization and political influence, these are not likely to be enough to counteract the public fears that Fukushima mobilized, or to avert the unfavorable economic prospects that the industry faces in the absence of state backing.

Given the carbon constraints on future energy systems and the risks and other costs inherent in nuclear power, most view significantly expanded renewable sources of energy as essential to meeting projected future energy demand. Indeed, as suggested by Jacobsen and Delucchi, some combination of wind, water, and solar-based energy offers the best prospect for designing sustainable energy systems, given finite mineral stocks, limited sink capacity for absorbing carbon emissions, and the above-noted limitations on nuclear energy. But even if it is technologically and economically possible to supply the world with energy from these sources alone, political difficulties rooted in various value conflicts still remain. As four contributors to this issue well illustrate, sustainable energy systems are far more difficult to attain in practice than they are to construct in theory, in part due to entrenched social and political resistance to transition away from carbon-based energy sources, and in part because the alternatives that they represent still generate opposition or introduce challenges based on their status as lesser evils. As suggested above, the politics of energy involves selecting from among a set of imperfect options, as demonstrated by the examinations in this volume of large-scale solar energy development, appliance energy efficiency standards, electricity supergrid design, and energy-based climate change mitigation strategies.

Christian Hunold and Steven Leitner example the 'Grand Solar Plan' proposal to build several large-scale thermal solar plants in California's Mojave desert, which promise to deliver clean and renewable energy to one of the United States' largest and fastest growing urban centers. Although touted by some environmentalists for its ambitious effort to wean the state from dependence upon fossil fuels and for its role in advancing the state's climate change mitigation goals, others have opposed it, largely because of its projected impacts on the region's fragile desert ecosystems. Hunold and Leitner use discourse analysis to view the competing positions in the public debate over the plan, finding the dominant discourse to rely upon a construction of the desert as barren and useless, which, when joined to the ecological modernization discourse of engaging in grand technological projects, identifies few costs to consider alongside the plan's climate and sustainable energy benefits. While not overtly critical of the plan itself, Hunold and Leitner compare it with other high-modernist narratives of the past century – including those on behalf of massive hydroelectric and water reclamation projects in the western United States – suggesting that such discourses often conceal the environmental repercussions of the projects they advocate for environmental reasons. Against this powerful combination of discourses, desert conservationists stand little chance. Examining the politics of large-scale solar development through this lens, Hunold and Leitner reveal the difficulties associated with designing sustainable energy systems when this involves least-bad options, especially when these still contain objectionable elements and require for their public assent a process of obscuring their true environmental costs, and embedded in language and imagery designed to appeal to cultural or emotional associations rather than objective analysis.

Similarly, Rachael Shwom examines the political processes that eventually led to the United States' adoption of energy efficiency standards for appliances, which as purely informational and voluntary measures nonetheless have a significant impact on reducing household energy use. Because they mobilize consumer interests in saving money on their utility bills and encourage appliance manufacturers to develop and implement efficient technologies in their products to meet this mobilized demand for green products, such standards are, as Shwom notes, often regarded as among the 'low-hanging fruit' of sustainable energy and climate policy, achievable without coercive regulation or economic costs (and, indeed, resulting in a net benefit for consumers and society). Rejecting the oversimplistic view of social progress toward environmental sustainability as driven by consumer preferences alone, Shwom begins by observing that 'structural changes in our production systems' are needed to for a transition to a low-carbon energy economy, and that enlightened consumer preferences or individual behavioral change is not enough to restructure a market that is controlled by manufacturers. Drawing on insights from 'treadmill of production' and ecological modernization theories, Shwom illustrates through a case study of the evolution of appliance efficiency standards that each of these theories captures some of the sociological dynamics of this process, with the former working best in accounting for resistance to the adoption of such standards during the Reagan years of the 1980s, and with the latter accounting for their eventual adoption during the Clinton administration in the 1990s. Shwom develops a 'middle range' approach that relaxes the assumptions of each and takes elements from both theories, explaining the social and political dynamics that often obstruct the design of sensible energy and environmental policies, and further illustrating the difficulties in bringing about what are often viewed as among the easiest and most effective sustainability policy strategies.

Anthony Patt, Nadejda Komendantova, Antonella Battaglini and Johan Lilliestam examine the technical and governance challenges associated with meeting the European Union's climate and renewable energy goals, focusing on the proposal to build an electricity 'Supergrid' that covers the European Union as well as North Africa. By including the vast solar capacity of North Africa within the grid, the system would take advantage of the best sites for renewable energy generation, and by covering a large population and wide geographic region, it could smooth supply and demand, enabling the least expensive and most efficient market penetration of clean and renewable power. But as the authors show through this incisive study of various political challenges to the Supergrid's construction and maintenance, the most rationally organized and efficiently designed system is not always the most politically feasible, and, indeed, political viability and ecological rationality are often at odds in large-scale projects like this. As Hunold and Leitner also note, decarbonization imperatives and ecological modernization discourses can lead policy-makers to think big, but big thinking that focuses only on a project's technical merits can often fail to take into account some its most pervasive obstacles and significant drawbacks. Relying upon model-based analysis and stakeholder interviews, Patt *et al.* offer a relatively optimistic assessment of the prospects for a European–North African Supergrid, but in highlighting the risks and security issues associated with the scale and international nature of the project, they call needed attention to the importance of considering political and governance challenges alongside technical ones. Even if those risks can be managed, doing so requires cultural awareness and political skill, casting sustainable energy as a social and political challenge as much as one for science and engineering, and effective governance plans as no less vital than infrastructural ones.

Finally, Karena Shaw examines recent energy and climate change politics in British Columbia, which has adopted a provincial carbon tax and in several respects has played an environmental leadership role within Canada, focusing on framing issues in debates over expanding renewable energy as a climate change mitigation measure. As other contributors also note, the way in which problems are framed carries significant consequences for the ways in which problems may be addressed, with any discursive focus highlighting some features and obscuring others. Shaw notes that, like many other efforts to develop effective climate policy, British Columbia environmentalists have focused upon reducing carbon emissions, which calls attention to end-of-pipe rather than source-based issues, and which Shaw faults for closing off 'much more diverse and robust' sustainability strategies. The problem, Shaw argues, is not with expanding renewable energy generation itself, but rather lies in the neglect of potentially more effective options when the focus is placed on energy production rather than conservation, and when concerns about the integrity of larger ecosystems are reduced to a singular decarbonizing imperative. In a case study that reinforces some lessons also on display in Hunold and Leitner's solar case, Shaw examines how the enthusiasm for expanded hydroelectric capacity can obscure more holistic concerns for energy sustainability and exclude stakeholders whose participation could benefit the initial support for and long-term viability of such projects. Because sustainability itself is a social, political, and economic concept in addition to an ecological one, her study suggests, the politics of defining and realizing its ideals must take account of more than simply the technical aspects or benchmarks of its achievement. Casting climate change as essentially an energy systems challenge makes it more inclusive of potentially useful strategies to address it, and viewing it as a social and political as well as technical and environmental challenge reveals the most daunting obstacles to as well as the most promising means to effective change.

Taken together, these eight studies of various aspects of contemporary energy politics provide a glimpse into the political challenges that complicate the design and construction of sustainable energy systems, yielding insights into the nature of ongoing resistance to change and highlighting several factors that frustrate 'rational-comprehensive' global planning and development of energy infrastructure and policy. Their collective lesson may be to dampen the naive optimism of those who believe that large-scale environmental problems can be solved by economists and engineers through equally large-scale engineering projects, as if all forms of resistance to them would evaporate once their technical superiority is publicly shown, and governance of those projects and the systems they create can be made immune to the pathologies of the flawed or outmoded systems they replace. But its lesson should not be pessimism, either, as these eight studies also inform more constructive analyses of energy politics than unguarded pessimism typically countenances, and point the way toward more viable means for choosing among least-bad options, mobilizing available mechanisms and constituencies of support, and navigating among various predictable or understandable forms of resistance to them.

References

Jacobsen, M.Z. and Delucchi, M.A., 2009. A path to sustainable energy by 2030. *Scientific American*, 301 (5), 58–65.
Lindblom, C.E., 1959. The 'science' of muddling through. *Public Administration Review*, 19, 79–88.
Tamminen, T., 2006. *Lives per gallon: the true cost of our oil addiction*. Washington, DC: Island Press.
US Energy Information Administration, 2010. *International energy outlook 2010*. Washington, DC: US Department of Energy.

Poor little rich countries: another look at the 'resource curse'
Sudhir Chella Rajan

Resource-rich countries are plagued by macroeconomic crises known as 'Dutch Disease', which is associated with the inflation of local currencies on account of a large influx of foreign exchange and a dip in labor supply for non-traded goods. In developing countries, the historical context of state formation is often such that the revenues generated by natural resource exports bolster the stability of authoritarian regimes, and the dominant state actors consolidate their power by managing boom–bust cycles to avert crises. In the context of oil resources, with their special geopolitical significance, relevance for the environment, and enclave character, the primary producers face even more challenges, especially if they are relatively new players and are buffeted by geopolitical power games. Using Mexico, Venezuela and Angola as paradigmatic cases, the relevance of outside forces, domestic policies, and the opportunistic forms of engagement with external power chosen by local actors that produced tragic outcomes in each of these instances are examined.

Introduction

A nation endowed with mineral wealth is far less privileged than one might imagine, especially if it is unlucky enough to be in an already underdeveloped region. Consider a poor country in Latin America or sub-Saharan Africa, with a history of exploitation by colonial rule and local elites, caught up in vicious circles of institutional decline, having inadequate access to healthcare, education and jobs, and already wholly dependent on foreign exchange revenue from marginal earnings from agricultural commodity exports. The sudden discovery of significant quantities of mineral resources under its control will jolt its political and economic elites into reorganizing themselves into stewards of an extractive economy that relies primarily on external expertise to manage investments, technology and planning. For speedy production of the resource and transfer into global commodity markets, large global corporations are brought in whose revenues may well exceed the country's domestic output. The contracts will almost undoubtedly have terms that are unfavorable to the public interest, but advance the private interests and power of a small elite network of public officials, local oligarchs, and representatives of the resource extraction industry.

When oil is the resource in question, there are several further complicating factors. Oil is probably the most closely watched international commodity, even though its share of global trade is less than 5%. It is concentrated in surprisingly large quantities in a few countries of the world but requires considerable human and financial capital and technology for exploration, extraction and distribution. Given the relatively inelastic worldwide demand for its products and the high entry barriers, there are opportunities for creating substantial rents rather than profits; that is to say, sellers have the ability to charge far more for the product than simply the costs of extraction and a reasonable rate of return. For technical reasons, however, it is relatively difficult to control changes in output very quickly because doing so will probably cause permanent damage to the integrity of wells. And finally, oil production has enormous environmental impacts, in the form of land clearance, construction of roads, pipelines and other infrastructure, major accidents such as blowouts and spills, local air pollution associated with flaring and exposure to toxic gases, and of course climate change.

Economists and political scientists have noted many of these features over the past two decades or so, and have coined the term 'resource curse' to characterize the challenges faced by countries relying on natural resource exports for their wealth. Much of the scholarly focus to date has been on the counter-intuitive finding that the extraction and export of natural resources has hindered rather than improved growth since the early 1970s (Sachs and Warner 2001). On the face of it, resource-rich countries also seem to share several disturbing institutional features with one another. The regimes controlling the resources are often corrupt, authoritarian or over-centralized, with weak state capacity and poor institutions. Their societies are fragmented, with vast disparities in income, poor education, and typically a growing class of skilled and unskilled workers as well as an elite group of experts serving as managers, most of whom who are foreign-born. Common to many resource-rich countries are stagnant growth, poor social welfare indicators, high levels of poverty, inequality, and unemployment, and social anomie in the midst of extraordinary wealth.

While there is a plethora of perspectives on the resource curse, ranging from skepticism over its existence through behaviorist, neo-Marxist, public choice and statist frameworks explaining its existence (for surveys, see Rosser 2006, Frankel 2010), a dominant position influential in shaping multilateral policy is starting to emerge, having both macroeconomic and institutional dimensions. According to Jeffrey Sachs and Andrew Warner (2001), increasing revenues from natural resource exports leads to a rise in the price of non-tradable goods because of the appreciation in the real exchange rate. This, in turn, leads to a decline in the competitiveness of other (say, non-oil) sectors, thereby increasing the country's overall risk exposure to volatility in the global price of the natural resource. The institutional aspects of the resource curse are associated with the generation of the unusually large revenues from resource extraction, having to do with the relatively low costs of production compared with prices in international markets (Karl 2004). Economic investments in oil production tend to be concentrated in enclaves, providing huge rents for a small elite and very few benefits for the rest of society. But the rents also distort the state's ability to pursue institutional development, such as democracy and the rule of law, by weakening 'agencies of restraint'. Oil states, in particular, tend to have expanding bureaucracies and otherwise become profligate at the expense of nurturing domestic institutions such as courts and civil service training centers. With substantial revenues that can be easily diverted for personal gain, the regimes tend to be corrupt and authoritarian.

Here, while registering my overall agreement with the central features of this explanation, I review the literature critically, in order to highlight what appears to be a prominent blind spot in the mainstream perspective. I argue that even though conventional accounts of the resource curse appear to be logical and consistent with the evidence, by eliding some crucial factors they systematically skew the institutional possibilities for reform in resource-rich countries. These factors are tied primarily to international geopolitics and the rent-seeking tendencies and power of global capital and new forms of mercantilism emergent in large oil-consuming states around the world, together with the hegemonic power of neoliberalism (Harvey 2005). I shall use cases from Africa and Latin America to show how the resource curse can be described alternatively, with perhaps different implications for national and international policy than those currently on offer by multilateral organizations and other donors.

I begin by describing the central arguments of resource curse theorists who use macroeconomic and domestic institutional attributes to characterize the problem. I then examine three cases from Latin America and Africa, which together lend credence to my claim that a systematic bias appears in most conventional explanations of the resource curse, which disregard the impact of the lopsided power relations of international political economy and the historical legacy of colonialism on the development of resource-rich countries. But dependency theory by itself is an inadequate framework to replace or supplement these theories because it simply points to the externally imposed conditions that have suppressed growth in many developing countries, and to the continuing barriers to actual global competitiveness of the developing world by unfair terms of trade and political bullying. Instead, I contend, one should not discount the role of domestic actors who engage in strategies of extraversion; that is to say, collaborative and sometimes independent means to engage in rent-seeking together with outsiders. Taken together, particularly in the context of oil-rich countries, the resource curse appears as a tragedy for ordinary people as a result of a grand collusion between the financial and political interests of domestic elite power networks and global capital, with even well-meaning political leadership helpless to make sound macroeconomic policy as a result of institutions damaged in the course of a long history of domestic and international intervention, especially in the context of boom–bust cycles of oil prices.

Characterizing the resource curse

The earliest intimations that the economic performance of low-income countries tends to be negatively correlated with their natural resource wealth came from economists such as Alan Gelb, James Mahon and Richard Auty, who introduced the term resource curse into the development lexicon. Their initial thesis has since been extended (Auty 2001, Sachs and Warner 2001) but the overall argument remains fairly straightforward. Over the past four or five decades, the median per-capita income of the resource-rich countries has reduced to levels far below that of the resource-poor countries, whereas in the previous half-century or so the situation was reversed. This pattern is also reflected in their relative growth rates; in the period 1960–1990, the growth rates of the resource-rich countries were less than one-half of those of resource-poor countries.

Resource-rich countries, especially if they are small, generate the bulk of their income from the sale of minerals abroad, which ends up raising their relative exchange rates (that is to say, their currencies become dearer). In the process, these countries lose the ability to build up a competitive industrial sector that is separate from those parts of their economy linked to resource extraction. With higher wages in the resource extraction sector, employment and entrepreneurial talent will converge towards it and crowd out any other possible growth-generating opportunities elsewhere in the economy. In addition, being high-price economies and in the midst of boom and bust cycles affecting their revenues from resource sales, they are likely to suffer the consequences of missing out on the standard advantages of export-led growth. All in all, the resource-rich countries end up having lower levels of growth, but with greater inequality. In contrast, resource-poor countries start to invest much earlier in labor-intensive competitive manufacturing, resulting in faster diversification, higher saving rates, and quicker capital accumulation. As mentioned earlier, oil is the emblematic instance of these problems, given its special importance in the global economy, its enclave character, and peculiar price cycles compared with most other commodities.

A parallel literature tries to explain the origins of the resource curse primarily in political and institutional terms (for example, Karl 1997, Auty 2001, Robinson *et al.* 2006). The main argument here is that it is the political leadership in resource-rich countries that shifts its priorities in managing revenues by engaging in rent-seeking for personal financial or political gains.

The state tends to be negligent about developing its industrial sector, in part because sufficiently large rents already accrue from exploiting the resource endowment. The rents are further derived from enclaves that are sufficiently delinked from the rest of the economy, which implies that windfall gains accrue primarily to select business entities and their political benefactors within the country. This in turn generates an incentive to maintain the *status quo*, since elites potentially have a great deal to lose by allowing a change in institutions that provides other sectors in the economy incentives to become more efficient. Together, these conditions lock in the endurance of institutions not conducive to development. There is some uncertainty as to whether pre-existing institutional conditions cause the resource curse or whether institutions are made worse by it. Karl seems to point to some ambiguity on this issue, but Robinson *et al.* (2006, p. 447) are quite insistent: 'Countries with institutions that promote accountability and state competence will tend to benefit from resource booms since these institutions ameliorate the perverse political incentives that such booms create. Countries without such institutions however may suffer from a resource curse.'

The resource-rich state is characterized by predatory regimes with weak, inept, or corrupt institutions, which are effective only to the extent that they control resource extraction and divert its revenue stream toward conferring wealth on elites. But the windfall revenues also diminish the need for the state to collect any taxes from its population, which in turn reduces political contact with the people in the form of accountability and representation. Rather, a generous welfare state on the one hand ensures that basic services function well and its populace remains politically docile, while, on the other hand, potential challengers to the regime are kept at bay through patronage networks. A disproportionate fraction of revenues tends to be spent on the military to protect the regime from internal as well as external threats, both perceived and real.

Three cases

Mexico: after the revolution, the drought

Mexico's case illustrates many of these conditions, particularly after the mid-1970s, when significant off-shore oil resources were discovered. Funds from oil seemed to contribute to an economic recovery of sorts, since the previous decade was characterized by a severe balance-of-payments crisis, which was itself resource driven, because it was precipitated by the global oil-shocks of 1973/74. Mexico became a choice candidate for receiving 'petro-dollars', providing it with cheap access to money from international financial institutions anxious to circulate the new liquidity generated by the spurt in oil revenues caused by the OPEC oil shocks. The loans were used to promote government-led investments in industrial development, on the basis of anticipated future oil revenues. Between 1977 and 1982, Mexico's public-sector external debt rose from about $23 billion to $85 billion. A major contribution to this problem came in 1979, when the US Federal Reserve decided to tighten interest rates significantly, which caused a sudden increase in debt servicing requirements for all developing countries that had borrowed heavily during the era of easy petro-dollars. In 1982, under the further pressure of falling oil prices, the government saw massive levels of capital flight and was forced to devalue the peso three times, furthering inflation and increasing interest payments on the debt.

Mexico's industrial development was largely state-led although the private sector was significant and highly concentrated. As John Minns (2006, p. 58) points out, two banking groups in the 1970s:

> controlled 72% of the total resources of the private sector and 51% of the total capital reserves of the economy as a whole. At the end of the developmental period in the early 1980s, Mexico had a level of industrial concentration similar to or higher than most advanced economies; just 0.82% of firms accounted for 64.3% of total production.

While the boom–bust cycles created by fluctuating oil prices generated substantial conflicts between domestic capitalists and the political establishment, it was clear that some private businesses benefited enormously from state-sponsored subsidies, contracts, very low corporate taxes, and so on. Mexico's special historical and geographical relationship with the United States, while generating a strong nationalist sentiment, did not preempt engagement with foreign capital. Until the 1980s, foreign investments were tempered by rules relating to majority ownership by Mexican firms and the state. Still, it was a narrow group of private business elites who benefitted from these arrangements, often with ties to foreign companies and to the state.

Since the 1980s, virtually the entire non-oil economy in Mexico has become heavily reliant on subsidies, so much so that oil export revenues pay for nearly 40% of government spending. The funds come from heavy taxes on the state oil monopoly Pemex, which is subsequently unable to capitalize its industry effectively. Oil's share of export earnings was as high as 70% in the early 1980s, but has since declined to about 20%. Between 1983 and 1988, the economy grew at about 0.1% annually, with 100% inflation and a declining share of non-oil output. In 1994, a second major currency crisis took place, which resulted in further devaluation of the peso and the loss of about $11 billion in foreign reserves in less than four weeks. In recent years, there has been a resumption of economic growth and stability in the currency, but the country continues to be saddled with substantial external debt, which effectively curtails the government's ability to manage its oil export earnings sustainably, which is especially troublesome with falling oil reserves and production at post-peak levels (Usui 1997, Minns 2006).

One explanation of Mexico's crisis is that it is the outcome of faulty fiscal, foreign borrowing and exchange rate policies inspired by its distinctive domestic politics of rent-seeking in the wake of windfall revenues from oil. Yet, it is important also to recognize the international political economy context of

Mexico's resource curse. As Peter Gowan (1999) and others have argued, while Federal Reserve Chairman Volcker's decision to raise interest rates sharply in 1979 might itself have been motivated by specific domestic US economic concerns, it also signaled a strong dollar strategy, with very specific foreign policy intentions. In the 1980s, the Reagan administration's ideological commitment to reducing state support for various programs initially indicated withdrawal from the International Monetary Fund (IMF), but it was subsequently recognized that the institution could be used for extending US influence over economic policy in other countries. When Mexico was saddled with dollar debt as a direct result of Volcker's moves (and a three-decade history of dollar hegemony starting with Bretton Woods), its rescue package came with conditions designed by the US Treasury and the IMF to cut welfare expenditures, relax labor laws, and promote privatization and open the door to foreign investors.

Domestic elites in Mexico, while not directly responsible for generating the crises, were often beneficiaries of the reforms that followed. But the active role played by these actors is most clearly seen in the negotiations around NAFTA, which could truly be considered the logical outcome of the series of structural adjustments that began in the 1980s:

> In the negotiations before 1994, Mexican business leaders played a major part – in some cases actually leading the formal discussions for the Mexican side. The Mexican bourgeoisie had entered the state directly and had done so through the PRI. They publicly lauded its approach. The multibillionaire media owner, Emilio Azcarraga, said that he had done so well as a result of the Salinas administration that he was willing to give US$75 million to the PRI. (Minns 2006, p. 115)

Venezuela: from patronage comes the revolution

Terry Lynn Karl points to Venezuela as the archetype of a resource-rich state getting caught up in institutional problems. When oil was discovered at the beginning of the twentieth century, Venezuela was characterized by extremely weak political and administrative institutions, with a military strongman, Juan Vicente Gomez, as ruler. Gomez negotiated the entry of foreign oil companies (principally Royal Dutch Shell and Standard Oil) into a country with virtually no institutional or economic infrastructure to manage its oil resources by itself. The ensuing:

> partnership between the oil companies and Gomez left little for the construction of an impersonal state bureaucracy or the development of the country, but it worked to the benefit of both parties: the companies achieved their central goal of capturing crude oil supplies; Gomez remained in power and managed to add to his considerable wealth. (Karl 1997, p. 78)

Institutional development was evidently in the interest of the oil companies in the early years to ensure their stable presence in the country, and they formed a new consensus with existing elite interests to reshape the Venezuelan state. The resulting laws provided the state with the sole authority to deal with exploration contracts, concentrated power in the hands of the executive, eased of controls on companies to own and manage property, and provided centralized authority for collecting and managing rents. Karl argues that in the years that followed the state became the desired locus of power, but without an impersonal and accountable bureaucracy, it became a patronage machine for distributing rents rather than a capable and legitimate administrative entity.

In 1973/74, with the first oil embargo, Venezuela saw an unexpected windfall as oil revenues quadrupled to $10 billion, giving the newly elected president, Carlos Andres Perez, a substantial political boost. Yet, the huge inflows of money into the treasury invited fears of inflation, which led to a series of decrees to curb costs, the invocation of special presidential powers, general weakening of democracy, and ironically, massive foreign borrowing to manage spending requests from different sectors. In other words, when the government received a major windfall, it tried to do too much too soon, and this tendency to overextend itself was accompanied by an attack by rent-seekers. The institutional outcome of this disastrous sequence is what Karl describes as a 'pacted' democracy, where the formal institutions of democracy overlay an elite arrangement of patronage through petro-dollars.

By 1976, the oil industry was entirely nationalized but the country, like Mexico, was seriously affected in the 1980s by a combination of spiraling expenditure from oil revenues followed by a precipitous drop in oil prices in 1983, in which the impact was magnified by the Volcker interest rate hikes. It attempted devaluations in its currency, import protection and producer and consumer subsidies to stave off major crisis until 1989, by which time it had experienced another steep drop in oil prices and a growing foreign debt burden. In 1989, Perez returned for a second term, replacing Jaime Lusinchi, whose economic populism was checkered by corruption scandals and the fiscal crisis. Immediately upon assuming the presidency, with a campaign slogan that the IMF was a 'bomb that only kills people', Perez adopted an IMF package of $4 billion, which was accompanied by measures to privatize state companies, substantially devalue the bolívar, withdraw most consumer and producer subsidies, reduce taxes and customs duties, and generally minimize the role of the state in the economy.

The February 1989 protests, which claimed close to 3000 lives as a result of police shooting, are marked as the 'Caracazo', and eventually generated the conditions to give Hugo Chávez the presidency a few years later. But 1989 was a dark year economically as well, with 44% of the population under the poverty line and inflation soaring to 81%. By 1991, even according to official estimates, nearly 80% of Venezuela's 19.5 million people lived in relative or critical poverty. According to George Schuyler (1996), the events of 1989 demolished whatever elite consensus had developed during previous decades, based on the idea of well-organized political parties and favored positions for powerful groups, when it became obvious that the government was unable or unwilling to respond to economic hardship for the majority of its population.

In the course of a single decade between 1981 and 1991, petroleum revenues per capita had declined about three and a half times. Yet, in just three years, between 1988 and 1991, the share of national income going to the richest 10% of the population had risen from 30.3% to 43%. The birth of the Bolivarian revolution was predicated on the reality and perception by the poor that an extraordinarily affluent global upper class had for quite a long time systematically mismanaged the country's oil wealth and its economy to suit their interests.

The Chávez presidency has managed to avoid some of the elements of the resource curse, although it remains to be seen whether these can be sustained. In the decade 2001–2010, the real average annual growth rate of Venezuela was 3.38%, compared with 1.83% during the previous decade and 0.92% a decade earlier. Given its explicit rejection of elite capture of the state as well as of externally imposed neoliberal policy, it is not surprising that the Bolivarian revolution has paid special attention to development, with an impressive record. The government renegotiated oil royalties with transnational corporations early on and also initiated a series of missions to promote health and education. By the end of 2007, unemployment levels were down to 6.3%, the number of people living in extreme poverty more than halved by comparison with the previous decade, and the infant mortality rate dropped from 25.6 per 1000 births in 1990 to 13.9 (Riggirozzi 2010). Nevertheless, it is not clear whether inequality *per se* has reverted even to pre-1991 levels, and official data are ambiguous on this score. Moreover, Venezuela's relationship with the United States has been tense for over a decade, although less so since the 2008 election of President Obama. Venezuela negotiated the purchase of $4 billion in arms from Russia in 2005 and has strengthened military ties with China, both of which are sore points for US foreign policy. At the same time, Venezuelan oil imports to the United States stand fourth in volume, after Saudi Arabia, Canada, and Mexico.

Angola: race to the bottom

The third case we consider is that of Angola, currently the second largest petroleum producer in sub-Saharan Africa, and until 1975 a Portuguese overseas territory for nearly four centuries. Colonialism in Angola was characterized from the seventeenth to the nineteenth centuries by the supply of slave labor to plantations in Brazil, Principe and Sao Tome by Portuguese entrepreneurs, with African chiefs and their slave-hunting tribes serving as their primary collaborators in providing a steady supply of slaves (Wolf 1982). Although Britain signed a treaty with Portugal in 1810 to cease slave trading, the King of Portugal did not finally abolish slavery in colonies until 1869 and the practice continued to take place illegally for decades afterward. In the second half of the nineteenth century, with the reduction in revenues from the slave trade, agriculture in the interior began to form the basis for surplus creation, managed largely by Portuguese and Brazilian merchants, with

Luanda becoming a major trading center and the site of an emerging Angolan bourgeoisie. The Berlin Conference of 1884 consolidated territory in the hinterlands under Portuguese control, but it also meant that the government needed to actually possess property in the interior, leading to new arrangements with local intermediaries.

Portuguese governance of the country was highly centralized, with Lisbon maintaining an iron hand over the territory. The Portuguese Colonial Act of 1930 further alienated the native-born population in Angola from civil or political rights, with the explicit language of race. It created two communities in the African colonies: natives and non-indigenous, the latter including whites, *mestiços*, and *assimilados*. It is in the last category that one can locate the especially pernicious element of divide-and-rule: the *assimilados* were those members of the black native population who were officially sanctioned as being 'assimilated' on the basis of their being able to dress, converse and behave like educated Portuguese. Furthermore, colonial territories were required to produce raw materials for Portuguese industry with low production and purchasing costs, to contribute to the equilibrium of the Portuguese balance of payments, to be financially self-sufficient, and to be politically and administratively centralized under the metropolitan government (cited in Cross 1987).

The discovery of diamonds in 1912 had already shifted the locus of economic and political interest in the region, but that of oil in 1950 was even more significant. Mineral exports, primarily diamonds, gold and copper, doubled in the 1960s, which precipitated a land-grab by ethnic European settlers in mineral-rich areas, while farm income dropped by more than one-half during this period. By the early 1970s, oil had turned into the primary revenue source from exports. The population of European settlers in Angola was by now nearly 10 times what it had been in the 1940s, marking new clusters of communities along racially defined lines. In 1968, Gulf Oil (now part of Chevron) was awarded exploration contracts in Cabinda province. By 1970, revenues from this province supported nearly one-third of the colonial government's $54 million military budget, which was largely used to fight a burgeoning civil war (LeBillion 2001).

In 1961, the Popular Movement launched an independence struggle for the Liberation of Angola (MPLA), a relatively small communist militant group at that time. Two other groups, the National Liberation Front of Angola (FNLA) and the more militant National Union for the Total Independence of Angola (UNITA), which was a bitter enemy of the MPLA, joined the attack on the colonial government, but the war turned into a three-way fight, with complex international alliances on each side. The FNLA and UNITA received assistance from the United States, France and Britain, but also support from the Republic of China, Romania, North Korea and South Africa against the MPLA, which was largely supported by the Soviet Union and Cuba, with the backing of Sweden, Denmark and Nigeria (Bender 1987). In 1975, a three-way negotiated settlement with Portugal led to a transitional government. But the post-independence situation was characterized by intense civil war until 2002, featuring conflict between the MPLA and UNITA. A third movement, the FLEC, an association of separatist militant groups, fought for the independence of Cabinda, an oil-rich exclave province. By the end of the war, an estimated 500,000 people had been killed.

Throughout this period, revenues from oil and diamonds were barely affected by the civil war, but grew at a robust pace of 8–10% annually, for the most part. In recent years, Angola has a booming economy, tied to high oil prices. China's Eximbank recently approved a $2 billion line of credit, intended to rebuild the country's infrastructure and bypassing the involvement of multilateral agencies like the IMF. Yet, the country's contradictions are clear: 70% of the population lives on the equivalent of less than $2 a day, the majority lack access to basic healthcare, and about one in four children die before their fifth birthday. The country ranks 157 out of 179 countries in terms of human development and, during the recent global financial crisis, GDP growth remained flat or negative. Oil exports account for nearly 90% of revenues to the government, which provides fuel subsidies to the poor, but not investments in education, healthcare and jobs. At the same time, the government is able to use oil as an economic sanctuary against military and political threats, primarily due the almost exclusively off-shore location of the oil-fields. The oil-fields themselves are secured, enclaved and globally networked with financial institutions, oil companies and intermediaries, with security provided by private military companies.

Angola's importance in the global political economy of oil is unmistakable. Currently producing nearly two million barrels per day, Angola is the largest producer in sub-Saharan Africa. The US imports 7% of its oil from Angola and considers the country an important strategic partner for energy cooperation and security (United States 2011). At the same time, China has vigorously pursued exploration contracts with Angola, making it now the second largest trading partner for oil in the 'new scramble for Africa'. While China and the United States have become the dominant players seeking contracts for oil in the continent, they are by no means alone: Brazil, India, Malaysia and South Korea are equally active in chasing after partnerships in the region (Frynas and Paulo 2006). The United States has used diplomatic instruments, economic incentives and military aid to promote its relationship with Angola, often assisting private firms to obtain concessions for oil exploration and production. China, in contrast, has adopted a bilateral approach, often securing concessions in exchange for aid to rebuild railways, government buildings, schools, hospitals and roads. In the process, it has provided an alternative to IMF aid, and thereby enabled Angola to avoid having to abide by neoliberal conditions for structural reform. China's entry is thereby providing Angola's leaders with new bargaining power for development aid. All in all, the current situation is yet another twist to the bizarre history of the country's elites managing different partners to negotiate the management of its oil resources with outsiders: for instance, in the mid-1970s, the government called Cuban troops to protect American oil interests in Cabinda (Bayart 2000, p. 232).

Is wealth really the curse?

The mainstream economic and institutional explanations of the resource curse go hand in hand by making the case that where prevailing institutions are weak, resource booms give rise to political opportunism and misallocation of economic gains through a tragic internal logic that leads directly to the resource curse. For those countries that appear to have escaped the resource curse, such as Indonesia and Botswana, it is simply good governance that needs to be credited:

> But the origins of good macroeconomic policy in Indonesia stemmed from the fact that Suharto staffed the relevant bureaucracies not with political appointees but rather with Berkeley-trained economists and technocrats hired on the basis of merit. (Robinson *et al.* 2006, p. 465)

There are several valuable features of these analyses, which need to be acknowledged. First and foremost, by characterizing a syndrome common to many resource-rich developing countries, they bring into focus the perils of the resource-rich, thereby creating the basis for further research in an important domain that might otherwise not receive much notice. Second, they provide useful models of the dynamics of endogenous factors involving the predatory pursuit of power and wealth by elites that reinforce the underdevelopment of resource-rich countries. Third, they help to characterize the peculiar conditions under which a revenue-rich country can turn into a fiscally insolvent one and provide some common basis for understanding these conditions even if the solutions proffered are not easily available.

At the same time, the cases we have seen above make clear that these explanations are incomplete, if not inadequate. In each instance, notwithstanding the messy internal politics and poor management of resources, it is clear that the countries followed trajectories that sometimes seemed to work against conventional expectations related to the resource curse, and, secondly, that their crises had a strong relation to external conditions and forces. Mexico's fiscal crises *preceded* the discovery of large amounts of oil, and Venezuela had an authoritarian government prior to the development of its resources and democratization took place *subsequently*. Angola's troubled history of colonialism and its long war afterwards were certainly connected to its resource wealth but by no means determined by it.

In other words, the timing and sequence of resource exploitation *vis-à-vis* institutional change are different in each case and out of odds with the conventional understanding of the resource curse. Mexico's first peso devaluation in 1982 was arguably the result of profligate spending arising from a combination of petro-dollar loans pushed by banks abroad in the preceding years and the government's unreasonable expectations of continued high revenues from oil sales, both of which were exacerbated by clientalism. The early institutional development of the Venezuelan state was determined in large part by the unhealthy coalition of foreign oil companies and domestic elites, whose rent-seeking interests dovetailed with each other to the detriment of the public good. As Karl points out, this feature is common to many resource-rich developing countries:

> In sum, all major exporting countries have faced the same external dilemma throughout their history. On the one hand, they have had to bargain hard, both individually and collectively, to emerge from the domination of the international companies that so profoundly affected their development paths. On the other hand, their gradual success paradoxically set the stage for sharp rises and falls in prices, a prolonged trough of lower prices, and an especially risky international environment. (Karl 1997, pp. 51–52)

Unfortunately, Karl does not pursue this line of research very far either in her original analysis of Venezuela or in subsequent work. With very few exceptions, other scholars on the topic also seem quite unmindful of the external pressures on resource-rich developing countries at various points in their history, treating the resource curse as an entirely indigenous problem that is also the logical outcome of a sequence of events linked primarily to two causal factors: the windfall revenues arising from resource sales and the poor quality of institutions in the country in question.

This logic and the evidence for this theory are far less unequivocal than is postulated. First, developing countries typically lack the ability to raise capital from abroad to finance their growth unless they are seen as boom economies to begin with, creating a self-fulfilling prophecy. During lean times, when the revenues from exports are low, resource-rich countries find it difficult to finance their spending commitments and investments made during boom times, which leads to the sort of fiscal tailspins Mexico and Venezuela found themselves in. This is not to say that the governments do not have themselves to blame for not anticipating downturns, but given poor infrastructure and very low development as their starting points, the appeal for spending during times of plenty should not necessarily be seen as reckless but as an anxiety to get the ball rolling when the going is good. When external funding for development programs as much as for patronage payments are not easily forthcoming on a regular basis, it is not surprising if resource-rich developing countries feel compelled to overspend during boom times.

Second, there is in fact inadequate evidence that resource rich countries tend to have poor democratic institutions. Haber and Menaldo (2011) have recently analyzed the long-term longitudinal relationship between countries' resource dependence and their regime type and found that oil and mineral reliance does not undermine democracy, preclude democratization, or protract democratic transitions. Nevertheless, this need not undermine the general case made that mineral rents provide incumbent politicians with the means to buy clientelistic support while keeping direct taxes on citizens low, thereby depressing participatory politics (Ross 2001). Where opportunities exist for consolidating these gains and preserving extant regimes, whether authoritarian or democratic, they tend to endure, but when other factors such as international geopolitics, domestic ethnic conflict or similar legacy issues gain importance, then political fortunes too may shift accordingly. The quality of pre-existing domestic institutions is certainly one of the relevant features influencing the country's political path, but only one among many.

Indeed, an entire sphere of influence about which surprisingly little analysis has been carried out in this context is the international political economy of resource demand. Popular culture is apparently far more mindful of the fervent geopolitical context of blood diamonds and oil than are mainstream political scientists and economists, judging by the latter's relative silence on the issue. Minerals, particularly oil, are of course produced primarily for an external market, and it is often because of the special enclave character of these resources that remote, otherwise uninteresting and desolate countries suddenly catch the public eye. Mineral resources are international commodities in great demand, but because there is often little or no local capacity to manage their extraction, a series of measures needs to be undertaken by interested parties to re-gear indigenous institutions that may already be caught up in complex prevailing arrangements, burdened with a post-colonial legacy, perhaps only recently emergent as a state, and already halfway on a development trajectory shaped by multilateral donors, domestic political interests and businesses.

Nevertheless, the strong version of dependency theory, which claims that the resource curse is directly the outcome of unequal exchange and the structure of the world economy, is too sweeping and unfocused a paradigm to add value to existing explanations. A broad-brush causal attribution of the resource curse to global capitalist structures that subordinate the needs of resource-rich developing countries to the interests of the powerful completely sidelines the dynamics of local circumstances in relation to global political economy. In particular, it erases the role of local agents and their active construction of and participation in the development of dependency, treating them rather as passive victims. Yet it is clear that an array of structural factors – for example, the political economy of global oil demand, the coercive influence of international banking and finance, and the threat of military intervention – are in fact utilized by the domestic political actors and other elites to consolidate personal wealth and power. In the process, the predilection for boom and bust cycles associated with global oil markets leads to faltering macroeconomic conditions but these are in turn complemented by the opportunistic behavior by elite networks, both domestic and international.

Jean-Francois Bayart's (2009) use of the term 'extraversion' is perhaps relevant in this context. Bayart argues that the participation of indigenous actors in such activities as the slave trade in Africa or colonial governmentality represents an internal stratification that aided and abetted external interests as well as certain local ones. Government policy in the colonial regime often coincided with the strategies of local actors and was in fact co-opted by the latter in those instances, or was effectively resisted by them when it went against their interests. Bayart describes six such strategies: coercion, trickery, flight, mediation, appropriation, and rejection. In the contemporary, post-colonial context, similar strategies are adopted by domestic actors who seek to mobilize rents by capitalizing on relationships with the outside world, including bankers, private corporations, multilateral organizations and governments. It is in this context and through such actions that they turn into 'elites', who may form state actors or remain outside the state, but it is important to note that their power is derived by the extent to which they form symbiotic relationships with powerful external interests, which could have little to do with their relative standing in their own societies prior to these conditions. Dependency is still present in this framework, but it is mediated by the extraverted rent-seeking actions of local players who are now seen as active agents rather than passive victims.

The notion of extraversion can help explain the peculiar challenge of the resource-rich developing country because it calls attention to the ways in which the discovery of mineral wealth puts into motion a set of strategies that are used to engage with developers and create a mutually reinforcing, although not necessarily cooperative, rent-seeking platform. Typically these manifest themselves as secretive contracts between extractive industries and the state, which may include corrupt side payments or indirectly provide political support to the regime in return for long-term and loosely regulated arrangements for resource extraction and revenue generation. The theory makes superfluous the question of whether bad pre-existing institutions generate the resource curse or whether it is the other way around (see Frankel 2010, p. 18). The institutions that build on the extraverted relationships are those of dictatorship and state control, secrecy and inequality, simply because these are deemed necessary to keep the relationships with the outside world going. As organizations such as Publish What You Pay, Global Witness and the Revenue Watch Institute are discovering, the resistance to increasing transparency or changing these institutions is equally strong from both the resource-rich state and the foreign corporations who are engaged with it as purveyors of mineral extraction.

The cases we have seen provide a window into the complex nexus of relationships that have developed between local elites and the external world, shaped by a history of colonial intervention that specified who could be assimilated and who not, followed by Cold War geopolitics, and finally a globalized network of rent extraction involving local elites as much as banks, multinational corporations and private security companies. The resource curse can be described as the long-term effects of local history and geography in external relationship with globalized interests coming into rent-seeking play over the extractive enterprise. The social consequences are indeed dependent on the pre-existing domestic institutions available to manage resources, but local agents as well as foreign interests enter into a dynamic political relationship with these institutions to exploit the situation for their needs.

References

Auty, R.M., ed., 2001. *Resource abundance and economic development*. Oxford: Oxford University Press.
Bayart, J.F., 2000. Africa in the world: a history of extraversion. *African Affairs*, 99 (395), 217.
Bayart, J.-F., 2009. *The state in Africa: the politics of the belly*. 2nd ed. Oxford: Polity.
Bender, G.J., 1987. The eagle and the bear in Angola. *The ANNALS of the American Academy of Political and Social Science*, 489, 123–132.
Cross, M., 1987. The political economy of colonial education: Mozambique, 1930–1975. *Comparative Education Review*, 31 (4), 550–569.
Frankel, J.A., 2010. *The natural resource curse: a survey*. NBER Working Paper 15836. Cambridge, MA: NBER.
Frynas, J.G. and Paulo, M., 2006. A new scramble for African oil? Historical, political, and business perspectives. *African Affairs*, 106 (423), 229.
Gowan, P., 1999. *The global gamble: Washington's Faustian bid for world dominance*. London: Verso.
Haber, S. and Menaldo, V.A., 2011. Do natural resources fuel authoritarianism? A reappraisal of the resource curse. *American Political Science Review*, 105 (1), 1–26.
Harvey, D., 2005. *A brief history of neoliberalism*. Oxford: Oxford University Press.
Karl, T.L., 1997. *The paradox of plenty: oil booms and petro-states*. Berkeley: University of California Press.
Karl, T.L., 2004. Oil-led development: social, political, and economic consequences. *In*: *Encyclopedia of energy*. New York: Elsevier, 661–672.
LeBillon, P., 2001. Angola's political economy of war: the role of oil and diamonds, 1975–2000. *African Affairs*, 100 (398), 55.
Minns, J., 2006. *The politics of developmentalism: the Midas states of Mexico, South Korea, and Taiwan*. New York: Palgrave Macmillan.
Riggirozzi, P., 2010. Social policy in post-neo-liberal Latin America: the cases of Argentina, Venezuela and Bolivia. *Development*, 53 (1), 70–76.
Robinson, J.A., et al., 2006. Political foundations of the resource curse. *Journal of Development Economics*, 79 (2), 447–468.
Ross, M., 2001. Does oil hinder democracy? *World Politics*, 53 (2), 325–361.
Rosser, A., 2006. *The political economy of the resource curse: a literature survey*. Sussex: IDS.
Sachs, J.D. and Warner, A.M., 2001. The curse of natural resources. *European Economic Review*, 45 (4–6), 827–838.
Schuyler, G.W., 1996. Perspectives on Venezuelan democracy. *Latin American Perspectives*, 23 (3), 10–29.
United States, 2011. Background note: Angola. Available from: http://www.state.gov/r/pa/ei/bgn/6619.htm [Accessed 3 July 2011].
Usui, N., 1997. Dutch disease and policy adjustments to the oil boom: a comparative study of Indonesia and Mexico. *Resources Policy*, 23 (4), 151–162.
Wolf, E.R., 1982. *Europe and the people without history*. Berkeley: University of California Press.

Energy and human ecology: a critical security approach

Shane Mulligan

Energy security has long been an important aspect of state security, but has only rarely been thought of as an environmental issue. Yet given our dependence on fossil fuels, a finite natural resource, energy security is fundamentally an ecological issue. Many observers see the impending 'peak' in world oil production as a greater threat to political order than climate change or terrorism, yet few governments are openly discussing peak oil, and there is virtually no international governance mechanism to address the issue. Building on the insights of Critical Security Studies, a case is made for reading peak oil as an important security issue for both importing and exporting states. The probable consequences of peak oil are examined in terms of three parameters that constitute 'security' issues – threats to freedom, uncertainty for the future, and the possibility of death – and it is shown that peak oil constitutes a compelling security threat in these terms. This formula suggests a novel perspective on energy security, approaching it as a problem of human ecology rather than merely one of state security.

Introduction

[A]side from military defense, there is no project of more central importance to national security and indeed independence as a sovereign nation than energy security. (Henry Kissinger cited in Stulberg 2007, p. 3)

The fundamental object of contention in the life-struggle, in the evolution of the organic world, is available energy. (Alfred Lotka 1922, p. 147)

Energy security has re-entered political discourse in recent years, although not with the urgency that accompanied the energy crisis of the 1970s. The inevitable decline of energy resources – fossil fuels, in particular – has been much neglected since the 'Limits to Growth' debates of the 1970s, while the problem of politically contrived scarcity ('the oil weapon') has faded as market forces have come to dominate distribution and supply. Yet as 'peak oil' appears to be on the horizon – perhaps soon to be followed by peak coal and peak natural gas – an emerging chorus is warning of the consequences of impending energy scarcity. This resurgent energy crisis is seen by some as likely to bring on a significant decline in human welfare and political stability, or what may constitute a 'collapse' of western or industrial civilization (Tainter 1990, Duncan 2005/06, Costanza et al. 2007, Homer-Dixon 2007).

Continuities and disruptions of the global order are a key theme of international relations, but images of ecologically induced systemic collapse have little place in scholarly international relations, and are notably absent from mainstream *security* literature. The scope of *environmental security* has generally been with regard to localized conflicts induced (in part) by scarcity of natural resources – which for most scholars seems to mean *renewable* resources (for example, Homer-Dixon 1999) – or tends toward conflicts based on acquisitive interests of states or rebel groups (Le Billon 2005). The study of *global* environmental (or ecological) security tends to see far greater threats in pollution effects than in resource constraints, and the focus today is largely on emissions from fossil fuels, rather than any concerns about these fuels 'running out' (Pirages 2005). On the other hand, the concept of *energy security* reflects a more traditional security focus on states and strategic concerns about resources, especially oil, in terms of state power and economic wealth (Kalicki and Goldwyn 2005). Moreover, energy security is marked by a focus on human agency, from recalcitrant states to manipulative market actors, while the discourse largely neglects questions of geology and the physical resource base. Fossil fuel depletion seems to have been largely bypassed in the security literature.

In what follows, I argue that the impending decline in available global net energy – what I refer to here as *energy descent* – might well be viewed as a serious threat to political order and human welfare, and that it therefore is highly amenable to securitization. Indeed, energy descent shares with other security issues a number of key characteristics that have emerged from the Critical Security Studies (CSS) literature. I proceed in four stages. First, I establish the meaning of energy descent, and survey some of the work suggesting that this condition is likely to occur in the near future. Second, I lay a foundation for looking at energy descent as a security issue, by outlining three major threads within the CSS literature: the themes of freedom, uncertainty, and death. Third, I show how energy descent represents a threat under each of these themes. Finally, I conclude with some reflections on the significance of an ecologically informed securitization of energy.

Energy descent: the end of an era?

Since the beginnings of the industrial revolution, human societies have steadily increased their consumption of energy, and especially fossil fuels, while this consumption has coincided with unprecedented increases in population and material well-being. The discovery of fossil fuels, and the development of technologies to exploit them, were decisive in enabling modernity, industrial society, and economic development as we know it (Keay 2007). As Vaclav Smil (1994, p. 1) suggests:

> the evolution of human societies has been dependent upon the conversion of ever larger amounts of ever more concentrated and more versatile forms of energy. From the perspective of natural science, both prehistoric human evolution and the course of history may be seen fundamentally as the quest for controlling greater energy stores and flows.

And Charlie Hall *et al.* (2003, p. 318) suggest that even 'the history of human culture can be viewed as the progressive development of new energy sources and their associated conversion technologies'. The density, portability, and profitability (in terms of net energy gain) of fossil fuels have been essential in making modern life, along with current population and consumption levels, possible. Fossil fuels are essential to modern agriculture, transportation and trade, even employment and the maintenance of family and social ties. They can thus be seen as an essential part of contemporary (industrial and globalized) human ecology, and especially of an economic system predicated on continued growth – growth that may well depend on continually increasing energy availability.

In recent years, however, a number of studies have emerged suggesting that the growth in the availability of energy, and especially of *net* energy, is drawing to a close. The most attention has been given to the impending 'peak' in global oil production (Goodstein 2004, Roberts 2004, Deffeyes 2005, Heinberg 2005), although other studies suggest that both coal (Energy Watch Group 2007) and natural gas (Darley 2004) may also soon reach their peak.[1] The concept of peak oil, first elaborated by the geologist M. King Hubbert in the 1950s, refers to a maximum rate of production – extraction, really – of crude oil from the earth. Hubbert's model is based on observations of a lag between the date of the peak in *discovery* of oil deposits in any oil field, and the peak in *production*. Discovery and production tend to rise from low levels more or less steadily to a peak, and then begin to decline. Subsequent to the natural peak, there is effectively no way to increase production to the peak levels: the decline in production in any given field (even a national territory) is generally irreversible.[2]

Historical data leave little doubt that Hubbert's model is accurate. The peak in discoveries in the continental USA, for example, occurred in the 1930s; US production peaked in 1970/71, and now stands at about half the peak rate. North Sea oil discoveries peaked in the early 1970s, while production peaked at the turn of the century (Heinberg 2005, pp. 97, 112). Indeed, according to the current President of ASPO, Kjell Aleklett (2005), some 50 of the top 64 oil-producing states have now peaked, including Mexico, Indonesia, Great Britain and Norway. A number of studies have estimated that the *global* oil production peak will occur sometime between now and 2020; and many believe that the peak has been reached, and that production will never exceed the levels reached in 2005–2008.

Since oil, natural gas and coal supply about 80% of the energy used in human industrial activity, the prospect of a near-term peak in production means that we may soon be facing an unprecedented *decline* in available energy, and moving into an era some refer to as 'energy descent' (Odum and Odum 2001, Holmgren 2003, Hopkins 2008). The general decline in net energy is due to the fact that, as readily accessible deposits of high-quality hydrocarbons are depleted, new supplies must be found in harder to reach areas (deep water, the Arctic), even while the quality of the resource declines (Alberta's tar sands). Both factors contribute to rising costs in terms of energy inputs, as more energy is used in the process of acquiring energy. Hence the tar sands require near the equivalent of one barrel of oil to produce four barrels of syncrude, leaving a *net* gain of only three barrels.[3]

Of course, a large part of net energy is dependent on technology, and many decry arguments for energy descent based on the claim that new discoveries, technological advances, and substitution in response to price incentives, will collectively offset the severity and impact of peak oil. This 'Cornucopian' view sees little reason to fear scarcity in essential resources, in large part because rising oil prices are sure to spur investments in substitutes (such as biofuels and unconventional oil) and conservation, as they did in the 1970s and 1980s. Yet the currently available alternatives are not cheap, and none are close to the scale, or share the characteristics, to make up for fossil energy use (Heinberg 2009). Moreover, these alternatives generally depend on higher prices, as well as higher energy inputs, per unit of energy: the available substitutes must command a larger portion of our economic surplus, and also larger energy inputs, thereby reducing the net energy available.

Moreover, as Prugh *et al.* (1999, p. 16) argue, there are inherent limits to the 'doctrine of infinite substitutability'. For ecological economists, nature is the foundation of economic activity, not simply another factor of production like labor and capital. Ecological economics recognizes the importance of energy (including net energy) in enabling economic activity, and not as simply a body of commodities that can be substituted at will. That 'natural capital' underpins human economies – and the ability of human societies to reproduce themselves over time – points to a fallacy in the politically popular notion of 'sustainable growth' in a finite world. The idea that consumption and population levels could stabilize at some (as yet undetermined) level in a steady-state economy, which might maintain itself in perpetuity, has been a popular theme among these scholars (Daly 1991). Yet even this may not be sustainable: as Georgescu-Roegen (1975, p. 4) argued, the 'crucial error [of the steady-state view] consists in not seeing that not only growth, but also a zero-growth state, nay, even a declining state which does not converge toward annihilation, cannot exist forever in a finite environment'. Yet as current human population and habits are already degrading resources at an unsustainable rate, it may be that we have already entered the realm of 'overshoot' – the emergence from which may well entail a sharp reduction of human numbers and activities (Catton 1980, Meadows *et al*. 2004, p. 5).

The debate over limits to growth is especially contentious with peak oil, in part because 'we heard this before' in the 1970s. That energy crisis, however, was largely political, and when the political problems were managed (for a time), the crisis dissolved. But the geological or ecological factors that left the United States (especially) vulnerable to the oil shocks did not change: despite the intense application of technology and capital, the United States decline from the 1970/71 peak has not abated. The Cornucopian vision was sorely tested, moreover, as the global oil price tripled from 2005 to 2008: despite massive investments into unconventional sources like Alberta's tar sands and biofuels, global production of 'liquids' remained flat for almost four years. According to data from the US Energy Information Administration, the monthly oil production peak of May 2005 was not exceeded again until July 2008, after which a decline is evident. Many believe that 2005–2008 represents the plateau – a blunted peak – of global oil production. Of course, the global economic crisis changes the context, and it may be some time before *demand* reaches that peak level again. Yet if supply is not forthcoming, it will be only the price that actually rises, and further economic contraction is likely. It may be that the limits to growth have now been reached, as the peak in available energy constrains human economic and reproductive activities (Hall and Day 2009). If so, as one popular website boldly states, 'Civilization as we know it is coming to an end soon'.[4] At the very least, energy descent suggests the possibility of serious disruptions within our modern integrated system of food and materials manufacturing, finance, and government services (including security). While images of collapse, 'die-off,' and the decline of civilization are hardly the stuff of public policy or even security studies, it is remarkable that peak oil (gas, coal) have been absent from the principal discourses that might be useful in preparing for the threat.

Securitization: the making of a security issue

There is of course no inherent reason why resource degradation, energy descent, or even the collapse of civilization should constitute a security concern. Security is not an objective category, but a form of discourse that enables (and insists upon) shared understandings of 'threats'. As Michael Williams (2003, p. 513) argues, '[i]ssues become "securitized", treated as security issues, through these speech-acts which do not simply describe an existing security situation, but bring it into being as a security situation by successfully representing it as such'. Energy descent must *be made into* a security issue if it is to be understood as one. The success of a securitizing move can be measured by the degree to which the relevant audience comes to accept the issue as a threat, and thus becomes willing to act upon it, or to accept or demand the state's use of exceptional measures to deal with it. Success may depend on a number of factors, including the quality of the representation of the threat, the epistemic or political authority of the agents who make the securitizing claim, and the empirical evidence that the threat is significant enough that a security response – entailing significant state resources and a claim for exceptional measures, including suspension of normal operating procedures – is appropriate (Balzacq 2005, Stritzel 2007).

Energy descent has not been taken up within the principal security literature. To what extent, then, is it susceptible to securitization? It surely fits within the broadened agenda of security studies – indeed, energy is relevant to a range of security issue-areas identified by the Copenhagen School: environmental, military–political, economic and societal security. But this tells us little in itself about how energy scarcity or descent qualifies as a security issue. As Huysmans (1998, p. 227) asks: 'what makes it possible to speak of 'security' in relation to very different questions?' Are there core or essential elements that make issues worthy of the attention and resources dedicated to security? While any effort to delineate the scope of the concept is limiting, I will here pursue three main ideas that circulate through much of the recent CSS literature: questions of freedom, uncertainty, and death.

Freedom, and especially freedom of choice, has long been associated with security. As Richard Ullman suggested, the security concerns of states encompass any situation or condition that 'threatens significantly to narrow the range of policy choices available to the government of a state or to private, nongovernmental entities ... within the state' (Ullman 1983, p. 133). Freedom itself – or the perception of freedom – is the quality that is threatened. For sovereign states, freedom may be best seen in terms of autonomy in making policy decisions, as autonomy is part of what it means to be sovereign (Litfin 1997). While traditional security concerns saw the threat of lost autonomy as one arising primarily from foreign (military) interference, the expanded security agenda allows that other factors and conditions – migration, disease, environmental factors – can similarly impact on states' ability to freely make policy.

Freedom from exploitation and repression, or 'emancipation', is also a central concept in CSS (Alker 2005), as well as in discourses of human security (Brauch 2008). Ken Booth, in his formulation of the Aberystwyth approach, argues for a conception of security in terms of 'life choices and chances'. Security thus refers to something beyond mere survival: 'Security ... is a means by which individuals and collectivities can invent and reinvent different ideas about being human' (Booth 2006, p. 23). The kind of freedom Booth argues for has much to do with human rights and liberal notions of the rights of citizens and collectives. It encompasses notions of autonomy, and even of 'power', in being free of (or able to overcome) constraints that might prevent one from freely choosing one's actions.

But from the perspective of the Copenhagen School, security takes on quite the opposite form: securitization entails the removal of an issue from the realm of 'normal' (that is,) politics, and into the realm of the exception, of sovereign prerogative. Action toward a security issue may entail the suspension of normal rules, or even an authoritarian approach that eschews deliberation or democratic participation (Williams 2003). Securitization is thus a tool that enables states to take exceptional measures, including repression or the suspension of the public freedoms considered normal in the West; this contrast with liberal expectations may reflect a rather Euro-centric vision of securitization and normality (Vuori 2008), but, as we will see, it is one with which the threat of energy scarcity/descent resonates.

A second feature common to much of the security discourse is the issue of life, or quality of life, and the specter of decline or even death. To cite Ullman (1983, p. 133) again, a threat to security 'threatens drastically or over a relatively brief span of time to degrade the quality of life for the inhabitants of a state'. This conception of security, or perhaps more precisely, of the *effects* of (in)security, was of course well stated by Thomas Hobbes in his trenchant (and durable) justification for the state. Hobbes argued that, in the absence of a strong state and the security it provides, 'the life of man' could only be 'solitary, poore, nasty, brutish, and short'. The range of security concerns in recent decades generally appeals, in one way or another, to concerns about welfare, whether due to military or terrorist activity, economic or cultural dislocation due to 'foreigners', health threats, or ecological decline. The task of security providers, in this view, is to uphold welfare, to protect a population from factors that threaten to degrade the quality of life.

This is nowhere more clear than in the association of security with survival itself. Indeed, the 'continuall feare, and danger of violent death', was what made life in the state of nature so utterly insecure. Security is in demand where there is a threat to life itself: the securitization of any issue involves its representation as something that threatens the very existence or identity of the subject of security, as an 'existential threat' to the state (or the human subject). '[T]he survival of the ... basic political unit ... is the key' (Wæver 1995, p. 52). Security, as Jef Huysmans (1998) describes, stands in as a 'thick signifier', mediating relations between life and death: security allows us to hold death at bay, or at least offers a discursive hook that enables us to discuss the terms through which death might be held at bay. According to Huysmans (1998, pp. 235–237), part of the effect of security is thus in offering a remedy (of sorts) to an *epistemological* fear, a fear of the unknown, the human fear of the 'void' that accompanies (the idea of) death.

This points to a third common feature of contemporary security concerns: the notion of uncertainty. Uncertainty, like security, is concerned with the future: security enables us to maintain certain *expectations* of that future. 'Security is about the future or fears about the future ... It is about control, certainty, and predictability in an uncertain world' (Dalby 2002, p. 163). The ability to project our will into the future, to control or influence future events or conditions via current actions, invites reflections on the concept of power and its longstanding relation to security.

The future that security enables is one in which we know who we are. Identity is increasingly seen, or portrayed, as something that needs to be protected against threats from the 'other': security is thus aimed at maintaining (a people's or state's) identity, whether in a material or relational sense (Mitzen 2006). While critics suggest this reification of identity contradicts the realities of historical human population dynamics, identity formation is nevertheless a powerful political tool, and security (namely, the threat of the other) plays an important part in creating and maintaining such identities: the discursive construction of threats is also a way of *fixing* identities (CASE Collective 2006, pp. 453–454). Thus identity concerns reflect another thread of the security fabric, intertwined with the concern for certainty: the notion of continuity, of maintenance into the future, of keeping a coherent identity or maintaining relationships in the face of change. Security is in this sense a matter of keeping things (at least roughly) as they are (McSweeney 1996, Mitzen 2006). States seek to maintain themselves and their operations, and to avoid dismantling, dismemberment, or conquest: for such changes threaten a further loss of power and control. Elites face security concerns when their relative positions are threatened and their futures less certain. And those who would change the *status quo* are sufficiently insecure that an uncertain future may be preferential to the certainty of their current condition.

These three security themes – freedom, life and death, and uncertainty – by no means cover the spectrum of contemporary ideas on security, but they do represent key concepts that help to unite some of those concerns labeled 'security'. As descriptors of the general nature of threats, they help to illustrate what it is that security is expected to provide, avoid, offset, or overcome. We can now turn to the question of how the decline of available energy invokes these concerns of freedom, uncertainty, and death.

Energy and/as security

Freedom

By many measures, the quality of life enjoyed in the industrialized world is unprecedented in human history. It is a life of abundance, and this abundance enables a wide range of luxuries, and a wide range of choices, from the shoes we wear to the cars we drive to our places of work and residence. But perhaps most importantly, it frees many of us from the burdens of providing for human needs through physical human labor.

> It is difficult to overestimate the degree to which the use of energy and the manipulation of materials has reduced the crushing burdens of physical work, lessened the concentration of human effort on food production, freed men for other pursuits, and extended to millions a wealth and opportunity formerly enjoyed by the smallest elite. (Ward and Dubos 1972, p. 16)

Thanks to the availability of fossil energy, we live like kings; indeed, Ward and Dubos estimated in 1972 that the average American has at his/her disposal the labor of some 400 'energy slaves' (a term coined by Buckminster Fuller to express the 'muscle power' embodied in modern machines). Much as with human slavery, the institution of energy slavery enables a degree of personal freedom for the masters that would be impossible in its absence.

These personal freedoms are not only embodied in the life expectations of many westerners, but also in the political ideology of liberalism. This is more than a coincidence, as liberalism is itself an ideology of abundance. In his seminal text, William Ophuls (1977, p. 9) suggests that 'virtually all the philosophies, values, and institutions typical of modern society are the luxuriant fruit of an era of apparently endless abundance', and argues that these cannot be expected to last beyond those conditions.

> Under conditions of ecological scarcity the individual, possessing an inalienable right to pursue happiness as he defines it and exercising his liberty in a basically laissez-faire system, will inevitably produce the ruin of the commons. Accordingly, the individualistic basis of society, the concept of inalienable rights, the purely self-defined pursuit of happiness, liberty as maximum freedom of action, and laissez-faire itself all become problematic, requiring major modification or even abandonment if we wish to avert inexorable environmental degradation and eventual extinction as a civilization. Certainly, democracy as we know it cannot conceivably survive. (Ophuls 1977, p. 9)

While Ophuls' argument may tend toward hyperbole, it represents a widely held view that what is necessary in order to avert catastrophe is the heavy hand of enlightened rulers. (One might argue, of course, that the loss of liberties, and of democracy as we know it, represents another kind of catastrophe.) The related question is whether governing institutions will be *compelled* to implement a range of coercive measures, and to curtail personal freedoms, in the interests of maintaining some degree of order under ecological constraints (Hardin 1968).

In a more profound sense, perhaps, the impending peaks in fossil fuel supply are not only a geophysical constraint, but also a psychological one. That is, we have long known that fossil fuels are limited, but we have continued to act as if they are not. Moreover, we have by and large pretended that the decline cannot follow – as John Peet (1992, p. 155) has noted:

> the standard politico-economic world view *denies the possibility* that humankind will not be able to achieve any technological feat that may be needed [to overcome energy constraints], and in the meantime, resources are being used without any thought for the future. (Emphasis added)

There is of course no end of debate on the inevitability of energy descent, and no shortage of alternative energy proposals, some of which are widely seen to offer a (more or less) easy way out of an energy dilemma. The history of cold fusion, for example, is a modern day quest for the perpetual motion machine (although under a different physic). Whether breeder reactors, shale oil, or large-scale solar collection can provide a way forth on the scale (and in the timeline) needed remains to be seen, but it is hardly reassuring that, even while certain technologies have been known for decades, it has not been economically feasible to develop them (Smil 2008). The ability to deny that an era of human history is ending, then, may be one of the more disturbing losses of the coming energy descent.

Uncertainty

But is all this really assured? The debate between Malthusians and Cornucopians shows the controversy with regard to our energy future. Ironically, the two sides in this debate seem remarkably certain in their estimations and expectations, at least in terms of whether or not the peak is coming, is a relevant concern, and indeed what kinds of conditions are likely to follow (Bardi 2009). Peak oil (let alone peak energy) is in many ways rife with uncertainty, from unreliable data (much of the reserves data are proprietary or even secret) to upcoming technological changes (ditto, and add the incentive of entrepreneurs and politicians to exaggerate potentials), and with regard to the date of the peak itself: most estimates range from 2005 to 2020, but some go to 2030 or beyond (Government Accountability Office 2007, p. 13, Fig. 5).

Even granted that peak oil is imminent, does this tell us much about what to expect in the future? For it is not only the timing of the peak that is uncertain (and contested), but the implications and effects as well. As Lester Brown (2008, p. 21) suggests: 'when [oil] production turns downward, it will be a seismic economic event, creating a world unlike any we have known during our lifetimes'. The Hirsch report, commissioned for the US Department of Energy in 2005, similarly argued that the consequences of not preparing for a peak would be 'unprecedented':

> The world has never faced a problem like this. Without massive mitigation more than a decade before the fact, the problem will be pervasive and will not be temporary. Previous energy transitions (wood to coal and coal to oil) were gradual and evolutionary. Oil peaking will be abrupt and revolutionary. (Hirsch *et al.* 2005, p. 64)

Thus even among those who feel certain that the peak is imminent, the post-peak future remains something of a void; there is no historical precedent. One US Army study admits of uncertainty, but suggests possibilities:

> Peak oil is at hand with low availability growth for the next 5 to 10 years. Once worldwide petroleum production peaks, geopolitics and market economics will result in even more significant price increases and security risks. To guess where this is all going to take us ... would be too speculative. Oil wars are certainly not out of the question. (Westervelt and Fournier 2005, p. 1)

It is widely held that energy descent poses a profound threat to the maintenance of complex systems like the state and global commerce, and associate it with some form of collapse in these systems, or in 'civilization' more generally (Tainter 1990, Homer-Dixon 2007). The specific effects of energy descent, however, are hard to envision precisely. A number of observers see the current economic slowdown as at least partially due to peak oil (if only via the oil price shock of 2008), while a more ecological view sees this decline as fully in line with expectations of energy scarcity (Hall and Day 2009, Hamilton 2009). Kenneth Deffeyes suggested in the 2005 film *The End of Suburbia* that the peak would result in 'ten billion dollars wiped from the stock market; two million American jobs GONE; state and municipal budget surpluses GONE'. (That his predictions are now headlines might suggest something about both the current economic condition, and peak oil 'prophets'.)

Whatever form collapse takes, it is likely to impact on the production, delivery and consumption of basic goods and services, including food and 'security'; a decline in population is widely expected (Meadows *et al.* 1972, Catton 1980, Tainter 1990). Yet what follows collapse – because something will – still remains an open question. Does collapse represent a state of widespread disorder that continues into the distant future? Will it affect all states, or will only some be losers in a negative sum game (Gurr 1985)? Does it entail, as Klare (2007, p. 7) suggests, the repudiation of international and domestic norms, as 'the struggle over energy' comes to 'override all other considerations' both nationally and internationally? Does it mean the rapid dissolution of complex systems in a catabolic collapse, leading to a rapid shutdown of electrical grids, transportation systems, commerce, and public order (Kunstler 2005)? Does collapse look like the Soviet Union in 1990? Rwanda in 1994? Zimbabwe in 2008? Or the USA in 2010? Will the future resemble the bloodied streets of Baghdad, or the barren anarchic world of *Mad Max*, or an eco-utopia where children ask 'Mommy, what was traffic?' If '[c]ivilization as we know it is coming to an end soon', well what then?

The uncertainties surrounding this future are exacerbated, it seems, by the paucity of attention given to the threat of peak oil by governments, and the apparent lack of preparation at the national or global level. As George Monbiot wrote – with some incredulity – in *The Guardian* (14 April 2009), politicians seem to hold it as 'a badge of honour' that *they have no plan* to deal with peak oil. 'The ... possibility of a huge, multifaceted failure of some substantial part of industrial civilization is so completely outside the understanding of our leaders that we are almost totally unprepared for it' (Hall and Day 2009, p. 237). Then again, it is hard to say how we could prepare, given the uncertainty in events and likely reactions. As Georgescu-Roegen argues:

> anyone who believes that he can draw a blueprint for the ecological salvation of the human species does not understand the nature of evolution, or even of history – which is the permanent struggle in continuously novel forms, not that of a predictable, controllable physico-chemical process, such as boiling an egg or launching a rocket to the moon. (Georgescu-Roegen 1975)

The prevailing notion with the post-peak world is one of uncertainty, and the human response to conditions of scarcity is a matter of much conjecture, hope, and attempts at conversion. We surely need to maintain some hope among the resounding tone of doom: but hope is neither certainty nor security.

Death

Perhaps the most profound uncertainty, however, is the epistemic 'void' represented by (the fear of) death (Huysmans 1998, pp. 235–237). The expectations of energy descent – uncertain as they are – clearly invite such fears, from the prospect of resource wars to the collapse of economies, food supplies, social orders, and even world views. The degree to which our daily comforts are indebted to energy is one thing. The dependence of our lifestyles, indeed of the ability of our economic system to support life itself, is also at issue. The economic importance of energy, and especially oil, is hard to overstate. Virtually all modern transportation is oil-driven, which makes it essential for employment, manufacturing and commercial activities, emergency services and social networks; a wide range of essential and non-essential products (pharmaceuticals, cosmetics, plastics) are manufactured from a petroleum base; and, along with natural gas, oil is a major input into our energy intensive agricultural system, especially through the manufacture of nitrogen fertilizers, extensive transportation, and (increasingly) its use in irrigation. The use of fossil energy to provide that most essential form of human energy, food, is viewed by some as the Achilles heel of fossil fuel dependence (Pfeiffer 2006). It is generally accepted that modern agricultural practices consume about 10 calories of fossil energy for every calorie of food energy produced (which is why many biofuels are a losing proposition). The ability of the human ecological system to produce sufficient food to meet the needs of over 6.5 billion humans (and the desires of many) may well be tested in the face of energy scarcity.

As Richard Dawkins (1995, p. 132) notes, the fossil fuel era contains the seeds of its own demise: '[i]f there is ever a time of plenty this very fact will automatically lead to an increase in population until the natural state of starvation and misery is restored'. Thomas Malthus is most famed for his claim that food production would be unable to keep up with population increases, but concerns about the ability of humans to capture enough energy to maintain population levels (let alone growth) was widespread among 'energy ecologists' in the 1800s (Bramwell 1988, pp. 64–91). William Catton (1980) argued that fossil fuels represent a wealth of 'ghost acreage' that provides the stored solar energy needed to sustain human numbers. Death is a pervasive theme in the ecological literature as well, and especially the literature of ecological collapse. 'The specter haunting scientists like [Rachel] Carson was death – the death of birds, of ecosystems, of nature itself, and, because of our dependence on nature, the death of humans as well' (Worster 1994, p. 353). It is the specter of death, perhaps more than any other, that makes ecological decline – and particularly energy descent – unavoidably security issues.

In more traditional security terms, concerns over the *survival* of states invite rumination on the prospects of the *death* of states and even civilizations.

Collapse scenarios frequently invoke the history of disappeared civilizations – from Easter Island to the Roman Empire and the Mayan civilization – rather than 'conquered' ones. But history is dynamic, and the death of one civilization will often sow the seeds of the future. The Roman Empire collapsed, but its language and laws live on, and its capital city has remained a vital cultural centre for millennia. The Indus valley civilization ended – and in doing so, began anew (Lawler 2008). The prospect of the death or collapse of civilization, however, reinforces our uncertainties – and insecurities – regarding the post-peak future.

Conclusion: on the ethics of securitization

To show the susceptibility of energy descent to securitization is not necessarily to endorse this approach. Securitization carries consequences, and as Wæver has argued, this puts 'an ethical question at the feet of analysts, decision-makers and political activists alike: why do you call this a security issue? What are the implications of doing this – or not doing it?' (cited in CASE Collective 2006, p. 474). As noted, securitization may entail a number of dubious effects, including the suspension of the 'normal rules' of the game, even a shift toward a more authoritarian politics that itself threatens the democratic institutions that have come to be so highly valued in the west (Wæver 1995, Williams 2003). Yet it is far from clear that the politics of energy actually subscribe to, or are much circumscribed by, the norms of international society at all. Coercive practices, the abrogation of contracts, and breaches of international law (including the UN Charter's prohibition against the threat or use of force) already seem to be very much a part of the energy game (Peters 2004) Some states are already using scarcity and supply monopolies to pressure others, as with Russia's natural gas politics (Stulberg 2007). China's oil diplomacy seems largely immune to human rights concerns, while resource wars are, according to many, already well underway. One might argue, then, that the securitization of energy is already well entrenched, and no further securitization is needed or likely to have much effect. The ethics of securitization thus becomes somewhat moot.

On the other hand, the possibility that states are already pursuing policies to deal with peak oil, while not discussing the reasons, suggests that this security issue – unlike terrorism, drugs and other issues – has been deemed something of a state secret. This may be a reflection of the secretive, exceptional, 'Schmittian' approach to politics that seems to be emerging in the twenty-first century (Williams 2003), and may be explained, to some extent, by looking on current trends in global politics as *responses* to the threats posed by energy descent. The high-level deception surrounding the invasion of Iraq, for instance, fits this model well, despite that the fact that 'energy security' was not widely invoked to justify the aggression. The claims of security threats demand exceptional responses, and 'Exceptionalism is from the outset fiendishly entangled in an authoritarian, decisionist politics that declares exceptional conditions (such as a state of emergency) in order to give legitimate authority to contentious policies and practices' (CASE Collective 2006, pp. 465–466). But even this may hold our expectations too high in terms of disclosure: 'The strategic or pragmatic action of discourse ... operates at the level of persuasion and uses various artifacts (metaphors, emotions, stereotypes, gestures, silence, and *even lies*) to reach its goals ... (Balzacq 2005, pp. 172–173; emphasis added). Why should we expect states to admit the true (security) thinking behind their actions, or to alert populations to urgent security concerns? If scholars must wait to be told about security threats – indeed, if our method *requires* discursive realization of security issues – then perhaps we are not really well equipped to analyze issues of government secrecy and the deliberate misrepresentation of issues and actions, which is an important component of governing effectively. If this is the case with peak oil and energy descent, then the open discussion of these issues might in fact undermine the secretive approach to security, while enhancing the discursive one.

Acknowledgements

An earlier version of this paper was presented at the CPSA Annual Conference, Carleton University, Ottawa, 27–29 May 2009.

Notes

1. Because natural gas is not easily transported outside pipelines, the concern here may be more with regional (rather than global) peaks.
2. This is not an absolute, of course. 'Above ground factors' sometimes reduce production well before geological constraints do (that is, Iraq), while sufficient investment and technology may rejuvenate a particular oilfield (at least temporarily).
3. Most of the energy inputs into tar sand are currently in the form of natural gas.
4. Matt Savinar, available from: www.lifeaftertheoilcrash.net [Accessed 1 March 2010].

References

Aleklett, K., 2005. The oil supply tsunami alert. ASPO, 25 April. Available from: www.energybulletin.net/node/5655 [Accessed 16 February 2009].
Alker, H., 2005. Emancipation in the critical security studies project. *In*: K. Booth, ed. *Critical security studies and world politics*. Boulder, CO: Lynne Rienner, 189–213.
Balzacq, T., 2005. The three faces of securitization: political agency, audience and context. *European Journal of International Relations*, 11 (2), 171–201.
Bardi, U., 2009. Peak oil: the four stages of a new idea. *Energy*, 34, 323–326.
Booth, K., 2006. *Theory of world security*. Cambridge: Cambridge University Press.
Bramwell, A., 1988. *Ecology in the twentieth century*. New Haven, CT: Yale University Press.
Brauch, H.G., 2008. Conceptualising the environmental dimension of human security in the UN. *International Social Science Journal*, 59 (1), 19–48.
Brown, L.R., 2008. *Plan B 3.0: mobilizing to save civilization*. London: Norton.

CASE Collective, 2006. Critical approaches to security in Europe: a networked manifesto *Security Dialogue*, 37 (4), 343–387.
Catton, W., 1980. *Overshoot: the ecological basis of revolutionary change*. Chicago: University of Illinois.
Costanza, R., Graumlich, L.J. and Steffen, W, eds, 2007. *Sustainability or collapse? An integrated history and future of people on earth*. Cambridge, MA: The MIT Press.
Dalby, S., 2002. *Environmental security*. Minneapolis, MN: University of Minnesota Press.
Daly, H.E., 1991. *Steady-state economics*. Washington, DC: Island Press.
Darley, J., 2004. *High noon for natural gas: the new energy crisis*. White River Junction, VT: Chelsea Green.
Dawkins, R., 1995. *River out of Eden: a Darwinian view of life*. New York: Basic Books.
Deffeyes, K., 2005. *Beyond oil: the view from Hubbert's Peak*. New York: Hill and Wang.
Duncan, R., 2005/06. The Olduvai theory. *The Social Contract*, Winter. Available from: http://www.thesocialcontract.com/artman2/publish/tsc1602/article_1362.shtml
Energy Watch Group, 2007. Coal: resources and future production. EWG-Series No. 1/07. Available from: http://www.energywatchgroup.org/fileadmin/global/pdf/EWG_Report_Coal_10-07-2007ms.pdf
Georgescu-Roegen, N., 1975. Energy and economic myths. *Southern Economic Journal*, 41 (3). Available from: www.eoearth.org/article/energy_and_economic_myths_(historical)
Goodstein, D., 2004. *Out of gas: the end of the age of oil*. New York: Norton.
Government Accountability Office, 2007. Crude oil: uncertainty about future oil supply makes it important to develop a strategy for addressing a peak and decline in oil production. GAO-07-283, 28 February. Available from: http://www.gao.gov/products/GAO-07-283
Greene, G (Director) and Silverthorn, B. (Producer), 2005. The End of Suburbia [film].
Gurr, T.R., 1985. On the political consequences of scarcity and economic decline. *International Studies Quarterly*, 29 (1), 51–75.
Hall, C.A.S. and Day, J.W., Jr, 2009. Revisiting the limits to growth after peak oil. *American Scientist*, 97 (May–June), 230–237.
Hall, C., et al., 2003. Hydrocarbons and the evolution of human culture. *Nature*, 426 (20 November), 318–322.
Hamilton, J., 2009. Causes and consequences of the oil shock of 2007–08. *Brookings Papers on Economic Activity*, Spring. Available from: www.brookings,edu/economics/bpea/bpea.aspx
Hardin, G., 1968. The tragedy of the commons. *Science*, 162, 1243–1248.
Heinberg, R., 2005. *The party's over: oil, war, and the fate of industrial societies*. Gabriola Island: New Society.
Heinberg, R., 2009. *Searching for a miracle: net energy limits and the fate of industrial society*. International Forum on Globalization/Post Carbon Institute, September. Available from: http://www.postcarbon.org/new-site-files/Reports/Searching_for_a_Miracle_web10nov09.pdf [Accessed 30 November 2009].
Hirsch, R.L., Bezdek, R. and Wendling, R., 2005. *Peaking of world oil production: impacts, mitigation, and risk management*. Washington, DC: US Department of Energy.
Holmgren, D., 2003. *Permaculture: principles & pathways beyond sustainability*. Halifax: Nimbus.
Homer-Dixon, T., 1999. *Environment, scarcity, and violence*. Princeton, NJ: Princeton University Press.
Homer-Dixon, T., 2007. *The upside of down: catastrophe, creativity and the renewal of civilization*. Toronto: Alfred Knopf.

Hopkins, R., 2008. *The transition handbook: from oil dependency to local resilience.* White River Junction, VT: Chelsea Green.
Huysmans, J., 1998. Security! What do you mean? From concept to thick signifier. *European Journal of International Relations*, 4 (2), 226–255.
Kalicki, J.H. and Goldwyn, D.L., eds, 2005. *Energy and security: toward a new foreign policy strategy.* Baltimore, MD: Johns Hopkins University Press.
Keay, M., 2007. Energy: the long view, October. Oxford Institute of Energy Studies, SP 20.
Klare, M.T., 2007. Beyond the age of petroleum. *The Nation*, 12 November. Available from: http://www.thenation.com/doc/20071112/klare
Kunstler, J.H., 2005. *The long emergency: surviving the converging catastrophes of the twenty-first century.* New York: Atlantic Monthly Press.
Lawler, A., 2008. Indus collapse: the end or the beginning of an Asian culture? *Science*, 320, 1281–1283.
Le Billon, P., ed., 2005. *The geopolitics of resource wars: resource dependence, governance and violence.* London: Frank Cass.
Litfin, K.T., 1997. Sovereignty in world ecopolitics. *Mershon International Studies Review*, 41, 167–204.
Lotka, A.J., 1922. Contribution to the energetics of evolution. *Proceedings of the National Academy of Science*, 8, 147–151.
McSweeney, B., 1996. Identity and security: Buzan and the Copenhagen school. *Review of International Studies*, 22 (1), 81–93.
Meadows, D.H., Meadows, D.L., Randers, J. and Behrens, W.W., 1972. *The limits to growth.* New York: Universe Books.
Meadows, D., Randers, J. and Meadows, D. 2004. *Limits to growth: the 30-year update.* White River Junction, VT: Chelsea Green.
Mitzen, J., 2006. Ontological security in world politics. state identity and the security dilemma. *European Journal of International Relations*, 12 (3), 341–370.
Mulligan, S., 2010. Energy, environment, and security: critical links in a post-peak world. *Global Environmental Politics*, 10 (4), 79–100.
Odum, H.T. and Odum, E.C., 2001. *The prosperous way down.* Boulder, CO: University of Colorado Press.
Ophuls, W., 1977. *Ecology and the politics of scarcity: prologue to a political theory of the steady state.* San Francisco, CA: W.H. Freeman.
Peet, J., 1992. *Energy and the ecological economics of sustainability.* Washington, DC: Island Press.
Peters, S., 2004. Coercive western energy security strategies: 'resource wars' as a new threat to global security. *Geopolitics*, 9 (1), 187–212.
Pfeiffer, D.A., 2006. *Eating fossil fuels: oil, food and the coming crisis in agriculture.* Gabriola Island, BC: New Society Publishers.
Pirages, D., 2005. From limits to growth to ecological security. *In*: D. Pirages and K. Cousins, eds. *From resource scarcity to ecological security: exploring new limits to growth.* Cambridge, MA: The MIT Press, 1–20.
Prugh, T., et al., 1999. *Natural capital and human economic survival.* 2nd ed. Boca Raton, FL: Lewis Publishers.
Roberts, P., 2004. *The end of oil: on the edge of a perilous new world.* Boston: Houghton Mifflin.
Smil, V., 1994. *Energy in world history.* Boulder, CO: Westview.
Smil, V., 2008. Moore's curse and the great energy delusion. *The American*, 2 (6). Available from: www.american.com
Stritzel, H., 2007. Towards a theory of securitization: Copenhagen and beyond. *European Journal of International Relations*, 13 (3), 357–383.

Stulberg, A.N., 2007. *Well-oiled diplomacy: strategic manipulation and Russia's energy statecraft in Eurasia*. Albany, NY: SUNY Press.
Tainter, J.A., 1990. *The collapse of complex societies*. Cambridge: Cambridge University Press.
Ullman, R., 1983. Redefining security. *International Security*, 8 (1), 129–153.
Vuori, J.A., 2008. Illocutionary logic and strands of securitization: applying the theory of securitization to the study of non-democratic political orders. *European Journal of International Relations*, 14 (1), 65–99.
Ward, B. and Dubos, R.J., 1972. *Only one Earth: the care and maintenance of a small plane*. Norton.
Wæver, O., 1995. Securitization and desecuritization. *In*: R.D. Lipschutz, ed. *On security*. New York: Columbia University Press, 46–86.
Westervelt, E.T. and Fournier, D., 2005. *Energy trends and implications for U.S. Army installations*, September. Engineering Research and Development Center, ERDC/CERL TN-05-1.
Williams, M.C., 2003. Words, images, enemies: securitization in international politics. *International Studies Quarterly*, 47 (4), 511–531.
Worster, D., 1994. *Nature's economy: a history of ecological ideas*. 2nd ed. Cambridge: Cambridge University Press.

Confronting risks: regulatory responsibility and nuclear energy

Steve Vanderheiden

The imperatives of contemporary environmental governance require the minimization and/or the redistribution of risk among persons, peoples, and generations, subject to various tradeoffs and based in several key principles of risk distribution. Especially in cases involving manufactured risks, justice requires that states and societies protect their vulnerable from avoidable anthropogenic risk, and this imperative forms the basis for regulatory responsibility. The ethical issues surrounding risk as they apply to nuclear energy, including those inherent in expanded nuclear development as well as in continued reliance upon non-nuclear sources of electrical generation, are examined. Of particular concern is comparison of the risks associated with nuclear energy and those related to reliance upon carbon-intensive energy sources, including issues of justice in the distribution of risk and the legitimacy of involuntarily imposed risks, such that the potential costs and benefits associated with each of these risk-laden options can be meaningfully compared and the proposal to expand nuclear power as a climate policy tool critically assessed.

Introduction

Ulrich Beck (1992) identifies the 'risk society' as resulting from the fact that human societies must increasingly be organized around distributing risks, including the *external risks* that arise without direct human causation (for example, from earthquakes or other 'natural disasters') as well as the *manufactured risks* that arise from human choices (for example, from pollution or other anthropogenic environmental hazards). Such risks to human health and welfare cannot be eliminated entirely, but they can be managed, and the threats that they pose can be reduced and redistributed. Risk, Beck (1992, p. 19) argues, is '*ascribed* by civilization' rather than being the product of good or bad fortune, and has overtaken scarcity as the core concern of modern social conflict such that the 'new paradigm' of risk society turns on the question: 'How can the risks and hazards systematically produced as part of modernization be prevented, minimized, dramatized, or channeled?' Indeed, contemporary environmental governance has largely become an imperative of minimizing and fairly distributing risk among persons, peoples, and generations, subject to various tradeoffs and normative principles. Where manufactured risks are involved, it is now regarded as an issue of basic justice that the vulnerable be protected from risk generated by human activities, forming the core imperative of regulatory responsibility.

Foremost among current challenges for environmental governance is anthropogenic climate change, which threatens manifold and momentous social and environmental disruptions unless human societies can significantly reduce their greenhouse gas emissions. While there remain considerable uncertainties concerning the relationships between increasing atmospheric concentrations of greenhouse gasses and the various consequences that have been predicted by climate scientists (Intergovernmental Panel on Climate Change [IPCC] 2007b), there remains little genuine doubt that the climatic instability caused by human dependence upon fossil fuels for energy constitutes a critical manufactured risk that demands a concerted and far-reaching human response, if one that defies conventional risk analysis (Pidgeon and Butler 2009). Most agree that this response must include a mix of conservation policy efforts designed to reduce demand for energy along with development of alternative sources of energy to replace carbon-intensive fossil fuels in electricity production and transport sectors. As national governments and environmental non-governmental organizations grapple with the challenges posed by climate change and weigh the policy options for minimizing its harmful consequences, and despite the March 2011 Fukushima Daiichi meltdown, one controversial policy option has reasserted itself into the debate over domestic and global energy and environmental policy: the proposal for significantly expanded reliance upon nuclear power.

The 'nuclear option' in climate policy is controversial for familiar reasons: it generates a set of manufactured risks that are comparable with – if also different from in some practically and conceptually significant ways – those posed by climate change itself. Both involve potentially grave risks for current and future generations, but with their respective risks distributed across different populations and entailing varying levels of probability and uncertainty. Climate change involves moderate and widely dispersed damage estimates at high levels of probability, with uncertainty about the range and extent of impacts, with both probability and severity increasing in a linear fashion with the increase in atmospheric greenhouse concentrations. By contrast, a reinvigorated nuclear energy program involves significantly less probable but more intensified, focused, and certain harm to fewer persons, and with a binary rather than linear risk scale, as risky outcomes either occur or they do not. Some of those threatened by climate change would also be placed at greater risk by expanded reliance upon nuclear energy, but the policy dilemma primarily involves displacing risk from one set of vulnerable subjects to another; that is, expanded reliance upon nuclear power could marginally decrease climate-related risk for large numbers of persons, at the cost of increasing nuclear-related risks for fewer persons. In weighing these two options, further assessment of these differently structured risks is needed so that a normatively defensible response to the dual risks inherent to reliance upon fossil fuels and nuclear energy for electrical generation can be crafted. Some relevant questions in this assessment are technical in nature, but the core of such exercises in risk assessment and response is irreducibly normative, requiring the critical examination of risk and the way that various social goods (including human health and welfare, environmental sustainability, and security) trade off against one another, and how various kinds of risks are balanced and distributed among human populations.

Since the social response to risk involves issues of its just distribution among persons and peoples – or as Beck (1992 p. 35) notes: 'wealth accumulates at the top, risks at the bottom' – its normative analysis requires the application of principles of distributive justice and not merely the standard consequentialist tools of conventional risk assessment. 'As the risk society develops,' Beck (1992, p. 46) notes, 'so does the antagonism between those *afflicted* by risks and those who *profit* with them'. Attention must therefore be paid to how the downside costs and upside benefits are allocated, since risk imposition often benefits some while placing others at greater risk. Processes of control over assignments of risk ought likewise to be considered, for as Kristin Shrader-Frechette (1985, p. 442) notes, standard forms of risk assessment tend to 'ignore the value dimension of policy analysis and to disenfranchise the public who, in a democracy, ought to control that policy'. By reducing all risk to expected aggregate costs and benefits, standard risk assessment ignores problems surrounding the distribution of risk and the asymmetries often involved in risk imposition (Sunstein 2004), and so requires additional evaluative criteria for its justified imposition. Here, I shall consider how the manufactured risks associated with climate change might be compared against those issuing from nuclear energy development, which has been offered as a remedy. In particular, my concern shall be with how these two sets of risks might be compared with one another, such that the potential costs and benefits associated with each of these risk-laden phenomena can be meaningfully compared and the proposal to expand nuclear power as a climate policy tool can be critically assessed. In so doing, I intend to offer an account of risk that takes on what Beck (1992, p. 21) describes as its core meaning, as 'a systematic way of dealing with hazards and insecurities induced and introduced by modernization itself'. Such hazards and insecurities must be dealt with in some manner, and a 'systematic way' of doing so requires that their current production and distribution be subjected to critical scrutiny.

The nuclear option

While nuclear energy production was once anathema to environmental activists, and indeed to the ideological left more generally (Rothman and Lichter 1987), concerns about climate change have led several high-profile green figures to rethink its prohibition. James Lovelock, the British atmospheric scientist that originated the Gaia theory, Stewart Brand of the *Whole Earth Catalog*, and Friends of the Earth founder and director Hugh Montefiore have all recently endorsed nuclear power as a climate-friendly energy option. Greenpeace founder Patrick Moore has done likewise, here summarizing the appeal of a carbon-free energy source in an electricity infrastructure dominated by fossil fuels:

> More than 600 coal-fired power plants in the United States produce 36 percent of US emissions – or nearly 10 percent of global emissions – of CO_2, the primary greenhouse gas responsible for climate change. Nuclear energy is the only large-scale cost-effective energy source that can reduce these emissions while continuing to satisfy a growing demand for power. And these days it can do so safely. (Moore 2006, p. B01)

Some of these claims are contestable, and both the safety and cost-effectiveness of nuclear power shall be further considered below, but the argument's force can be found in its contrast between the climate impacts of nuclear power and that of coal, on which the United States currently relies for the bulk of its electricity production and which nuclear power could potentially replace. Expanded nuclear energy is recommended as the lesser evil, with continued reliance upon coal for electrical generation very likely to bring about catastrophic climate impacts and the downside risks of nuclear accidents seen as worse but less probable. As Bernard Cohen (1983) also argues, Moore suggests that the risks inherent in nuclear energy have been overstated and those associated with climate change understated, such that proper risk analysis would endorse nuclear expansion.

But would it? Clearly, the risks associated with unmitigated climate change are serious ones, and taking them seriously requires fundamentally rethinking the way that humans generate and use electricity, now and in the future. Scientists estimate that cuts of 80–95% from 2000 emissions levels will be required by 2050 in order to stabilize atmospheric concentrations of greenhouse gases at a level that would prevent the 'dangerous anthropogenic interference with the climate system' that was identified as the objective of the 1992 UN Framework Convention on Climate Change (IPCC 2007a, Hansen *et al.* 2008). Updating scientific assessments prior to the 2009 climate meetings in Copenhagen, the International Scientific Congress on Climate Change warned in June 2009 that 'recent observations show that greenhouse gas emissions and many aspects of the climate are changing near the upper boundary of the IPCC range of projections' (Richardson *et al.* 2009, p. 6), raising the prospect of crossing irreversible 'tipping points' in climate impacts earlier than previous forecasts projected. Given the threat of catastrophic and irreversible climate disturbances, with the profound social, political, economic, and ecological costs that these are expected to bring about, all options for decarbonizing the economy must now be placed on the table for consideration, including an expanded US and global nuclear energy program. Eliminating risk altogether, as Beck argues, is no longer a viable option. Both climate change itself and the primary strategies for mitigating its effects involve risk imposition, albeit of different kinds and degrees. Charting the most defensible course between a risky environmental phenomenon and risky decarbonization policy requires the ability to meaningfully compare and effectively manage risk, which in turn requires understanding its normative dimensions.

Proposals to expand nuclear energy are often framed in terms of their potential climate benefits, compared with fossil fuel-intensive electrical generation, and the new landscape of public and elite opinion concerning 'the nuclear option' owes largely to its potential source of 'green' power. To explicate relevant tradeoffs and comparative risks, I shall focus on the case of nuclear energy expansion in the United States, where large-scale electrical generation now accounts for one-third of all greenhouse emissions, where low-carbon energy sources are urgently needed to replace coal-fired power plants, but where nuclear energy development has long been stalled by concern about its risks – a concern that began to cede some ground to worries about climate change mitigation before the Fukushima disaster. There, fossil fuels account for 86% of total energy use and 71% of electricity generation, while nuclear energy accounts for 8% of overall energy, and renewable sources (including hydro, wind, solar and geothermal) together account for 6%. The United States currently operates 103 nuclear reactors, with no new domestic reactor orders since 1978 and the newest reactor (the Tennessee Valley Authority Watts Bar 1, ordered in 1970) coming online in 1996. Reactors are initially granted 40-year operating licenses, but can apply for 20-year license renewals, so if no new reactors are constructed then the first of these 103 nuclear facilities will be decommissioned after its 60-year life-span ends in 2030 and the last US reactor will cease operations in 2056 (Ferguson 2007). Holding energy use and the proportions of non-nuclear domestic electrical generation sources constant, the loss of the power loads of these 103 nuclear plants would increase domestic greenhouse emissions by 6–7%, while a doubling of reactor capacity by 2050 would reduce them by the same amount (Union of Concerned Scientists 2007). While an expanded US nuclear energy program cannot by itself adequately address the threat of serious climate change, it could make a significant dent in its current carbon-based energy portfolio, and in so doing play some role in a larger domestic and international climate policy.

Compared with coal and natural gas-fired power plants, nuclear energy has a significantly higher capitalization cost, a longer lead time to bring new plants online, and approximately 50% higher per-kilowatt generation costs. Barring accidents, it is much lower polluting, both in terms of greenhouse pollutants and other air-borne and water-borne hazardous particulates, but in the event of an accident the potential costs of nuclear power are much higher, and long-term storage needs for spent nuclear fuel generates leakage and security concerns that the US government has yet to adequately address (Rogers and Kingsley 2004). Absent significant government subsidies and possibly unjustified liability limits for nuclear facilities, along with a viable long-term storage solution for depleted uranium, nuclear power cannot compete with the relatively inexpensive fossil fuel technologies in terms of startup and operating costs. Not surprisingly, such subsidies and protections have been aggressively advocated by the nuclear industry, often with climate-related benefits as a primary selling point, and both the 1992 and 2005 Energy Policy Acts have offered billions of dollars in incentives in an effort to jump-start the domestic nuclear industry, thus far to no avail (Ferguson 2007). But the US government *could* provide additional incentives and remove more regulatory obstacles, making expanded nuclear energy an economically viable energy source, if the benefits of doing so outweigh the costs of those incentives and the risks that relegated nuclear energy to pariah status throughout much of the world following the accidents at Chernobyl, Three Mile Island, and now also Fukushima. The question is: *should* they do so? Is the 'nuclear option' worth its several downside costs, the most serious of which involve low probabilities of major harm? On what bases might such a decision be made, and how can the risks associated with nuclear energy be commensurably compared against those of intensified climate change?

Several safety concerns are typically cited in opposition to expanded nuclear energy programs, and a precautionary approach – here understood as a moratorium on further nuclear plant construction until safety concerns can be adequately addressed – is typically defended in light of the uncertainty that surrounds those safety issues. Worries about safety emanating from public opinion have thus far supported what Kerry Whiteside terms a 'precautionary idea' in the context of expanded nuclear energy development, manifesting 'whenever authorities take early preventative measures to forestall a potential, irreversible danger, even though causal links in the chain leading to that danger have not yet been firmly established' (2006, p. 65). US climate change policy, by contrast, has largely followed what Whiteside describes as the 'reflexively anti-precautionary' posture characteristic of its regulatory politics. With nuclear energy, safety concerns – including risks of a reactor meltdown, nuclear material proliferation, contamination from stored nuclear wastes, and terrorist attack – involve the potential for catastrophic and irreversible harm, warranting the precautionary imperative to minimize impositions of risk in light of the potential for catastrophic outcomes. These risks would increase with an expanded nuclear energy program, whether as the result of increases in facilities and volume of materials or through the deregulatory incentives that government has created in order to re-start reactor construction,[1] and must be assessed as such. But similar risks arise from climate change, and such risks would be exacerbated by mothballing existing nuclear facilities and could be reduced by expanding them. In the tradeoff between nuclear energy and fossil fuels, risk is ubiquitous and inescapable; as Beck (1992, p. 31) suggests 'there occurs, so to speak, an overproduction of risks, which sometimes relativize, sometimes supplement and sometimes outdo one another'. No longer can simple precaution point the way toward a defensible resolution of this dilemma, and standard imperatives to minimize risk or maximize expected value are confounded by the way that risks are distributed among parties and over time by both options. If Beck's (1992, p. 80) risk society 'harbors a tendency to a legitimate totalitarianism of hazard prevention', it also suggests that risk itself, along with the goods that make it inevitable, are subject to justice in their distribution. In addition, it points the way to identifying acceptable risks and the compensatory measures needed to justify imposing risk where such imposition is unavoidable. To such issues we shall now turn.

Weighing opposing risks and uncertainties

Anti-nuclear activists frequently point to the possibility of some very bad outcome in defense of a strong precautionary stance against the further development of nuclear power, implicitly claiming that this low-probability but high-cost outcome justifies the rejection of any potential benefits. But does it? At issue is how to compare the high-probability climate benefits of expanded nuclear energy against the small chance of catastrophic harm that expansion risks, and when to forego likely benefits in anticipation of merely possible costs. A precautionary stance against nuclear energy focuses upon its downside risks, foregoing potential benefits in light of those possible costs, and John Harsanyi challenges such a stance in principle. Arguing against the *maximin* decision rule found in the Rawlsian difference principle, he criticizes the decision rule to 'evaluate every policy available to you in terms of the *worst possibility* that can occur to you if you follow that particular policy' (Harsanyi 1975, p. 595), ranking alternatives not in terms of expected benefits but of worst case outcomes. To illustrate the irrationality of a precautionary stance, Harsanyi posits that you live in New York and must choose between a dull and poorly paid job there and an interesting and well-paid position in Chicago. If you take the Chicago job, you would have to fly there the next day, in which case there is a small chance that you would be killed in a plane crash in transit. Presumably, that is your only risk. Your options are thus as presented in Table 1.

Your best and worst options are both possible if you take the Chicago job, but some uncertainty prevents you from knowing which of the two will obtain,

Table 1. Risk option example.

	Chicago plane crashes	Chicago plane does not crash
You choose the New York job	You will have a poor job in New York but will be alive	You will have a poor job in New York but be alive
You choose the Chicago job	You will die	You will have a good job in Chicago and will not die

while you would be certain to have a suboptimal but not worst-case outcome if you opt to remain in New York. If you choose based upon worst possible outcomes, you would have to forfeit the best possible outcome in order to avoid the worst one. Harsanyi (1975, p. 595) argues: 'it is extremely irrational to make your behavior wholly dependent on some unlikely unfavorable contingencies, regardless of how little probability you are willing to assign to them', and indeed this claim as stated is plausible. While it may *sometimes* be rational to sacrifice the potential gains from risk in order to avoid worst cases that are also made possible by it, he is right to claim that it is not *always* so, at least in the type of case he describes here. A sufficiently low probability of the plane crash would lead to higher expected value with the Chicago job, and, just as surely, a high enough probability for the crash would make the New York job a more rational option. Probability is the key to expected value.

Rather than making decisions on the basis of the worst possible outcome, Harsanyi argues that it would be rational for you to employ a Bayesian decision rule and maximize your expected utility. Given the very low probability of your being killed in a plane crash *en route*, he suggests, you should 'take your chances and choose the Chicago job' (Harsanyi 1975, p. 595). The expected value of that option includes the sum of the disvalue of being killed in a plane crash heavily discounted by its very low probability, combined with the value of the better job. If, as Harsanyi suggests, the expected net value of moving to Chicago exceeds that of remaining in New York, it would be irrational to choose otherwise. Here, Harsanyi accurately captures how standard risk analysis is conducted, where outcomes are discounted by probabilities of their occurrence. But what follows from his analysis? Does it provide the requisite analytical tool for comparing the divergent risks inherent in climate change and expanded nuclear energy? As he characterizes the precautionary stance of the maximin decision rule:

> If you took the maximin principle seriously then you could not ever cross a street (after all, you might be hit by a car); you could never drive over a bridge (after all, it might collapse); you could never get married (after all, it might end in disaster), etc. If anybody really acted in this way he would soon end up in a mental institution. (Harsanyi 1975, p. 595)

Presumably, Harsanyi does not mean to entirely disregard the possibility of that worst outcome, but rather proposes that it be discounted for its low probability. Some do in fact recommend that low-probability risks be ignored entirely rather than being discounted in this way, but as Shrader-Frechette (1985) has shown, this conflicts with the terms of risk analysis itself, particularly with low probability but high-cost risks like nuclear meltdowns. Harsanyi implies that the expected value of the Chicago job is higher than the New York job even after subtracting the discounted disvalue of your being killed in a plane crash in invoking expected utility, although he never specifically addresses probabilities or discounting. So long as probabilities can be estimated in this way, however and so long as agents are able to attach a finite disvalue to their being killed,[2] risky individual choices are at least sometimes warranted. In such cases, Harsanyi's point begs the question but is reasonable: in so far as we understand rationality in terms of expected utility maximization, the rational choice would be to maximize expected utility, not to minimize risk or avoid worst cases. Your choice to take the Chicago job would be the rational one, no matter whether you arrive there safely, since rationality lies in the prospective estimate of the respective values of various outcomes, not in the retrospective assessment of how things in fact turn out. Risk-taking, in this sense, involves *ex ante* acceptance of downside risks in light of their upside payoffs, and is sometimes warranted despite risks of very bad outcomes.

But this sort of analysis applies only to a limited range of decisions, excluding the social distribution of resources that is the subject of Rawls's principle, since maximin involves actual bad outcomes for someone and not the merely possible worst cases that he alleges. Individuals might validly rely upon expected value in making risky decisions that affect only themselves, as in Harsanyi's example, but cannot use it when choosing whether to impose risk upon others. In individual cases, persons accept risks when they choose the prospect of better outcomes despite the possibility of worse ones, and so harm only themselves if the bad outcome obtains. Even in such individual cases, persons tend not to employ the expected value approach of standard risk analysis, with most preferring to avoid certain losses by risking greater losses (for example, preferring a 50% chance of losing $3 to a certain loss of $1) but preferring certain gains over chances for greater ones (for example, preferring $1 over a 50% chance at $3). Risk tolerance and aversion varies across persons and decisions, and typically involves personal dispositions and contexts rather than quantitative expected value analysis (Jarvis Thomson 1986). Rather than presuming consent to risk acceptance when expected value analysis declares it rational for persons to take a given risk, an autonomy-focused approach to risk would give persons the opportunity to make informed decisions about the risks they will take. If you take the Chicago job, then you accept the risks of being killed in exchange for the upside benefits. If someone else puts you on that plane without your consent, based perhaps on Harsanyi's analysis, then you have not accepted that risk, and you can object to the risk imposition even if your plane arrives safely.

Personal risk-taking may sometimes be imprudent, but it is never wrong or unjust, at least where it involves the informed consent of rational agents. Societal risk-taking, by contrast, often involves imposed rather than freely-accepted risk, as Shrader-Frechette notes. 'In the individual case', she writes, 'the risk is freely chosen by one person, but in the societal instance, it is often involuntarily imposed on a group, without consent' (Shrader-Frechette 1988, p. 506). While societal risk could in principle be democratically accepted by an entire community, several considerations undermine the legitimacy of a popular plebiscite on the kinds of risk involved in nuclear energy expansion or climate change. First, in a society of any significant size, the likelihood of unanimous support for either option is extremely small, and majority rule decisions in cases involving risk allow for the imposition of risk upon a minority for the benefit of the majority. To avoid objections about risk imposition, all must freely accept that risk. Where a society is required to choose between two alternative risks, as with the climate–nuclear dilemma, a consensus decision rule for nuclear expansion would surely result in heightened climate-related risks, absent the requisite consensus on behalf of rejecting the *status quo* option. Moreover, the relevant polity depends on the scope of the risks involved, and differs between the climate and nuclear cases. Since climate change is expected to adversely affect residents of developing countries and future generations much more than current Americans, any plebiscite on accepting climate-related risks would have to include non-residents and future persons (Vanderheiden 2008), else it risks objectionably imposing risks onto others for the benefit of those allowed to control that imposition. Those most affected by the nuclear decision include residents whose utility rates or taxes stand to be increased by the decision to subsidize nuclear over fossil fuel-based power, along with those whose proximity to nuclear facilities renders them vulnerable to nuclear accidents. No polity constituted around the affectedness principle (Goodin 2007) can validly choose between these two risk sets, since those asked to accept one set would not be the same as those asked to accept the other.

To illustrate the difficulties involved in making societal risk decisions, Shrader-Frechette considers whether to disband or maintain a country's nuclear energy program, where there exists a low-probability but high-cost outcome in which nuclear reactor operators commit serious errors that result in a meltdown akin to that at Three Mile Island. As some nuclear plants are currently online, the decision to mothball them from safety concerns would result in substantial foregone energy production, but this would prevent the worst-case outcome. Maintaining rather than disbanding the current nuclear program results in either the best or worst outcome, depending on whether or not reactor operators make serious errors. The decision set is therefore as presented in Table 2.

As before, the maximin rule counsels that the nuclear program be disbanded in order to avoid the worst possible outcome, but it remains unclear which of the two options would yield maximum expected utility. Shrader-Frechette's point here is that the Bayesian decision depends upon how

Table 2. Nuclear program decision set.

	Nuclear reactor operators make serious errors	Nuclear reactor operators do not make serious errors
Nuclear program maintained	Serious accident in which many people die	Higher energy production and lower energy costs
Nuclear program disbanded	Accident avoided, but financial loss from lower energy supply	Financial loss from lower energy supply

the probability of reactor operator mistakes is calculated, but a more fundamental objection to the use of either standard risk analysis or democratically accepted risk is suggested by this case. Using standard risk analysis, the potential costs of a nuclear accident are discounted by their probability and then compared against the costs associated with disbanding the nuclear program. Depending upon that probability, maintaining the program may yield higher expected value, but through an objectionable displacement of risks. The benefits of maintaining the nuclear program are widely distributed, through lower energy costs (in her example), but the potential costs are narrowly concentrated among those residing near nuclear facilities. Even if the overall expected benefits exceed overall expected costs, the opposite is likely to be true for those most vulnerable to nuclear accidents, whose lives would be risked so that others could save money on their power bills. This hardly seems fair to them, but this unfairness cannot be captured by standard forms of risk analysis, which take no account of the distribution of risks across a population. Likewise, if the decision was made by majority rule rather than authoritatively imposed by a risk-minimizing state guided by Bayesian risk analysis, the same displacement of risk onto those most vulnerable could occur, raising the same objections.

The moral illegitimacy of risking someone else's welfare for benefits to oneself can be illustrated by another thought experiment: suppose that I make a wager that will pay each of us $1000 if we win but will cost you your life if we lose. Here, risk's upside benefits are equally shared but its potential costs are concentrated on you. The bet is a good one for me, since I would be insulated from its downside risks but not its upside rewards, but you would look at it (and probably also me, for wagering your life like this) with reasonable suspicion. It would be irrational for you to agree to that payoff structure, but it would be worse if I was to make this wager on your behalf without your consent. In the case above, it is difficult to imagine how anyone could rationally accept the risks of being killed in a reactor meltdown, no matter how improbable this possibility, for some marginal savings off their monthly utility bill. At some low probability, however, the tradeoff would be rational to accept, in expected utility terms. There is nothing unjust about persons taking irrational risks in order to potentially gain upside rewards, but its imposition without the consent of those whose lives are jeopardized by it would still be objectionable even if their consent would be rational. Risk-taking is a cornerstone of much of modern life, and Harsanyi is justified in ridiculing the extremely risk-averse as excessively and even viciously timid. Refusing to accept even minute risks makes extremely risk-averse persons a tremendous burden to others, who will be forced to incur risks on their behalf. However, the voluntary acceptance of risk differs from its imposition, even with the same payoff structure, and the concern here lies with the circumstances under which risk can be imposed upon some people in exchange for benefits that accrue to others.

In many cases of societal risk, it is untenable to require the prior informed and unanimous consent of all those subjected to downside risk, granting all potentially affected persons a veto over risky decisions. The imposition of risk on others is sometimes justified, where consent is impossible or impractical to obtain, where collective benefits require that all are subjected to some risk if any are, where the risky decision equitably allocates the costs and benefits of risk, and where the expected benefits outweigh expected costs for each. Here, risk is viewed as one kind of cost that is sometimes necessary for procuring important social benefits, but which must be equitably assigned in view of those benefits. Displacing risks onto some so that others may benefit in this sense constitutes a distributive injustice, but justly distributed risks and benefits may in some cases be assigned without the express consent of those affected by them. My 401K manager can legitimately purchase a volatile stock at some low price without every shareholder giving their consent in advance, even though investors are thereby placed at some financial risk as a consequence, since the potential costs and benefits of this decision are equitably distributed among investors. Those with more shares stand to gain or lose in proportion to their holdings. But that manager could not place all investors at greater risk in exchange for benefits that accrue only to some, as this would amount to an unjust transfer of costs in one direction and benefits in the other. Trustees, like fund managers, typically take such calculated risks on behalf of their clients, and it is expected that they do so, although their judgment may reasonably be called into question later if risky decisions repeatedly go wrong. Governments act as trustees on behalf of their citizens, and must impose some risks in order to provide collective goods. Where this risk imposition appears imprudent or inequitable in its exchange of upside benefits for downside risks, its legitimacy as a trustee of the public comes under scrutiny, and rightly so.

Polities can accept risk through democratic processes, which are analogous to informed consent in individuals, and as Shrader-Frechette (1988, p. 506) notes: 'democratic *process* is probably *more important* in cases of societal risk under uncertainty'. But majority-rule processes that subject minorities to risk of serious harm in exchange for benefits that accrue primarily to the majority, when such risks would be irrational for that minority to accept, cannot be justified in this way. Trusteeship implies that decisions made on behalf of others without their consent are expected to benefit those others, and *could* be the subject of their consent even if they are not in fact. Imposing risks upon others that do not meet this criterion instead involves *risk displacement*, violating the rights of those placed at unjustified risk in a way that *ex ante* compensation cannot fully correct (McKerlie 1986). Given the unavoidability of some societal risk-taking, the question must be: under what circumstances can some imposition of risk be justified? Since the 'nuclear option' involves exchanging one set of risks for another, and thus also placing a different set of subjects at risk, criteria for acceptable societal risk-taking must be able to meaningfully compare alterative risk sets, with their distributed costs and benefits, and prescribe compensatory measures for those made worse off by the best option.

Commensurable risks?

We can now return to evaluating the decision to expand nuclear power programs in light of imperatives to mitigate anthropogenic climate change. Here, the potential costs and benefits of two separate but related categories of risk tradeoff, although the probabilities and magnitudes of each kind of risk are shrouded in uncertainty. As noted above, the United States would increase its greenhouse emissions by 6–7% and global emissions by 2%, holding other variables constant, if it was to decommission all of its currently-operating nuclear plants, increasing one kind of risk while decreasing another. Likewise, a significantly expanded US nuclear energy program could reduce national and global emissions by a similar amount, reducing climate risks but at the expense of nuclear ones. While these marginal changes correspond with non-trivial increases and reductions in climate-related risk, the US 'nuclear option' falls well short of what scientists estimate will be necessary in order to avoid 'dangerous anthropogenic interference' with the earth's climate system, and it is impossible to know what specific hazards this would avoid, but it should reduce climate-related risks at the expense of higher nuclear-related ones. Unlike the above analysis, in which low-probability but high cost outcomes were compared against certain intermediate ones, the tradeoff involves low-probability but high cost outcomes becoming slightly higher-probability (with nuclear expansion) in order to marginally reduce high-probability but intermediate cost outcomes. The decision looks something like that presented in Table 3.

Here, the top right sextant is plainly the best-case scenario, and the middle left one is the worst. But we cannot meaningfully compare the three options on the basis of either sextant on its own, without knowing how our choices affect the probability of an accident occurring. Comparing both expansion and disbandment of the nuclear program against the *status quo*, we need to know how rising expected climate benefits affect rising accident risks and how reducing accident risks increases those from climate. If we could be certain to

Table 3. Risk tradeoff decision.

	Nuclear accident occurs with existing nuclear program	No nuclear-related harm
Expand nuclear program	Maximum climate benefits (but climate-related harm only marginally diminished), but nuclear catastrophe outweighs	Maximum climate benefits, and no harm from raised risk of nuclear catastrophe
Maintain nuclear program	Foregone climate benefits, and catastrophic nuclear accident occurs anyway	Higher climate risks, with no corresponding safety benefit
Disband nuclear program	Averted catastrophic harm, but higher climate-related harm	No catastrophic harm, but none averted to justify the opportunity costs for climate

remain in the right-hand column – that no harm would result from our nuclear program, should we maintain or expand it – better results come from being higher in the column, but moving higher also raises the probability of moving into the left-hand column, in which case we would prefer to be lower. Given uncertainty about this tradeoff between two risky courses of action, how do we compare our three options?

Analytic decision theories are stumped by tradeoffs of this sort. There is no dominant game theory option in this trilemma, which differs from prisoners' dilemmas in that outcomes depend on a chance element rather than decisions of others. The worst outcome above results from maintaining current programs when an accident occurs, but maintaining is superior to disbanding if the accident does not occur, although it increases the probability of the accident occurring. While expanding the program is superior to either of the other options whether or not accidents occur, it also increases the likelihood of such accidents, compared with maintaining or disbanding the program. One might instead employ a Bayesian risk analysis, but absent more robust probability estimates for accidents occurring at various levels of nuclear energy use, it would be impossible to reliably estimate the expected value of each option. Moreover, options are linear rather than threefold, since expansion or reduction from current levels can be by one plant or several, and expected values for all possible levels of nuclear power deployment would need to be calculated in order to be meaningfully compared. The optimum level of nuclear power production comes just below the threshold at which an accident occurs – at which point it would have been better to use just less – but this threshold cannot be calculated in advance, and may not even be a function of overall use rates. Decision theory must be prospective, rendering it useless where the primary variable needed to rank options cannot be known in advance and its probability in each option cannot be accurately estimated. In short, game theory and quantitative risk analysis both fail to resolve the climate–nuclear dilemma, prescribing an appropriate role for nuclear power in the decarbonizing imperatives of climate change mitigation policies.

Procedural democratic theories fare no better. As suggested above, risky decisions must take account of public preferences where possible. As J.E.J. Altham notes, persons are willing to accept much higher levels of risk when given the choice to do so, as opposed to when such risks are imposed, making democracy a means of managing risk as well as a procedure for choosing among risky options. He writes: 'The risk of smoking twenty cigarettes a day is reckoned to be pretty high. A risk of similar magnitude to the general public from an industrial process, even a very beneficial one, would be regarded as quite intolerable' (Altham 1984, p. 29). Absent full consensus by all those who stand to be affected by the dual risks of nuclear energy and climate change – a consensus that depends on the participation of future persons in decision-making processes and which would necessarily oppose the rational interests of those on whom greater risk is imposed than they receive in upside benefits – majority rule decision rules invite charges of unfairness and illegitimately imposed risk. Indeed, rights against imposed risk are regarded as necessary protections against majority tyranny, but raise problems of their own in cases like this one where some risk is unavoidable, since inequitably imposed risk can in principle be corrected through compensation schemes but rights violations cannot (McCarthy 1996, Zimmerman 2006). As Shrader-Frechette notes of the effort to address fundamentally democratic questions through analytic decision theories rather than political contestation:

> All risk questions are ultimately philosophical questions. To attempt to reduce them to purely scientific issues ... is to ignore the value dimension of policy analysis and to disenfranchise the public who, in a democracy, ought to control that policy. (1985, p. 442)

But in this case, neither democratic nor analytic resolution to the climate–nuclear dilemma appears possible, given inherent limits of each process.

Conclusion: seeking traction in a third way

One strategy for resolving alleged dilemmas in which both horns offer incommensurably bad options is to show that there is actually a third option that is clearly superior to either of the other two. Indeed, this has been the strategy of those opposing the nuclear option as a response to the predicted hazards of climate change, who point to potential benefits of conservation and the combination of safety and efficiency available through expanded deployment of renewable energy technologies, including solar, wind, hydroelectric and geothermal power (World Information Services on Energy 2005).[3] By this analysis, the supposed choice between accepting the risks associated with expanded reliance upon nuclear power or intensified climate change is a false one, given that greenhouse emissions can be reduced by the same amount through far less risky electrical generation technologies and conservation options. Such proposals are obviously appealing in that they avoid the dilemma of apparently incommensurable risks discussed above by offering comparable but clearly preferable options. If the data concerning the relative safety and cost-effectiveness of renewable energy technologies compared with nuclear power are accurate, they obviously present a compelling policy alternative to either of the unattractive options posed against each other above. No doubt, these renewable energy options can go a long way toward decarbonizing the energy economy, and they may together someday replace fossil fuels entirely in providing an electricity infrastructure. In the meantime, existing nuclear facilities are nearing the expiration of their operating licenses, and some argue for their replacement with new nuclear facilities rather than with the coal-fired plants that would otherwise be brought online to 'bridge the gap' between energy supply and demand, further entrenching fossil fuels in the energy infrastructure for decades to come. Given the urgent imperative to start decarbonizing now, what can be said for or against the claim that nuclear power must remain an energy source into the intermediate future, until such time as renewable sources are able to meet the world's full energy needs?

While a full accounting of the distributive implications of climate change and nuclear energy is beyond the scope of this paper, a tentative response to this challenge can be ventured by revisiting Beck's notion that the distribution of risk rather than scarce resources is now the most fundamental role of the state and the most basic task of justice: when our demand for energy forces us to choose between placing some at risk of being killed in a nuclear accident or devastated by climate change, we must consider whether the activities that create this demand benefit those whose welfare has been offered in collateral for the wager in which we benefit ourselves through the imposition of risks onto others. Even if it is not certain that they will be harmed, the fact that we subject others to substantially higher risks of being harmed requires some justification. Do these same activities also make them better off in some tangible way? Is the circumstance under which they are placed at greater risk of harm something to which they would give their informed consent, in that they stand to benefit by the upside rewards of a risky activity as well as the downside risks? Or are we merely displacing the costs of our affluent lifestyles onto those made vulnerable to nuclear accidents or climate change, whether in the near or more distant future? If the latter, we must think seriously about the fair distribution of risks and rewards, and the distributive injustice of insulating ourselves from the risks while those made vulnerable to it are largely insulated from its rewards. And we must act accordingly.

Resolving the nuclear–climate dilemma by finding a third alternative that avoids the hard choice between its two unpalatable horns may be policy savvy, and the ecological modernization discourse on which it rests offers an attractive narrative of a relatively painless decarbonization path. Certainly, 'clean energy' technologies should be developed and deployed in replacement of the fossil fuel-based plants that the planet cannot much longer tolerate, and we must not pretend that there would not be a climate-related cost to the decision to disband existing nuclear power facilities, or an opportunity cost to climate in not expanding them. This cost must be borne by those who benefit by the activities that make it necessary, as climate-related costs are unlikely to be. For this reason, we cannot merely displace such risks through climate change or expanded nuclear power, for the downside costs of these options are borne primarily by their non-beneficiaries. If we significantly injure or kill those who are made more vulnerable as the result of risks that we impose upon them as the result of choices from which we primarily benefit, then we cannot adequately compensate them for their injury. Modernization, as Beck argues, begat the risk society in which we live and to which we contribute risk, so it cannot also be expected to fully remedy that situation. Ultimately, greater attention to the distribution of risks and the rewards that attach to them ought to persuade us not only to avoid the risks of severe and irreversible harm where possible, but also to assign far more of the risks to ourselves rather than others in cases where we are also the primary beneficiaries of risky activities, so that we may displace fewer onto others. We should, in other words, strive to live more sustainably in order to act justly toward others, given the mutually reinforcing nature these dual imperatives.

Notes

1. As the Union of Concerned Scientists (2007, p. 29) notes: 'the Price-Anderson liability limit therefore serves as a disincentive for industry to develop and use additional safety features, or to adopt reactor designs that are safer but more expensive'.
2. If, on the other hand, one attaches infinite disvalue to being killed, even a very low probability of that outcome makes it irrational, since a discounted infinity remains infinite. Quantitative risk assessment cannot accommodate infinite value, and so is easier to use in assessing risks to others than for risks to self.
3. See, for example, World Information Services on Energy (2005).

References

Altham, J.E.J., 1984. Ethics of risk. *Proceedings of the Aristotelian Society*, 84, 15–29.
Beck, U., 1992. *Risk society: towards a new modernity*. Trans. M. Ritter. Newbury Park, CA: Sage.
Cohen, B.L., 1983. *Before it's too late: a scientist's case for nuclear energy*. New York: Plenum Press.
Ferguson, C.D., 2007. *Nuclear energy: balancing benefits and risks*, April, CSR No. 28. New York: Council on Foreign Relations.
Goodin, R.E., 2007. Enfranchising all affected interests, and its alternatives. *Philosophy and Public Affairs*, 35 (1), 40–68.
Hansen, J., et al., 2008. Target atmospheric CO_2: where should humanity aim? *Open Atmospheric Sciences Journal*, 2, 217–231.
Harsanyi, J.C., 1975. Can the maximin principle serve as a basis for morality? A critique of John Rawls's theory. *American Political Science Review*, 69 (2), 594–606.
Intergovernmental Panel on Climate Change, 2007a. *Climate change 2007: the physical science basis*. Ed. S. Solomon, D. Qin and M. Manning. Geneva: IPCC.
Intergovernmental Panel on Climate Change, 2007b. *Climate change 2007: synthesis report*. Ed. R.K. Pachauri, A. Reisinger, and the Core Writing Team. Geneva: IPCC.
Jarvis Thomson, J. 1986. *Rights, restitution, and risk: essays in moral theory*. Ed. W. Parent. Cambridge, MA: Harvard University Press.
McCarthy, D., 1996. Liability and risk. *Philosophy and Public Affairs*, 25 (3), 238–262.
McKerlie, D., 1986. Rights and risk. *Canadian Journal of Philosophy*, 16 (2), 239–251.
Moore, P., 2006. Going nuclear: a green makes the case. *The Washington Post*, 16 April, B01.
Pidgeon, N. and Butler, C., 2009. Risk analysis and climate change. *Environmental Politics*, 18 (5), 670–688.
Richardson, K., et al., 2009. *Climate change: global risks, challenges & decisions*. 2nd ed. Available from: www.climatecongress.ku.dk
Rogers, K.A. and Kingsley, M.G., 2004. The politics of interim radioactive waste storage: the United States. *Environmental Politics*, 13(3), 590–611.
Rothman, S. and Lichter, S.R., 1987. Elite ideology and risk perception in nuclear energy policy. *American Political Science Review*, 81 (2), 383–404.
Shrader-Frechette, K., 1985. Technological risk and small probabilities. *Journal of Business Ethics*, 4 (6), 431–445.
Shrader-Frechette, K. 1988. Risk assessment and uncertainty. *Philosophy of Science Association*, 2, 504–517.

Sunstein, C., 2004. *Risk and reason: safety, law, and the environment*. New York: Cambridge University Press.
Union of Concerned Scientists, 2007. *Nuclear power in a warming world*. Cambridge, MA: UCS Publications. Available from: http://www.ucsusa.org/assets/documents/nuclear_power/nuclear-power-in-a-warming-world.pdf
Vanderheiden, S., 2008. *Atmospheric justice: a political theory of climate change*. New York: Oxford University Press.
Whiteside, K., 2006. *Precautionary politics: principle and practice in confronting environmental risk*. Cambridge, MA: The MIT Press.
World Information Services on Energy, 2005. *Nuclear power: no solution to climate change*. Available from: http://www.nirs.org/climate/climate.htm
Zimmerman, M.J., 2006. Risk, rights, and restitution. *Philosophical Studies*, 128, 285–311.

Déjà vu all over again: climate change and the prospects for a nuclear power renaissance

Robert Duffy

> Drawing upon data from congressional statutes, federal agencies, the nuclear industry, and a range of secondary sources, the prospects for a nuclear resurgence in the United States in the aftermath of the Fukushima disaster are evaluated. Before the accident, several factors seemed to favor a nuclear revival: the rise of climate change as an issue; dramatic swings in the price of oil and natural gas; streamlined licensing procedures established in the Energy Policy Act of 1992; a variety of new economic incentives in the Energy Policy Act of 2005; and the shift to new, standardized reactor designs. Despite these changes, the chances of a nuclear revival in the United Stated were slim even before Fukushima; lingering public concerns over nuclear waste disposal, reactor safety and, most importantly, economic viability were serious obstacles.

Introduction

Can commercial nuclear power be an economically viable and timely option for addressing climate change? This may seem an odd question to ask in the aftermath of the triple meltdowns in March 2011 at the Fukushima Daiichi reactors in Japan, which has lead a number of nations to rethink their nuclear plans (Dempsey 2011, Morales 2011, Yang and Mufson 2011). Before the accident, the industry and its supporters in and out of government loudly trumpeted the possibility of a 'nuclear renaissance' fueled primarily by rising concerns over climate change, dramatic swings in the price of fossil fuels, and a host of federal subsidies (Snyder 2010, Whitten 2010). Although such talk now seems fanciful, it is worth noting that a nuclear revival was unlikely even before Fukushima. For nuclear power to make a significant contribution to the climate change problem, the United States and others would have had to embark on an unprecedented program of reactor building, and sustain it for decades. For that to happen, however, fossil fuels would have to become much more expensive (perhaps through an increase in the price of carbon) and the nuclear industry would have to overcome some familiar but significant political and economic obstacles, all of which were made worse by the Fukushima accident.

Here I shall review the prospects for nuclear power in the United States. I begin with an overview of the status of nuclear power today, and then consider the factors that had sparked talk of a nuclear revival: the rise of climate change to the agenda, volatility in the price of fossil fuels, the desire for energy security, new economic subsidies, and a streamlined licensing process. I then proceed to a discussion of the factors that have long plagued the industry, and that have been exacerbated by the disaster in Japan: public concerns over waste disposal and reactor safety, environmental contamination, licensing problems, and high costs.

The current status of commercial nuclear power

No reactors have been ordered in the United States since 1978 – and every reactor ordered since 1973 has been cancelled. Before the Japanese meltdowns, however, the future of nuclear power seemed brighter than at any point in the prior 20 years. In September 2007 NRG Energy filed the first full application to build a reactor since 1979, and by 2010 the US Nuclear Regulatory Commission (NRC) had received 18 applications for a total of 28 reactors, involving five different reactor designs (US NRC 2010a). In an effort to skirt public opposition, all but one of the proposed projects sought to build new reactors at existing nuclear sites. As recently as the summer of 2010, the US NRC's licensing schedule showed that it could issue a license as early as 2011, and that the first new reactors could begin operation in 2018. Exactly how many of these projects will actually be built, however, remains highly uncertain, and is dependent on many factors, including construction and financing costs, fossil fuel prices, federal incentives, climate change policy (Holt 2009) and, of course, public support, which has eroded after Fukushima (Craighill and Cohen 2011). In fact, just a month after the accident, NRG pulled the plug on its two South Texas reactors and wrote off its $331 million investment (Wald 2011).

The Energy Information Administration projects that US electricity demands will increase by 31% by 2035 (US Energy Information Administration 2009). Nuclear generation currently provides just under 20% of the nation's electricity while coal, by far the largest source of electricity, accounts for about one-half of the nation's supply. There are now 104 reactors in operation at 65 sites in the United States. The average reactor, originally licensed for 40 years, has been operating for 30 years, although 57 reactors have received 20-year license extensions. The US NRC is currently reviewing extensions for another 20 reactors (Holt 2009). Clearly, then, for nuclear power to make a substantial contribution to combating climate change, the United States would not only need to build many more reactors, it would also need to replace most of its aging reactors. To increase nuclear's share of electricity generation, the United States would need to embark on an exceedingly ambitious building program. According to calculations by the Keystone Center, the United States would need to build reactors at the rate of the 1980s, when 20 GWe year of nuclear capacity was added, and sustain it for 50 years (Keystone Center 2007). Such an outcome was highly unlikely even before Fukushima, because it would require construction at a rate higher than the industry's average historical growth rate and is much higher than forecast by the US Energy Information Administration (2009).

The outlook for nuclear power globally was mixed even before Fukushima. There are now 436 nuclear plants operating worldwide, producing about 370 GWe of electricity. Prior to the accident, there were 56 reactors under construction worldwide: 21 in China, nine in Russia, six in South Korea, and five in India (International Atomic Energy Agency 2010). Just as in the United States, increasing nuclear power's share of the world's electricity would require an unprecedented construction program, but that is exceedingly unlikely now. Indeed, after Fukushima the International Energy Agency reduced by one-half its estimate of new nuclear installations over the next 25 years, citing greater public scrutiny and the prospects of enhanced safety requirements (Morales 2011). Japan, Germany, and Switzerland have subsequently announced plans to phase out their reactors, and the European Union announced plans to test 143 reactors in its 27 member states (Dempsey 2011, Dempsey and Ewing 2011).

What explains renewed interest in nuclear power?
The emergence of climate change as an issue

The rise of climate change as an issue boosted the outlook for commercial nuclear power, both in the United States and around the world. Instead of being perceived as a 'problem' to be solved, the industry and its supporters seized the opportunity to argue that nuclear power is the 'solution' to the 'problem' of climate change. Indeed, in 2007 the Nuclear Energy Institute launched an advert campaign proclaiming nuclear power as the 'clean air energy' and as 'today's solution' to our future energy needs; the Institute's website currently touts nuclear power as 'America's largest source of clean-air electricity' (Nuclear Energy Institute, 2010a).

Of particular importance to a nuclear revival are the prospects of policy shifts resulting from the focus on climate change, notably those imposing a price on carbon emissions, which would make fossil fuel generation more costly, or a clean energy standard, which could create quotas for nuclear generation. Until Republicans captured control of the House of Representatives in November 2010, perceptions that the US government was likely to adopt a carbon tax or a cap and trade system had grown, leading utility executives to at least consider the possibility of installing new nuclear capacity. Of course, a tax or limit on carbon emissions would improve the position of all low greenhouse gas energy sources, including a variety of renewable sources, coal with carbon sequestration, and investments in energy efficiency. The more costly emitting carbon becomes, the greater the advantage of low carbon emitting technologies relative to fossil fuels. And because nuclear is an important source of base load generating capacity, it would stand to benefit if its chief competitors – coal and natural gas – became more expensive.

Volatility in fossil fuel prices

Rising gas and oil prices in 2006–2008 were another factor in utilities' renewed interest in nuclear power. Although natural gas plants are cheaper to build than either coal or nuclear plants, fuel costs are much more critical to their economic viability over the long term. Sharp swings in the price of natural gas thus injected a great deal of uncertainty into utility planning, a notoriously tricky business. US utilities no longer burn oil to generate electricity, so increases in oil prices do not directly affect the price of electricity, although price spikes stemming from peak oil could certainly affect nuclear economics. Rising oil prices do, moreover, have the unrivalled ability to focus attention on energy policy generally. As in the 1970s, rising gasoline prices thrust energy matters into the public eye, and forced policy-makers to again confront questions of energy security and the nation's mix of energy supplies. Nuclear proponents argue that it would be wise to diversify our energy mix, and that nuclear is both reliable and domestic and would thus advance the quest for energy independence.

New reactor designs

Claims of new and improved reactor designs have also played a role in reviving interest in commercial nuclear power. The industry has been dogged by safety concerns since the early 1970s, and knows that any hope for a comeback depends on convincing regulators and the public that new plants can be operated safely and with minimal risk. Reactor vendors have claimed that new plants will feature advanced designs that incorporate many passive safety features and, because they utilize fewer components, will have lower material and construction costs. Westinghouse, for example, claims that in the event of a loss of coolant accident, the pressurized water tanks in its new AP 1000 reactor would quickly and automatically bring water to the reactor core, because the pressure in the tanks is higher than that in the core. The company also says the AP 1000 will cost less to build and operate than the current generation of reactors, because the design features fewer motors, pumps, and pipes, theoretically reducing the potential for accidents while also reducing construction and maintenance costs (Nuclear Energy Institute 2010b).

Economic incentives

The most important factor in the utility industry's renewed interest in nuclear power are the economic incentives contained in the Energy Policy Act of 2005

(Public Law 109–58). The law provides 1.8 cents per kilowatt hour tax credit for the first 6000 megawatts of new capacity for the first eight years of operation, up to $125 million annually per 1000 megawatts. Because each of the reactors currently under consideration average just over 1000 megawatts, only the first few reactors through the licensing process would be eligible. For this reason, the Nuclear Energy Institute has been urging Congress to remove the capacity limit, index it for inflation, and extend the deadline for plants to begin operation to 2025 (Holt 2009).

The Energy Policy Act of 2005 also provided $18.5 billion in loan guarantees for new reactors – up to 80% of the construction costs for advanced energy projects that reduce greenhouse gases. In February 2010 President Obama proposed an additional $36 billion in guarantees, for a total of $54.5 billion (Clayton 2010, Stuckey 2010). The guarantees were announced in President Obama's 2011 budget proposal, and followed up on his State of Union call for 'building a new generation of safe, clean nuclear power plants in this country'. Energy Secretary Steven Chu said the loan guarantees could fund seven to 10 reactors (Whitten 2010).

The Energy Policy Act of 2005 also provided reactor operators with $2 billion of insurance against regulatory delays and litigation for the first six reactors ($500 million each for the first two plants, and up to $250 million each for the next four). The insurance would cover the utility's principal and interest on loans and any extra costs for purchasing power from other sources because of regulatory delays.

Finally, under the DOE's Nuclear Power 2010 program, the agency will pay up to one-half of the applicant's costs of seeking regulatory approval for reactor design certification, early site approval, and a combined operating license (COL). The DOE is providing the funding in order to encourage utilities to order new reactors and to demonstrate that the US NRC's new licensing procedures will streamline the review process. To date, DOE has funded a portion of the costs to support applications for early site permits for three reactors.

A streamlined licensing process

Until 1989, reactor licensing had been a two-step process. First, utilities would apply to the Atomic Energy Commission (later the US NRC) for a construction permit to build a reactor. Then, after construction was completed, the utility would apply for an operating license. Citizen participation, including public hearings, was allowed at both stages. The problem was that regulators typically issued construction permits for plants based on preliminary designs; as a result, safety issues often remained unresolved until the plant was mostly complete (Duffy 1997). If regulators uncovered issues, plant owners could be required to make expensive 'retrofits' and operations could be delayed for long periods. In a bit of understatement, the nuclear industry later called this a 'process flaw that had substantial financial implications' (Nuclear Energy Institute 2009).

After years of trying, the nuclear industry in 1989 persuaded the US NRC to significantly revise its licensing procedures (10 CFR Part 52). The new procedures, largely ratified by Congress in the 1992 Energy Policy Act, allow for design certification of reactors, early site approval, and a combined construction permit and operating license (COL). In a critical departure, the US NRC would only hold hearings on the adequacy of plant construction in certain, rare circumstances (Holt 2009). Moreover, once the US NRC issues the COL, it considers all safety issues resolved. The new process thus eliminates one stage of the licensing process and one opportunity for citizen participation. Fewer opportunities for citizen input means fewer chances to delay or block licensing and construction – which was the industry's primary goal in seeking the changes.

One key rule change was designed to encourage standardization in reactor design, which would, in turn, reduce construction and operating costs and licensing review times (US NRC 2010b). Previously, one of the industry's biggest problems had been that no two reactors designs were alike, so that neither the industry nor its regulators could learn from experience. Expensive construction fixes and licensing delays were the result. The new rule allows reactor manufacturers to apply to the US NRC for a design certification independent of an actual application to construct or operate a plant (10 CFR Part 52). In issuing a design certification, the agency approves the design and considers all safety issues associated with it resolved. Design certifications are valid for 15 years from the date of issuance, but can be renewed for an additional 10–15 years (US NRC 2010c). Once the US NRC certifies a design, utilities can order these designs 'off the shelf,' and seek to license them for particular sites. Moreover, once the US NRC certifies a design, potential opponents cannot challenge the adequacy of the design in subsequent proceedings.

Another change allows utilities to apply to the US NRC for approval for a plant site before applying to actually build a plant. This 'early site approval' includes a site safety analysis, an environmental report, and emergency planning information. Early site permits are valid for 10–20 years from the date of issuance, and may be renewed for an additional 10–20 years (US NRC 2010c). For the utility, early site approval resolves potentially contentious siting issues before they have committed significant sums to a project, which could save time and money once they actually seek to build a plant at the site (Nuclear Energy Institute 2010d). As with reactor design certification, the US NRC approves sites for a nuclear power facility independent of an actual application for a construction permit, so utilities may apply for a site permit as much as 20 years before they announce the site would be used for a nuclear plant. And once the US NRC approves a site, potential opponents will not be allowed to challenge its suitability.

These two rule changes effectively bypass local opposition to nuclear plants by shifting critical decisions to rulemaking proceedings in Washington and divorcing them from individual plant applications. Beginning in the late 1960s, most opposition to nuclear power was local in nature, stemming from citizens concerned about the construction of a particular plant. Under the new rules, decisions about reactor design and site suitability will have been made up to 20 years before a utility announces its intentions to build a reactor in a specific location. At that point, however, citizens will be unable to contest the adequacy of the design or the site, because the US NRC has already deemed those issues 'resolved'.

A third change allows the US NRC to issue a combined construction permit and operating license (COL). In a COL application, the US NRC staff reviews the applicant's qualifications, and information pertaining to design safety, environmental impacts, operational programs, and site safety. The review process also specifies the inspections, tests, analyses and acceptance criteria (ITAAC) that will be used to assess the plant. The ITAAC elements are agreed upon during the design certification process and in the combined license; they are then used during construction to determine whether the plant conforms to the requirements (US NRC 2010a). Once the US NRC issues a COL, it considers all safety issues associated with the plant to be resolved.

According to US NRC Commissioner Karen Svinicki, the combined licensing process was intended to spur reactor vendors to develop a few standard designs and get them certified by the US NRC. Separately, utilities would identify and analyze candidate sites, get them approved by the US NRC, and bank them for future use. Ideally, utilities would then select a certified design, and apply to build at an already approved site. Once issued, the combined license would both authorize construction and provide conditional authority to operate the plant. The primary advantage of the new process, she said, is that:

> it is designed to provide issue finality on a great number of design and siting issues that would not need to be revisited during the combined license application process. Further, it was thought that the variability and customization that resulted from two-step licensing would be greatly reduced. Since the US NRC would already have reviewed and approved both the site and the plant design, and the staff would be dealing with, at most, a handful of fairly uniform designs, the combined license reviews would be reduced in scope and would also have the effect of reducing the scope of a post-licensing hearing. (Svinicki 2009)

The US NRC estimates that the new licensing process could take as little as 42 months, and that plant construction time will be five to seven years (Nuclear Energy institute 2010d).

In the end, the rule changes are designed to streamline the licensing process and speed the construction of nuclear plants. Given the problems that plagued the industry for most of its existence, these changes are sensible. They do, however, come with a price in reduced citizen involvement. Simply put, there are fewer opportunities for citizen input, and those that do exist have been removed from the context of specific reactors. Should utilities decide to build reactors, citizen groups will find that the new rules leave them little ground to challenge US NRC decisions.

Obstacles to a nuclear renaissance
Waste disposal

The lack of a solution for the disposal of high-level nuclear waste remains a serious problem for the nuclear industry, one made worse by the Fukushima Daiichi accident. The waste issue has dogged the industry for decades, and the failure to address it in the interim is a stunning policy failure, especially because everyone knows how important it is to the industry's future growth. In fact, the future of the waste issue has never been more in doubt, now that the Obama administration has effectively pulled the plug on the nation's only high-level nuclear waste repository, and the Fukushima disaster highlighted the safety problems of storing spent reactor fuel at operating reactors (Bradsher and Tabuchi 2011).

The Nuclear Waste Policy Act of 1982 (P.L. 97-425; 42 USC. 10101) made the federal government responsible for the disposal of spent reactor fuel. As amended in 1987 the law, which critics referred to as the 'screw Nevada bill,' required the DOE to conduct a site characterization of Yucca Mountain, Nevada as the nation's sole high-level waste repository. Under the law, the Yucca Mountain site was to begin accepting waste from the nation's nuclear plants by 1998, a date that in retrospect now seems wildly optimistic. Stymied by the gridlock over Yucca Mountain, the nuclear industry has relied on 'temporary' storage at reactor sites. As a result, spent reactor fuel is stockpiled in cooling ponds at the nation's nuclear plants, fanning concerns about cost and safety. In fact, the release of large amounts of radiation from the exposed spent fuel in the Fukushima reactors sparked a debate about similar practices at US facilities, which will undoubtedly lead to enhanced regulatory controls.

Because most utilities are required to seek state regulatory approval for expanding their on-site storage facilities, the fight over waste disposal eventually involved state officials too. Both nuclear utilities and states sued the DOE over its failure to meet the 1998 deadline, arguing that the Nuclear Waste Policy Act required the DOE to assume ownership of the waste, and sought refunds from the Nuclear Waste Fund. One state attorney general said that forcing consumers to pay for a site and then not building one was a 'high-level swindle' by the federal government (Suplee 1995). The DOE lost two federal court cases on the issue, and later estimated that its liability payments would total $11 billion if the agency were forced to begin removing waste from reactor sites by 2020 (Holt 2009).

Each US reactor generates approximately 20 metric tons of used nuclear fuel annually. All told, the industry generates a total of 2300 metric tons of used fuel per year and, over the past four decades, has produced about 62,500 metric tons of used nuclear fuel. According to the Nuclear Energy Institute (2010e), if used fuel assemblies were stacked end-to-end and side-by-side they would cover a football field about seven yards deep. The volume of waste is such, in fact, that even if the Yucca Mountain nuclear waste facility was to open, it would be too small to hold the waste that has already accumulated. If the United States was to build more reactors, then, it would also need to site and build additional waste repositories. Given the controversy over Yucca Mountain, and the radioactive releases at Fukushima, the political obstacles to siting these facilities would be enormous. In short, questions about what to do with nuclear waste would only get worse if nuclear power was to make a comeback.

As noted above, the Obama administration has announced its intention to 'terminate the Yucca Mountain program while developing above ground disposal alternatives', which would be evaluated by a panel of experts convened by the White House. Although congressional Republicans opposed the move, the 2011 budget compromise eliminated funding for the project. At this date, the Yucca Mountain project seems dead (Broder and Wald 2011).

Licensing, siting, and safety concerns

With the rush of applications noted above, the US NRC was poised to embark on a new era. The agency had granted five early site permits (Schneider *et al.* 2009), and in February 2010 President Obama announced the first loan guarantees authorized under the Energy Policy Act of 2005 – $8.3 billion to the Southern Company for its two Vogtle reactors in Georgia. Before Fukushima, it seemed likely that these would be the first reactors to test the US NRC's new licensing procedures (Harder 2009a). They still may, but it is worth remembering that nuclear power was undercut previously by rushing to bring reactors to market, by changing regulatory requirements, and by constantly changing rector designs (Duffy 1997), as well as by public concerns about their environmental consequences and about their safety. There are no guarantees that those problems will not reappear and, in fact, it appears that they already have.

Let us begin with the effort to certify and standardize reactor designs. For all of their possible virtues, the fact is that the new reactor designs are largely untested, so no one really knows if they will work as claimed, and, as noted below, no one knows if they really will be cheaper to build and operate. To date, the US NRC has received five applications for certified designs, and has approved two – the Westinghouse AP 1000 and the GE-Hitachi Advanced Boiling Water Reactor. Four of the GE-Hitachi reactors have been built in Japan, and two are under construction in Taiwan. The GE-Hitachi certification expires in 2012 and will require major changes to be re-certified (Schneider *et al.* 2009). The Southern Company plans to build two AP 1000 reactors at the Vogtle site, but the US NRC recently ruled that one component was inadequate to withstand earthquakes (Wald 2010). According to US NRC Chairman Greg Jazcko, the agency's staff had concerns with a 'novel design feature that had never been reviewed by the US NRC before' (Harder 2009b).

For a variety of reasons, the licensing process has not gone as smoothly as nuclear advocates had hoped. As one example, utilities are now required to submit complete designs before construction can begin, but this has created an approval bottleneck, which the agency insists will only apply to the initial round of applications. US NRC Commissioner Dale Klein said 'After we do a few of these plants where design certifications are totally complete and after we go through a few joint construction and operating applications, we will reduce our time significantly without compromise to safety' (Harder 2009a). A US Government Accountability Office (2007) report concluded, however, that although the US NRC has taken a number of steps to prepare its staff for new licensing reviews, many uncertainties remained about the agency's ability to manage its workload.

The US NRC has estimated that the new licensing procedures (early site permits, certified reactor designs, and combined construction and operating licenses) could take about 30 months to review a combined license application, plus an additional 12 months for hearings. According to US NRC Commission Kristine Svinicki, the process has not been allowed to 'realize its full potential'. As a case in point, applicants have referenced five different reactor designs in the combined license applications submitted to the US NRC, but only the GE-Hitachi design has completed the certification process, and it is only referenced in one application. All of the other designs are either still going through the certification process, or the applicant has amended the design, forcing the US NRC to suspend its review. Indeed, the US NRC has suspended work on four applications involving five reactors, after the applicants indicated they were considering alternative reactor designs. None of the applications currently before the US NRC reference both a certified design and an approved early site permit. As a result, in most cases the agency is simultaneously reviewing the reactor design and the combined license application. In Svinicki's (2009) words: 'The problem with this, clearly, is that the finality that the process was designed to ensure is significantly reduced, increasing both the complexity of the review and the time it takes the US NRC to complete that review'. Clearly, then, the revised licensing process has not realized its full potential in large part because the industry is repeating its earlier mistakes. And the claims of a streamlined review process seem naïve in the aftermath of Fukushima; the US NRC will be under tremendous pressure in reviewing new reactor applications.

Despite the streamlined licensing process, Fukushima makes siting one new reactor politically problematic, never mind dozens (Zeller 2011a–c). Virtually all of the applications for new plants are at locations that already have reactors; most of them are in the southeastern United States, a region that is uniquely supportive of nuclear power. To substantially increase nuclear generation, however, utilities would eventually have to build reactors in other regions that are either not as supportive or that have no experience with nuclear reactors. Public opinion polls in the months following the accident in Japan suggest that public support for nuclear plants has once again dissipated, particularly if respondents are asked about the potential of siting a reactor close to their own homes (Craighill and Cohen 2011). The volatility of public opinion reveals how vulnerable the nuclear industry is to concerns about reactor safety and about the environmental consequences of nuclear technology (Sovacool 2011). The Fukushima accident reminded those who had lived through Three Mile Island and Chernobyl why they disliked the technology; and for others too young to remember those events, it surely gave them pause.

History has shown us that perceptions of risk, plant safety, and nuclear power's costs and benefits will have a profound effect on its future. One of the reasons nuclear policy changed in the 1970s was because public and policy-maker's perceptions of nuclear power changed from positive to negative (Duffy 1997). The industry has subsequently devoted much time and money over the years to undoing those perceptions. If nuclear power advocates are to take advantage of the new licensing procedures, it is imperative that the public believe in the integrity of the process, and that the technology is safe. After Fukushima, it seems certain that the industry and its supporters have their work cut out for them.

Nuclear economics: fact and fiction

Nuclear advocates rightly note that average reactor operating costs have dropped significantly in recent years, in large part because reactors are now operating at much higher capacity levels – nearly 92% of total capacity in 2009, up from just 56% in 1980 (Nuclear Energy Institute 2010c). But for new nuclear plants, the critical issue, at least in the short term, is how much they cost to build, not how much they cost to operate. Even before Fukushima, the problems facing the industry were the very same problems that derailed it in the 1970s, most notably escalating costs (Mufson 2007, Romm 2008b). Out-of-control construction costs brought the nuclear industry to its knees in the late 1970s, and could very well derail any comeback before it even starts. From the industry's standpoint, the early evidence is not encouraging – construction costs are much higher than initial estimates, and will continue to climb after Fukushima as the public demands, and regulators adopt, stricter regulatory standards. Shockingly, in the United States a good deal of the explanation for escalating costs rests with the industry itself, which appears to have learned nothing from its earlier failures.

Nuclear power has never been able to survive in the free market – it is and has always been heavily subsidized (Romm 2009a, Cooper 2009a, b, Koplow 2009). In addition to the subsidies contained in the Energy Policy Act of 2005, the nuclear industry has enjoyed an enviable list of taxpayer support since its inception. For example, the federal government provided industry with nuclear materials and research during its formative years, and protection from liability in the event of an accident. Today, the federal government continues to spend billions on research for advanced reactors, fuel cycle technology and facilities, and waste disposal (Holt 2009). The DOE has also been paying up to half the cost of combined construction permits and operating licenses for two reactors, in order to demonstrate the efficiency of the new licensing process. The bottom line is that nuclear power is simply not competitive without huge government subsidies, and if these subsidies were withdrawn, all talk of a nuclear renaissance would immediately cease.

The various subsidies offered in the 2005 Energy Policy Act are critical to any industry rebirth, but they will only be available to the first few reactors built. And unless they are expanded, it is likely that only a handful of new reactors will be built. According to the Congressional Budget Office (US CBO 2008), the first few nuclear plants could be competitive if they received the maximum benefits allowed under the 2005 Act. Most of the reductions in the cost of those plants would come from the loan guarantees, and from the production tax credit, which would reduce by almost 15% the levels of nuclear electricity. Because the tax credit is limited to the first 6000 megawatts of new capacity, however, the value of the tax credit would be diluted if utilities tried to build many reactors because it would be spread out over more plants (US CBO 2008).

The loan guarantees authorized under the Energy Policy Act of 2005 are also critical to the industry's future. As of September 2009, utilities had submitted 19 applications for 21 reactors seeking loan guarantees totaling $122 billion. The DOE ultimately announced that four companies had made the short list; Southern Company for two AP-1000 reactors at its Vogtle site in Georgia; South Carolina Electric and Gas for two AP-1000s at its Summer site; NRG Energy for two Advanced Boiling Water Reactors (ABWR) in Texas; and Constellation Energy Group for one Evolutionary Power Reactor (EPR) at Calvert Cliffs, Maryland.[1] On 16 February 2010 President Obama announced the first loan guarantees of $8.3 billion for Southern Company's plan to build two reactors at its Georgia site (Wald 2010). In a clear sign of how important the loan guarantees are to the industry, some companies that were not selected later announced that they would delay or cancel their projects (Schneider *et al.* 2009).

Even before the meltdowns in Japan, the reality is that in the absence of loan guarantees banks will not lend money to utilities seeking to build nuclear plants. Jim Clarkson, a consultant who advises companies on how to reduce their energy costs, said: 'We've had decades of subsidies for nuclear plants and all sorts of preferential treatment. They still require loan guarantees because the smart money won't touch them' (Mufson 2010). Indeed, banks are reluctant to lend because nuclear construction costs are so high that a single reactor could amount to most of the market capitalization of many utilities. As evidence, six of the nation's largest investment banks told the DOE that they would not issue loans for new nuclear plants unless taxpayers bore 100% percent of the risk, citing acute concerns 'about a number of political, regulatory, and litigation-related risks that are unique to nuclear power, including the possibility of delays' (Schlissel *et al.* 2009). In the words of two industry critics: 'If building new nuclear power plants is such a good idea, why won't anyone put their own money at risk without government loan guarantees?' (Van Doren and Taylor 2010).

The nuclear industry has an abysmal track record with respect to predicting construction costs. A study by the US CBO (2008) reveals that cost overruns at US nuclear plants in the 1970s averaged 207%. For the more than 40 plants completed between 1979 and 1986, the construction cost overruns exceeded 250% (US CBO 2008). In short, the historical evidence shows that construction costs increased as the size of plants increased and as more plants were being built. Nuclear advocates argue that it will be different this time, but there is little in the record to suggest that such claims will be accurate.

Cambridge Energy Research Associates (2009) reported that construction costs for power plants of all types increased dramatically in the past 10 years, but especially for nuclear plants, which increased 15% annually. In 2002 DOE and industry sources projected the costs of new reactors at $1200–1500 per kilowatt, or about $2–3 billion per reactor. Today, those numbers seem surreally optimistic. In its 2007 update of its Future of Nuclear Power report, Massachusetts Institute of Technology (MIT) cited a doubling of overnight costs from $2000 to $4000 per kilowatt. In reality, however, costs have gone even higher. A report by the Keystone Center estimated capital costs for nuclear of $3600–4000 per kilowatt, and noted 'the power isn't cheap: 8.3 to 11.1 cents per kilowatt hour'. One year later one of the report's authors said 'a reasonable estimate for levelized cost range ... is 12 to 17 cents per kilowatt hour' (Romm 2008b). To put that into perspective, the overnight cost for new coal plants was $2300, and just $850 for new natural gas plants. The average cost per kilowatt hour for nuclear was 8.4 cents, for coal 6.2 cents, and for gas 6.5 cents (MIT 2009).

To be sure, new nuclear plants could be competitive if construction costs can be reduced, and if plants can be built faster than in the past, thus reducing financing costs as well. But there is little evidence of that to date. In fact, in the United States and around the world, reactor costs have again skyrocketed beyond original predictions. Areva's reactor in Finland is three years behind schedule and 75% over budget, at a total cost of $7.6 billion, or close to $4800 per kilowatt (Schneider *et al.* 2009). In the United States, the cost of the two-unit South Texas project has jumped from $6 billion to more than $17 billion (Stuckey 2010). Similarly, Progress Energy informed Florida regulators that its two-unit project would cost $14 billion, triple the estimate offered just one year earlier. The company also said that its transmission project would add another $3 billion to the cost. In October 2007, Florida Power and Light estimated that its two planned units could cost about $13–14 billion, or $5550–8100 per kilowatt. Lew Hay, chairman of the company, said:

> If our cost estimates are even close to being right, the cost of a two-unit plant will be on the order of magnitude of $13 to $14 billion. That's bigger than the total market capitalization of many companies in the US utility industry and 50 percent or more the market capitalization of all companies in our industry with the exception of Exelon ... This is a huge bet for any CEO to take to his or her board. (Romm 2008b)

Regulatory uncertainty can also add significantly to construction costs. Utilities in Georgia, Florida, and South Carolina are allowed to charge customers for construction work in progress, which saves the utilities money by shifting the costs to ratepayers. Georgia's law, passed in 2000, is projected to save Georgia Power nearly $2 billion of the cost of two reactors. In a statement of remarkable candor, Suzanne Grant, a spokesperson for Progress Energy, a Florida utility, said of construction work in progress that, 'Without this legislation, we would not be considering building new nuclear generation in Florida' (Mufson 2010). Not surprisingly, consumer groups and some affected businesses have balked at paying higher electricity rates up front, noting that the reactors have not been approved by the US NRC and may never be approved. In fact, Progress Energy later delayed its nuclear project for 20 months, because the regulatory review was taking longer than expected; ratepayer opposition was also a factor (Plumer 2009). Florida Power and Light suspended its proposed Florida project when state regulators approved a fraction of their rate request (Whitten 2010).

Some independent analysts have also raised questions about potential materials and labor shortages should there be a rush to nuclear power, suggesting that there are not enough nuclear science and engineering students, or nuclear technicians, to staff additional plants (Keystone Center 2007). Others have suggested that a limited global supply of key reactor components like pressure vessels, steam generators, and cooling pumps could create procurement and manufacturing bottlenecks that would result in higher than projected construction costs. Because nuclear plants are capital intensive and have long lead times, this is a potentially serious problem. To cite one example, the Japan Steel Works Lt Facility in Hokkaido, Japan is the only plant in the world capable of manufacturing the central component for reactor containment vessels in one piece. Although the company has announced plans to double its manufacturing capacity, it would still be insufficient to meet projected demand. Even though the US NRC has not given the green light to any of the proposed reactors, several US utilities have already reserved slots at the facility (Takemoto and Katz 2008).

Nuclear power, and all other low greenhouse gas energy sources, would undoubtedly be much more attractive economically if some form of carbon tax was established. A 2008 report by the US CBO found that, in the long run, a carbon tax would increase the competitiveness of nuclear power, and 'could make it the least expensive source of new base-load capacity' (US CBO 2008, p. 2). More specifically, the US CBO (2008, p. 29) concluded that carbon charges of about $45 per metric ton 'would probably make nuclear generation competitive with conventional fossil-fuel technologies as a source of new capacity, even without EPAct incentives. At charges below that level, conventional gas technology would probably be a more economic choice'. For example, if the tax was between $20 and $45 per metric ton, nuclear generation as an option for new capacity would probably be preferred over coal but not natural gas. The US CBO (2008) noted that utilities would probably opt to continue operating existing coal plants until carbon charges reached about $45 per ton. In other words, nuclear plants would not displace emissions from coal plants unless and until a fairly sizable carbon tax was enacted. Given implacable Republican opposition to most carbon pricing options, however, it is highly unlikely that one will be enacted at any point in the foreseeable future. This is exceedingly ironic, given broad Republican support for nuclear power generally.

Conclusion

A study by MIT (2003) concluded that for nuclear power to become a significant option for reducing greenhouse gas emissions and meeting projected demands for electricity, current worldwide nuclear capacity would need to be expanded by a factor of three by the year 2050. A 2007 update to that report noted, however, that 'even if all the announced plans for new nuclear power plant construction are realized, the total will be well behind that needed for reaching a thousand gigawatts of new capacity worldwide by 2050' (MIT 2009). The report concluded that 'the sober warning is that if more is not done, nuclear power will diminish as a practical and timely option for deployment at a scale that would constitute a material contribution to climate change risk mitigation' (MIT 2009).

To state the obvious, it is hard to predict the future. Energy forecasts are notoriously unreliable. In the 1960s and early 1970s, projections of rapid growth in the demand for electricity lead many utilities to order reactors. Then the oil shocks in 1970s slowed economic growth dramatically, and the projected demand never materialized and utilities cancelled the reactors.

The meltdowns in Japan have clearly complicated the chances of a nuclear revival in the United States and around the world, at least in the short term. But there were already several longstanding, significant obstacles nuclear power had to overcome. One is the lack of progress in addressing concerns about waste disposal. With the Obama administration's decision to terminate work on the Yucca Mountain nuclear waste repository, there is no viable option on the horizon for dealing with nuclear waste in the United States, a problem only made worse by the problems with spent fuel at the Daiichi reactors. The industry is also plagued by lingering public concerns over reactor safety and environmental contamination, which could greatly complicate efforts to site nuclear plants, especially outside of the Southeast. The industry and its supporters point to the advantages of new, simplified reactor designs featuring passive safety features, fewer components, and lower material and construction costs. For all of their possible virtues, however, most of the new reactor designs are untested, so we do not know whether they really will work as claimed; nor do we know whether such reactors will actually be cheaper to build and operate. History has shown us that the claims of industry supporters about nuclear economics were wildly optimistic and the public is now more skeptical of the industry's commitment to safety.

If the nuclear industry was somehow able to reduce construction, operation, and maintenance costs significantly from previous levels, their product would be more competitive with other fuel sources. Similarly, nuclear power would certainly benefit in the longer term if emitting carbon became more costly, although it is unclear whether policy-makers have the stomach to enact policies that would raise the price of carbon enough to help nuclear. The US CBO has estimated that:

> Even if carbon dioxide charges over $45 per metric ton were implemented, it would take decades for sufficient nuclear capacity to be put in place before most utilities could consider substituting new nuclear capacity for existing coal plants. Replacing the 300,000 megawatts of existing coal capacity would require hundreds of new nuclear plants, a virtual impossibility in the aftermath of Fukushima. The capacity of the industry that builds nuclear plants and its suppliers of components is currently constrained and unlikely to expand rapidly enough for even tens of plants to be built in the next decade. (2008, p. 29)

Finally, nuclear power has been a poor choice economically, and in the United States has never been competitive without huge government subsidies. Although the economic incentives offered in the 2005 Energy Policy Act are significant, they apply to only a handful of reactors. While it is conceivable that a few reactors will be built, a broad revitalization will require fundamental shifts in nuclear economics, including a significant expansion of subsidies, and a resolution of the lingering concerns with waste disposal and reactor safety. Ultimately, the real question is whether investments in nuclear make more sense than investments in other technologies, which pose far fewer problems and which yield quicker returns.

Note

1. In October 2010, Constellation Energy announced that it was unable to agree to terms with the Department of Energy on the $7.5 billion loan guarantee (Behr 2010). Following the Fukushima meltdowns, NRG cited financing issues in announcing that it was suspending work on its South Texas project; Tokyo Electric and Power Company, which owns the Fukushima reactors, was one of the investors (Wald 2011).

References

Behr, P., 2010. Constellation pullout from Md. Nuclear venture leaves industry future uncertain. *New York Times*, 11 October. Available from: http://www.nytimes.com/cwire/2010/10/11/11climatewire-constellation-pullout-from-md-nuclear-ventur-82774.html [Accessed 5 June 2011].

Bradsher, K. and Tabuchi, H., 2011. Greater danger lies in spent fuel than in reactors. *New York Times*, 17 March. Available from: http://www.nytimes.com/2011/03/18/world/asia/18spent.html?scp=1&sq=bradsher%20+%20tabuchi%20+%20greater%20danger&st=cse [Accessed 17 March 2011].

Broder, J.M. and Wald, M.L., 2011. Report blasts management style of Nuclear Regulatory Commission Chairman. *New York Times*, 10 June. Available from: http://www.nytimes.com/2011/06/11/science/earth/11nuclear.html?_r=1&hpw [Accessed 11 June 2011].

Cambridge Energy Research Associates, 2009. Press release, 23 June. Available from: http://www.cera.com/aspx/cda/public1/news/pressReleases/pressReleaseDetails.aspx?CID=10429 [Accessed 4 March 2010].

Clayton, M., 2010. Obama's nuclear power policy: a study in contradictions? *Christian Science Monitor*, 4 February. Available from: http://www.csmonitor.com [Accessed 11 February 2010].

Cooper, M., 2009a. *All risk, no reward for taxpayers and ratepayers: the economics of subsidizing the 'nuclear renaissance' with loan guarantees and construction work in progress*. South Royalton, VT: Institute for Energy and the Environment.

Cooper, M., 2009b. *The economics of nuclear reactors: renaissance or relapse*. South Royalton, VT: Institute for Energy and the Environment.

Craighill, P.M. and Cohen, J., 2011. Slim majority of Americans see nuclear plants as safe energy source, poll finds. *Washington Post*, 19 April. Available from: http://www.washingtonpost.com/politics/slim-majority-of-americans-see-nuclear-plants-as-safe-energy-sources-poll-finds/2011/04/19/AFRnZG9D_story.html?wpisrc=emailtoafriend [Accessed 1 June 2011].

Dempsey, J., 2011. Germany shuts 7 plants as Europe plans safety tests. *New York Times*, 15 March. Available from: http://www.nytimes.com/2011/03/16/business/global/16euronuke.html?scp=7&sq=dempsey%20+%20germany&st=cse [Accessed 16 March 2011].

Dempsey, J. and Ewing, J., 2011. Germany, in reversal, will close nuclear plants by 2022. *New York Times*, 31 May. Available from: http://www.nytimes.com/2011/05/31/world/europe/31germany.html?_r=1&emc=eta1 [Accessed 31 May 2011].

Duffy, R.J., 1997. *Nuclear politics in America: a history and theory of government regulation*. Lawrence, KS: University Press of Kansas.

Harder, A., 2009a. Nuclear industry faces bottleneck. *National Journal Magazine*, 12 September. Available from: http://www.nationaljournal.com/njmagazine/id_20090912_1485.php?mrefid=site_search [Accessed 20 February 2010].

Harder, A., 2009b. NRC at center of nuclear regulatory bottleneck. *National Journal*. Available from: http://insiderinterviews.nationaljournal.com/2009/09/nrc-at-center-of-nuclear-regul.php [Accessed 20 February 2010].

Holt, M., 2009. *Nuclear energy policy*. Washington, DC: Congressional Research Service, RL33558.

International Atomic Energy Agency, 2010. *Latest news related to PRIS and the status of nuclear power plants*. Available from: http://www.iaea.or.at/programmes/a2/ [Accessed 17 February 2010].

Keystone Center, 2007. *Nuclear power joint fact-finding*. Keystone, CO: Keystone Center.

Koplow, D., 2009. *Nuclear power as taxpayer patronage: a case study of subsidies to Calvert Cliffs Unit 3*, 7 July. Arlington, VA: Nonproliferation Policy Education Center.

Massachusetts Institute of Technology, 2003. The future of nuclear power: an interdisciplinary study. Available from: http://web.mit.edu/nuclearpower/ [Accessed 14 January 2010].

Massachusetts Institute of Technology, 2009. Update of the MIT 2003 future of nuclear power study. Available from: http://web.mit.edu/nuclearpower/pdf/nuclearpower-update2009.pdf [Accessed 7 April 2010].

Morales, A., 2011. Nuclear curbs will hurt climate, energy security goal, IEA economist says. *Bloomberg News*, 30 March. Available from: http://www.bloomberg.com/news/2011-03-30/nuclear-curbs-will-hurt-climate-energy=security=goal-iea-econo mist-says.html [Accessed 2 June 2011].

Mufson, S., 2007. Nuclear power primed for comeback: demand, subsidies spur US utilities. *Washington Post*, 8 October, A1.

Mufson, S., 2010. Nuclear projects face financial obstacles. *Washington Post*, 2 March. Available from: http://www.washingtonpost.com/wp-dyn/content/article/2010/03/01/AR2010030103975.html?hpid=moreheadlines

Nuclear Energy Institute, 2009. New nuclear plant licensing. Available from: http://www.nei.org/keyissues/newnuclearplants/newnuclearplantlicensing [Accessed 26 February 2010].
Nuclear Energy Institute, 2010a. Clean-air benefits of nuclear energy. Available from: http://www.nei.org/keyissues/protectingtheenvironment/cleanair/ [Accessed 26 February 2010].
Nuclear Energy Institute, 2010b. New reactor designs. Available from: http://www.nei.org/keyissues/newnuclearplants/newreactordesigns/ [Accessed 26 February 2010].
Nuclear Energy Institute, 2010c. US nuclear industry capacity factors, 1971–2008. Available from: http://www.nei.org/resourcesandstats/documentlibrary/reliableandaffordableenergy/graphicsandcharts/usnuclearindustrycapacityfactors/ [Accessed 15 February 2010].
Nuclear Energy Institute, 2010d. Licensing new nuclear power plants. Available from: http://www.nei.org/keyissues/newnuclearplants/factsheets/licensingnewnuclearpowerplants [Accessed 15 February 2010].
Nuclear Energy Institute, 2010e. Nuclear waste: amounts and on-site storage. Available from: http://www.nei.org/resourcesandstats/nuclear_statistics/nuclearwasteamountsandonsitestorage/ [Accessed 10 March 2010].
Plumer, B., 2009. The future of nuclear, revised. *The New Republic*, 21 May. Available from: http://www.tnr.com/blog/the-vine-the-future-nuclear-revised [Accessed 29 October 2009].
Romm, J., 2008a. *The self-limiting future of nuclear power*. Washington, DC: Center for American Progress Action Fund.
Romm, J., 2008b. Nuclear power, part 2: the price is not right. Climate progress, 13 June. Available from: http://climateprogress.org/2008/06/13/nuclear-power-part-2-the-price-is-not-right/ [Accessed 15 February 2010].
Sovacool, B.K., 2011. *Contesting the future of nuclear power: a critical global assessment of atomic energy*. London: World Scientific.
Schlissel, D., Mullett, M. and Alvarez, R., 2009. *Nuclear loan guarantees: another taxpayer bailout ahead?*, March Union of Concerned Scientists. Available from: http://www.ucsusa.org/assets/documents/nuclear_power/nuclear-loan-guarantees.pdf [Accessed 10 February 2010].
Schneider, M., et al., 2009. 2009 World nuclear industry status report. *Bulletin of the Atomic Scientists*, November/December, 1–19.
Snyder, J., 2010. Nuclear's revival. *The Hill*, 3 March. Available from: http:ww//thehill.com/business-a-lobbying/84595-nuclears-revival [Accessed 3 March 2010].
Stuckey, M., 2010. Loan guarantees recharge nuclear debate. MSNBC.com, 9 February. Available from: http://www.msnbc.msn.com/id/35236957/ns/politics/ [Accessed 9 February 2010].
Suplee, C., 1995. A nuclear problem keeps growing. *Washington Post*, 31 December, A1.
Svinicki, K., 2009. Remarks of Commissioner Kristine L. Svinicki, US Nuclear Regulatory Commission, to the French Institute for International Relations, 4 May. Available from: http://www.nrc.gov/reading-rm/doc-collections/commission/speeches/2009/s-09-011.html [Accessed 9 March 2010].
Takemoto, Y. and Katz, A., 2008. Samurai-sword maker's reactor monopoly may cool nuclear revival. *Bloomberg.com*, 13 March. Available from: http://www.bloomberg.com/apps/news?pid=20601109&sid=aaVMzCTMz3ms [Accessed 17 February 2010].
US Congressional Budget Office, 2008. *Nuclear power's role in generating electricity*. Washington, DC: US CBO.
US Department of Energy, 2010. Department of energy files motion to withdraw Yucca Mountain license application. Available from: http://www.energy.gov/news/8707.htm [Accessed 5 March 2010].

US Energy Information Administration, 2011. Report No. DOE/EIA-0383: annual energy outlook 2011. Available from: http://www.eia.gov/oiaf/aeo/pdf/0383%282011%29.pdf [Accessed 25 August 2011].

US Government Accountability Office, 2007. *Nuclear energy: NRC's workforce and processes for new reactor licensing are generally in place, but uncertainties remain as industry begins to submit applications*, 21 September. Washington, DC: US GAO, GAO-07-1129.

US Nuclear Regulatory Commission, 2010a. Combined license applications for new reactors. Available from: http://www.nrc.gov/reactors/new-reactors/col.html [Accessed 5 March 2010].

US Nuclear Regulatory Commission, 2010b. Design certification applications for new reactors. http://www.nrc.gov/reactors/new-reactors/design-cert.html [Accessed 5 March 2010].

US Nuclear Regulatory Commission, 2010c. Early site permit applications for new reactors. Available from: http://www.nrc.gov/reactors/new-reactors/esp.html [Accessed 5 March 2010].

Van Doren, P. and Taylor, J., 2010. Stop nuclear welfare. New York Times.com room for debate blog: a comeback for nuclear power?, 16 February. Available from: http://roomfordebate.blogs.nytimes.com/2010/02/16/a-comeback-for-nuclear-power/?scp=1&sq=comebackpercent20forpercent20nuclearpercent20power?&st=cse [Accessed 16 February 2010].

Wald, M., 2010. US supports new nuclear reactors in Georgia. *New York Times*, 17 February. Available from: http://www.nytimes.com/2010/02/17/business/energy-environment/17nukes.html?scp=1&sq=inpercent20bidpercent20topercent20revive&st=cse [Accessed 17 February 2010].

Wald, M., 2011. NRG abandons project for 2 reactors in Texas. *New York Times*, 19 April. Available from: http://www.nytimes.com/2011/04/20/business/energy-environment/20nuke.html [Accessed 7 June 2011].

Whitten, D., 2010. Nuclear industry gets lift, no 'renaissance' from aid (update 1). *Bloomberg.com*, 17 February. Available from: http://www.bloomberg.com/apps/news?pid=newsarchive&sid=aBuB0XcbLLkE# [Accessed 17 February 2010].

Yang, J.L. and Mufson, S., 2011. Japan quake puts spotlight on aging US nuclear reactors, cost of building new ones. *Washington Post*, 16 March, A1.

Zeller, T., 2011a. US nuclear plants have same risks, and backups, as Japan counterparts. *New York Times*, 13 March. Available from: http://www.nytimes.com/2011/03/14/world/asia/14industry.html?scp=3&sq=zeller%20+%20US%20Nuclear&st=cse [Accessed 14 March 2011].

Zeller, T., 2011b. Experts had long criticized potential weakness in design of stricken reactor. *New York Times*, 15 March. Available from: http://www.nytimes.com/2011/0316/world/asia. Available from: http://www.nytimes.com/2011/03/16/world/asia/16contain.html?hp [Accessed 16 March 2011].

Zeller, T., 2011c. With US nuclear plants under scrutiny, too, a report raises safety concerns. *New York Times*, 17 March. Available from: http://www.nytimes.com/2011/03/18/science/earth/18scientists.html?scp=4&sq=zeller%20+%20US%20Nuclear&st=cse [Accessed 18 March 2011].

'Hasta la vista, baby!' The Solar Grand Plan, environmentalism, and social constructions of the Mojave Desert

Christian Hunold and Steven Leitner

> Proposals for large-scale solar thermal plants in Southern California have won enthusiastic government support. Public debate on this technology's environmental consequences has been notably muted, however. Why have environmentalists found it so difficult to secure ecologically sound siting processes for large-scale solar thermal plants? Instead of representing a shift toward environmental stewardship and sustainability, the discourse of the 'Solar Grand Plan' to develop renewable energy in Southwestern deserts parallels high-modernist narratives of the past century. Using discourse analysis, three different conceptions of space and place that shape the debate are identified. The Grand Solar Plan champions solar development as clean energy. This has generated a conservationist narrative that seeks to minimize habitat and landscape destruction but has yet to have a substantial impact on policy – although this may be starting to change. This lack of impact is explicable in terms of a third, culturally dominant discourse of the desert as barren and useless.

Introduction

Reducing greenhouse gas emission by making energy systems less carbon-intensive is a goal of governments everywhere in the industrialized world. One approach that is gaining ground in California is the development of large-scale solar thermal plants in the Mojave Desert. Energy companies have won federal and state government support in the form of expedited permitting procedures and financial subsidies. Technological and financial barriers to building solar thermal plants with generation capacities in excess of 500 MW are no longer insurmountable, and public support for expanding renewable energy production is strong. The construction of such plants is being advanced as part of a 'Solar Grand Plan' according to which a large fraction of US electricity needs would be produced in the southwest deserts and exported to population centers via high voltage transmission lines (Zweibel *et al.* 2007). Organized local opposition, however, is emerging as a major barrier to expanding solar power generation in California.

Southern California's solar thermal plants are to be built in remote, scarcely populated areas of the Mojave Desert. As envisioned by the 'Solar Grand Plan', deserts figure chiefly as solar resources to be harnessed for human energy needs. In the public imagination, deserts often signify lifelessness rather than wilderness worthy of protection; in the United States, they are also among the most despoiled landscapes (Kuletz 1998). Seen from this perspective, the surfacing of opposition to the siting of large-scale renewable energy projects in the deserts and semi-deserts of the American Southwest requires explanation. In this paper, we describe and analyze the claims, arguments, and rhetorical strategies advanced by competing actors on behalf of and against the siting of solar thermal plants in the Mojave Desert.

Our main argument is this: instead of representing a fundamental shift toward environmental stewardship and sustainability, the discourse of the 'Solar Grand Plan' (Zweibel *et al.* 2007) to develop renewable energy installations in the deserts or semi-deserts of the American Southwest closely parallels high-modernist narratives of the past century – initiatives intended to promote grand technological projects while legitimating or concealing their true environmental repercussions, often through specific constructions of the land, resources, and ecosystems at issue. Partisans in the Grand Solar Plan construct their positions on the basis of very different conceptions of space and place. Following an overview of the presently unfolding 'Solar Renaissance' across the American Southwest, we identify three discourses that intersect, compete, and coexist to shape the contours of the debate.

The Grand Solar Plan, as articulated by its proponents, comprises interlocking policy-making and public relations discourses to present the case for solar development to the public. In opposition to the Grand Solar Plan, an environmentalist counter-narrative that seeks to minimize habitat and landscape destruction has arisen. This counter-narrative, first advanced by desert conservationist groups based in southern California, has been slow to capture the imagination of national environmental organizations such as the Sierra Club and the Natural Resources Defense Council, which have resisted embracing environmentalist critiques of solar energy projects out of concern for compromising their own climate protection agenda (Mieszkowski 2009). What has made the Grand Solar Plan so persuasive to many, including many leaders of the US environmental movement? We account for this persuasiveness in terms of a third discourse that precedes the arrival of solar energy technology by many decades and that provides the cultural backdrop against which proponents and opponents of the Grand Solar Plan confront one another. This is a persistent view of the desert as a barren, useless, and undifferentiated wasteland – a culturally dominant view that complicates efforts to protect pristine wilderness from the incursion of renewable energy projects.

Explaining the 'Solar Renaissance'
Technological progress

California's Renewables Portfolio Standard Program, amended in 2006, mirrors the renewable energy portfolio standards (RPS) adopted by 25 other states at the time of this writing. RPS are a market-based approach to climate change, part of a broader trend of environmental policy innovation and diffusion at the state level as a response to inaction at the federal level. RPS legislation seeks to reduce emissions of greenhouse gases, especially carbon dioxide, by providing a guaranteed market to the renewable energy industry. The use of mandated percentages or megawatts is intended to help the industry establish a 'foothold' in the economy (Becker 2008). Some states have included in their RPS tradable credits programs and direct financial incentives; all are set up to have gradually increasing renewables requirements. California's legislation requires that, by 2010, 20% of the state's retail electricity will come from renewable sources, which are defined as 'biomass, solar thermal, photovoltaic, wind, geothermal, fuel cells using renewable fuels, small hydroelectric generation of 30 megawatts or less, digester gas, municipal solid waste conversion, landfill gas, ocean wave, ocean thermal, or tidal current' (SB 107 2006, p. 8). Of all these sources, solar energy will probably be among the primary means to meet California's 2010 goals. In November 2008, then-governor Arnold Schwarzenegger issued an executive order mandating 33% renewable energy by the year 2020.

Converting solar energy into significant amounts of electricity is a relatively recent development. A distinction should be made here between two types of solar technology – photovoltaic (PV) and concentrating solar power (CSP). Solar PV is the technology found in calculators and rooftop panels and is the type most widely known by the public. CSP or solar thermal differs from PV in at least two fundamental respects. First, unlike PV technology, CSP may be used efficiently in large-scale installations to generate considerable output. 'Large-scale' in this context means areas of up to several square miles. Although recently there has been renewed interest in utility-scale PV farms (the California utility PG&E contracted in August 2008 for two of such plants to produce a total of 800 MW), even the largest PV facility in existence is substantially smaller than the biggest CSP – although the size and price disadvantages of PV are subject to technological change and may be disappearing fairly quickly. Second, unlike solar PV, which generates energy from capturing the sun's photons, CSP does not directly convert sunlight into electricity but concentrates solar heat by way of a system of mirrors. The heat is then converted to electricity using a gas-driven or steam-driven turbine (Solar Power and Sun Lab n.d.).

Land-use considerations

Beyond technological progress, the present 'Solar Renaissance' is made possible by the opening up of public lands for leasing for construction and ongoing operation of solar power plants. In late 2004 spokespeople for the US Department of the Interior announced the intention of the Bush administration to create favorable terms for the leasing of Bureau of Land Management (BLM) land to solar developers (Environment News Service 2004). The Federal Land Policy and Management Act of 1976 served as the general basis to achieve this end, with 'right-of-way' leases the specific mechanism. All such leases would be situated on BLM land.

The right-of-way concept was originally created to allow transmission lines to move through public land along narrow corridors; these involve relatively small amounts of land, even for a transmission corridor with several lines providing energy to millions of customers. Because of the relatively limited impacts of such corridors, the leasing mechanisms are simplified and require only limited environmental review compared with leases for larger, higher-impact activities. Solar thermal fields, however, require single plots of thousands of acres to be cleared of vegetation. A framework establishing the details of obtaining right-of-way permits, and what these permits allowed, was outlined in a 2004 BLM memo, updated in 2007 (BLM 2007).

The status of large-scale solar projects in California

For evidence of a true race to cash in on solar opportunities in California, one needs look no further than the California Energy Commission's website on 'Large Scale Solar Projects in California':

> Many large solar energy projects are being proposed in California's desert area on federal Bureau of Land Management (BLM) land. BLM has received right-of-way requests encompassing more than 300,000 acres for the development of approximately 34 large solar thermal power plants totaling approximately 24,000 megawatts. (California Energy Commission 2008)

These requests represent a vast increase in generating capacity. If all these plants were actually built, California would have roughly 50% more electricity and solar reflectors would cover a combined area the size of the sprawling city of Los Angeles. Even if some of these right-of-way requests are speculative in nature, the potential habitat destruction implied by these solar applications is significant and explains the alarm being expressed by Mojave Desert advocates.

Large-scale solar CSP projects must go through a long and expensive review process before construction, requiring approval from both the BLM and the California Energy Commission, which entails acceptance under the National Environmental Protection Act (requires a publicly available environmental impact statement) and the California Environmental Quality

Act (CEQA). The final stage is the Application for Certification with the California Energy Commission (2008).

All environmental impacts of the proposed solar power plant must be accounted for in the project's Application for Certification. If the chosen site is habitat for federally listed threatened or endangered species environmental mitigation agreements must be reached. But whether mitigation can meaningfully lessen the destruction inflicted on a species is dubious and strongly contested by environmentalists. Mitigation in the case of a solar siting in the Mojave, as with any development on public land, means that the developer must purchase known habitat on private land for the species in question. This area is then dedicated as a no-development preserve for that animal or plant. The population on the site to be developed is not transferred and not likely to survive (even if animals were to be moved, it is unlikely there would be a high rate of survival). Environmentalists object to mitigation in the current siting process because the populations of the two primary species of concern, the desert tortoise and Mohave ground squirrel, are already so low.

Environmental advocates have offered alternatives. In the *Desert Report*, a Sierra Club-associated newsletter, widespread adoption of rooftop PV is presented as the ecologically ideal application of solar technology, since it uses fully developed sites, and generates electricity where it is needed, rather than being transmitted hundreds of miles, with its own environmental effects and resulting loss of electricity. PV is 'locally generated renewable power' and suggested as 'the better alternative'. Still, one author admits, 'that means either government incentives fostering its development or technological breakthroughs' (Taylor 2008, p. 5).

Another line of thinking may be more promising: siting CSP plants on privately owned former agricultural land throughout the sun-drenched areas of Southern California. This land has been leveled and cleared of vegetation; often the land has been abandoned due to groundwater depletion and is no longer usable. Build on that land, say supporters of this compromise, and leave the wild and undisturbed habitat for rare and endangered species. 'What would be the reaction if it were proposed to cut down vast areas of old-growth forest and permanently commit the land to production of renewable energy?' asks a concerned wildlife biologist in a letter to Rick York, Senior Biologist at the CEC (Leitner 2008, p. 1).

The question is an evocative one. Certainly 'paving over' old growth forest for energy production would not, by and large, be viewed as a viable option. So why then has the 'Solar Renaissance' proceeded with virtually no contestation of its proponents' claims that it is entirely 'environmentally friendly' (Nanosonic and Department of Energy n.d.)? We offer the following explanation: a symbolic and literal 'hierarchy of ecosystems' (Kuletz 1998, p. 254) that places the desert last on a ranking by human value and a pre-existing discursive construction of the desert (and the American West generally) lending itself to effortless salesmanship in the media have converged to legitimize the building of massive CSP solar fields in the Mojave Desert with a minimum of environmental consideration. The strength of this pre-existing construction also has rendered significantly more difficult the task of advancing environmentalist policy alternatives and counter-narratives, such as those introduced above. We now examine each layer of discourse in turn, starting with the underlying construction of the desert that has structured more recent events.

Barren deserts and grand technological projects
Widely held beliefs in the barrenness of desert lands in general, and specific deserts of the Southwest in particular, have established certain patterns of thinking and behavior that have persisted for over a century and influence the current debate over solar siting. Related closely both in genealogy and the ideological purposes served are the American discourses of the grand technological project: the great dams of the West, massive irrigation systems, the railroads, and even nuclear power. The two – the construction of wild 'nature' to be transformed into useful resources and the modernist discourses of monumental or nation-defining technology projects – are inextricably linked. Historically, the former has been used as a foundational narrative to justify the latter. Both discourses are culturally deeply embedded, and are drawn upon both to fit the ideological needs of different interests under present circumstances. Landscape studies as well as political science accounts inspired by the spatial and constructivist turns in the social sciences offer insights and useful models for investigating the solar energy debate. In what follows, we rely on the work of authors that has helped us unearth the various meanings attached to 'nature' and 'desert'.

John Beck (2001, pp. 64–65) identifies five central 'rhetorical tropes' embedded within the 'overarching conception of the desert as vacancy'. First, the notion of emptiness is connected to a fundamental *uselessness*, which is the basis, perhaps, for legitimizing all kinds of destruction of and experimentation on the desert. This uselessness can be understood as arising from the western perspective that acknowledges and values only human subjectivity – and, as many scholars have pointed out, traditionally it is only the subjectivity of particular, privileged groups of humans that really counts (Kuletz 1998, p. 207). Second, 'the desert is a metaphor of apocalypse, evidence of the ultimate wasteland' (Beck 2001). Third, there is a sense that the desert represents the boundaries of reason, with 'its tendency to alter habits of perception' and association with a primordial chaos, especially in the Judaic/Hebraic tradition (for example, the Book of Genesis; the Hebrew word for desert has connotations of chaos and confusion). Fourth, these qualities also become coupled with modernist ideology: the desert becomes the ultimate test for humans' capacity to impose reason and rationality on chaos and disorder. Finally, and perhaps less convincingly, Beck (2001, 65) finds a parallel between the vastness and boundarylessness of the desert and contemporary, globalizing capitalism.

Valerie Kuletz (1998) begins her study with a similarly articulated set of constructed attributes of the desert through which she understands the legitimacy of the 'nuclear discourse' that she claims represents the epitome of environmental degradation perpetrated against the American desert. The principal uses in the past 50 years of the Southwestern deserts have been as military bases, weapons testing grounds, clandestine science laboratories (sanctioned by the government and not), and nuclear dumping grounds. Indeed, Kuletz (1998, 7) writes, the desert landscape has been filled with residue of this 'internal colonialism'. Everywhere:

> 'signs' of power: high-wire fences, radar antennae, massive satellite communications dishes tilted up toward the stars, sonic bombs, stealth aircrafts, well-maintained roads in the middle of 'nowhere' leading to various 'installations', earth-shaking explosions, military trucks and personnel, unmarked trucks carrying 'explosives', jet trails across the bright blue sky, guard towers, fencing and more fencing, and everywhere government signs that read 'DO NOT ENTER'. (Kuletz 1998, 40)

Kevin Wehr (2004) captures the discourse of the great western dams and the construction of nature that legitimized them. Nature, in the form of large and rushing rivers, was, time and again, portrayed as a 'natural menace' that could be, nevertheless, through human technological ingenuity, 'convert[ed] ... into a natural asset' (Wehr 2004, 64). The notion of redemption for a somehow 'failed' landscape is an idea that reappears in the contemporary desert discourse. The destructive river becomes useful to humans (Wehr 2004, 70). Or, 'irrational' nature made rational (2004, 129). A common theme Wehr explores is the way in which agency is projected onto nature (2004, 65), requiring 'taming' (2004, 72). Yet contradictorily, these rivers would also be described in terms that suggest they were created precisely *for* human use (Wehr 2004, 82). Rivers 'had' to be 'harnessed' for the sustained economic growth of the southwestern United States (Wehr 2004, 110–111).

Technology was often brought to the desert in the shape of grand water projects: irrigation systems and dams. The Hoover Dam paved the way for the Glen Canyon Dam, which promised: 'The desert will bloom and great cities sparkle with light if only we would set our machines in motion' (James, Jr 1994, p. 4). Irrigation systems were heralded as a means to expand agriculture and settlement far beyond what as previously thought possible. There is a sense in the texts that Wehr draws upon that it would be a profound moral injustice to allow the 'natural wealth' to be wasted, by leaving it untransformed by technology (2004, 157). Social problems could and should be solved by technical means (Wehr 2004, 175). Water would be redirected by these dams for agricultural use in 'sub-marginal' (Wehr 2004, 175) arid regions, thus 'creating a 'prosperous and productive region' out of a sagebrush desert' (2004, 174). An additional section describes the cooption of the burgeoning environmental discourse: nature would be *improved* by these grand technological projects (Wehr 2004, 219). The Solar Grand Plan, we argue, harnesses the rhetoric of sustainable development to similar effect today.

The Solar Grand Plan[1]

Discourse analysis begins with the premise that actors' discursive constructs, imagery, stated and unstated values and assumptions are fundamental to understanding politics; our analysis of the solar discourses of supporters and critics of building solar power plants in the desert starts from this insight. Drawing on the environmental discourse analysis literature (Dryzek 2005, Barry *et al.* 2008) and textual analysis of policy documents produced by government agencies (BLM, California Energy Commission, California Governor's Office, Department of Energy, Western Governors' Association); promotional materials produced by the energy industry; campaign literature published by desert advocacy groups; and national and local media reports about solar energy policy and development in the Mojave Desert, we have identified four themes that anchor the Solar Grand Plan and the environmentalist counter-narratives: construction of desert space and its inhabitants; assumed values and relationships, including the appropriate relationship between humans and rest of the planet; the tension between renewable energy development and conservation; and the construction of the politics of renewable energy, including proponents/opponents of solar development in the Mojave Desert, and these agents' proposals for better policy alternatives. These themes broadly mirror each other across the discourses of solar proponents and their desert conservationists. To better understand the role that constructions of the desert play in the politics of solar energy in California, one of the authors of this study conducted, in July and August 2008, open-ended, semi-structured telephone interviews with seven environmental activists and energy industry representatives.

This Solar Grand Plan leaves intact and seeks to build on dominant constructions of the desert. The Plan has been articulated in a slew of policy documents, industry PR campaigns, and media coverage of the push for solar energy development in the Mojave Desert. There appears to be a close connection between the public relations campaigns of the State of California and the solar industry; the media have, more or less uncritically, adopted the phrases and vocabulary that originally appeared in these PR campaigns. There is a remarkable degree of consistency in the words, phrases, and ideas applied to solar technology and its potential uses in government and industry documents and media reports about solar energy. These include electricity price stability for sustained growth as the primary reason for pursuing solar technology; a concern with regulatory innovations to promote solar industry interests (implicitly as a means to get around environmental regulations); and portraits of renewables generally – and solar specifically – as economic boons to states through job creation. References to the environmental benefits of solar energy, such as limiting climate change by reducing greenhouse gas emissions, are decidedly secondary in these documents (for example, Solar Task Force 2006). In a sense, in the logic of the Solar Grand Plan and its proponents, CSP technology has become essentially self-justifying: it is good because it is renewable. This discursive constellation is consistent with observations about the growing acceptance in the United States of 'weak' ecological modernization discourses that emphasize 'green' technology development and job creation while giving a cold shoulder to the precautionary principle and ideas of nature as intrinsically valuable (Schlosberg and Rinfret 2008).

The *Scientific American Magazine* article that introduced the term 'Solar Grand Plan' exemplifies how solar energy proponents minimize environmental impacts. Mentioning studies by the National Renewable Energy Laboratory, the article asserts 'that more than enough land in the Southwest is available without requiring use of environmentally sensitive areas, population centers or difficult terrain' (Zweibel et al. 2007, p. 65). For example, a 2002 National Renewable Energy Laboratory report prepared for the US Department of Energy entitled 'Fuel from the Sky' claims that: 'Solar resources are optimal in the Desert Southwest and—given the geographic and climatic conditions— potentially the best in the world' (Leitner 2002, 43). The desert represents 'vast expanses of unused land' (Leitner 2002, 47): 'Premium solar resource areas, for example, are typically hot plains with little or no vegetation' (2002, 47). Described as 'scorching' and thus basically lifeless (Leitner 2002, 95), the southwestern deserts offer vast areas of 'empty' land. Their apparent uselessness to humans and non-humans alike serves to downplay the environmental impacts associated with building and operating solar power plants. Deserts, on this basically utilitarian view, are resources that offer plenty of space and sunlight and few significant problems for power plant development. Environmental impacts and political opposition are thought to be minimal because solar power plants use little water and emit no pollution— and the land on which they are to be built is widely thought of as having little value to anyone. Further, it is suggested that environmentalist activists are self-contradictory and impossible to satisfy – first calling for ways to address climate change and then rejecting 'reasonable solutions' such as large-scale solar power plants.

Consistent with our expectation that deserts occupy the bottom rungs on a ladder of natural ecosystems, the discourse of the Solar Grand Plan has no patience for valuing deserts precisely *because* they are (relatively) undisturbed landscapes. At most, there are half-hearted appeals to a sort of commonsense environmentalism: 'The desert ecology deserves protection, but the best locations for solar power plants are on land for which there might be few other uses' (Leitner 2002, 97). Imagining deserts as barren landscapes devoid of (valuable) life seeks to erase contradictions between solar power and wilderness preservation. It is not clear, at any rate, which aspects of desert ecology might deserve protection, or why. Rather, the prevailing tone suggests there may not be very much desert ecology worth conserving to begin with – an impression apparently shared by the Governor of California. Celebrated for his proposals to combat climate change, then-Governor Schwarzenegger in a *60 Minutes* interview nonetheless staunchly championed human needs over those of an inherently fragile ecosystem:

> The Mojave Desert is the best place to have a solar field because it has the most sun. [...] You have sun all year round. It's the best place. But there are some that want to hold it up because they think that it would endanger some animal life. That is going overboard. (Quoted in Mieszkowski 2009)[2]

In fact, when the California Department of Fish and Game is doing its job enforcing endangered species regulations, the governor seeks to resolve the tension between development and conservation by declaring the species in question imaginary!

> Now, the department wants the power company to buy three acres of land to protect these little creatures for every acre of solar land that is being used so that the squirrel could be saved if it exists. So a squirrel that may not exist is holding up environmental progress on a larger and more pressing fight against global warming. What they have here is a case of environmental regulations holding up environmental progress. I don't know whether this is ironic or absurd. But, I mean, if we cannot put solar power plants in the Mojave Desert, I don't know where the hell we can put it [*sic*]. (Schwarzenegger 2008)

Additionally, the 'if not here then where?' device employed above is often typical of the proponent discourse in logic and tone. It can be read both as an objective statement of the desert's high levels of solar radiation *and* an affirming of its otherwise useless and empty nature, while simultaneously suggesting that any dissent would be unreasonable.

We should note that many solar developers are quick to emphasize their concern and awareness of environmental issues regarding siting. Many people who work for these developers identify as environmentalists. Renewable energy companies are often formed with some commitment to 'the environment' written into their mission statement. When representatives of developers speak, they could be seen as saying all the right things from an environmentalist perspective:

> The responsibility is not lost on this company. We recognize that we have to do this right. We're setting a precedent for other solar plants to come. And we know that doing it right is going have a tremendous impact on the wildlife there. [...] We really recognize and understand the concerns of the environment groups there. (Scher, personal interview)

Increasingly, also, it seems, solar developers are pushing messages about their environmental responsibility. Conservationist counter-narratives may be having an effect here. When pressed about environmental impacts during interviews, on several occasions representatives from the solar industry would respond by asserting the desirability but also *inevitability* of the construction of large-scale solar installations in the Mojave, and with the notion that 'trade-offs' are necessary (Flatow, personal interview; Anonymous, personal interview).

Conservationist counter-narratives

Interviews with members and representatives of environmental organizations concerned about solar development in the Mojave confirm the significant obstruction to the goal of ecologically oriented siting posed by the pre-existing constructions of the desert, which cast the ecosystem in hostile, pejorative, devaluing terms. These interviews, combined with textual analysis of advocacy documents and press releases, also yield insight into the strategies adopted by desert environmentalists, including burgeoning attempts to forward counter-narratives, both about the desert itself and environmentalists' own preferences for policy, social values, and the human–environment relationship. Additionally, activists we encountered were careful in navigating the tension between 'big-picture' environmental goals – namely, the transition away from a fossil fuel-based economy – and their interest in the local conservation in the Mojave Desert.

For desert environmental activists, the anthropocentric hierarchy of ecosystems and the desert-as-a-wasteland construction are pervasive, everyday realities. Desert conservation is 'just more difficult', said Monica Argandoña, Desert Program Director for California Wilderness Coalition (personal interview). While activists decry the culturally dominant, negative conception of the desert upon which rests much of the strength of the case for rapid and unquestioned development, some have attempted to offer a direct counter-narrative about the Mojave. These activists hope that if the currently 'empty' desert space was to be discursively 'filled' with valuable natural entities, the entire orientation toward the desert by renewables developers and policy-makers – characterized by environmentalists as largely exploitative – would require dramatic reconfiguration. Various means have been employed to this end. Argandoña, for example, recalls an occasion where the *Los Angeles Times* published an article about the Mojave Preserve that drew on all the familiar desert constructions (Anton 2008):

> I felt like I was reading something that could have been printed 25 years ago. You think we've come a long ways in the desert but this article was about, again, 'the desert is a wasteland', all the murders that happen out there, illegal drug trade, train robberies ... It was such an exaggerated, horrible article. We all sent in letters to the *Times*. The National Parks Conservation Association, who represents the Mojave Preserve and Death Valley, submitted an editorial. None of it ever got published. (Argandoña, personal interview)

The article is essentially one cliché after another ('The desert is good at keeping secrets', reads its final line); what is more interesting and relevant is the content of the National Parks Conservation Association's response. Indeed, a brief, four-paragraph statement captures perfectly the main themes of the desert value discourses that exist as part of the broader environmentalist counter-narratives, emphasizing magnificent landscapes and pristine, unique ecosystems containing a multitude of interesting creatures and vegetation:

> Though deserts are often perceived as barren landscapes, these ecosystems sustain a considerable diversity of flora and fauna, including 100 year-old tortoises, 12,000 year-old creosote bushes, vibrant wildflowers, bighorn sheep, lizards, snakes, and other uniquely adapted plant and animal species [...] cactus gardens and Joshua tree forests, hidden springs and palm oases, impressive rock formations, sand dunes that dwarf skyscrapers, rugged mountain ranges, fields of wildflowers, and multihued canyons. (NPCA)

Similar language appears on a number of other websites, press releases, and educational videos, all seeking to forward a new construction of the desert as a worthwhile and special place (for example, California Wilderness Coalition 2005, Talamo 2008).

A notable exception to those approaches is a 2007 report released by Defenders of Wildlife, an environmental organization primarily concerned with habitat conservation and biodiversity (Kroeger and Manalo 2007). In *Economic Benefits Provided by Natural Lands: Case Study of California's Mojave Desert*, the authors use benefit–cost analysis to quantify the value the desert economic terms. While the stated goal of the report is the same as the other attempts in the valuing discourses – that is, to minimize all kinds of development in the Mojave – we observe a significant contrast not just in tone, but also in basic assumptions that underlie the authors' methods. The Defenders of Wildlife document is useful, therefore, in uncovering the divergences between the majority of the environmentalist positions and the Solar Grand Plan discourse. In the latter, discussed above, two basic assumed values were that human interests trump all others (and further, it would be absurd to suggest otherwise) and that there is nothing intrinsically worthy of special protection in undisturbed habitats. By these measures, the benefit–cost report is linked closely to the assumption of the solar proponents. First, only human utility is considered, if for no other reason than it is the only interest that can be satisfactorily quantified. Second, the entire purpose of the analysis for Defenders of Wildlife is reaching a justification for protecting undisturbed habitat while still relying on anthropocentric value claims, which generally characterize the orientation of most policy-makers.

The conservationist counter-narratives, on the other hand, begin from the assumption that the desert and its inhabitants are already valuable, that non-human interests are valid and worthy of representation – in contrast to the Solar Grand Plan proponents' general lack of recognition for anything of value existing in the desert other than 'world class solar resources'. While solar proponents are often unclear about what aspects of the desert *would be* deserving of protection, and on what grounds, desert conservationists are clear about their priorities and goals.

Some activists nonetheless acknowledge the limitations of their attempts at discursive reshaping, especially considering the degree to which the pejorative constructions of the desert are entrenched. D'Anne Albers, California Desert Associate for Defenders of Wildlife, expresses resignation at the prospect of a serious messaging campaign against misconceptions regarding the desert given the Sierra Club's longstanding support of the Solar Grand Plan (Albers, personal interview). Argandoña suggests, more hopefully, that initially skeptical individuals need to experience the desert firsthand to understand that the desert is inhabited and dramatically different from place to place (personal interview). How such experiences may be practically arranged for large numbers of people who do not already enjoy visiting – and have the means to visit – southwestern deserts remains an open question.

In political debates, how one depicts the other side can sometimes be a source of power stronger than one's rational argument or even material resources. We have already discussed the proponents' characterization of (particularly the less moderate) desert environmental advocates as irrational, obstructionist, hypocritical; and how that characterization mostly follows a common script for casting environmental groups in the United States in a negative light. As elsewhere, opponents are uncritically characterized as 'NIMBYs' as a strategy to denigrate and belittle (see also Barry *et al.* 2008). The activist construction of their opponents is often similar in this respect, reflecting an equally common script for the environmentalists against the monolithic corporation. In the present case, however, there is a twist: the industry involved, although it remains capitalist (see also Jessup 2010), has a reasonably fair claim to working in the pursuit of environmental aims. This added complication puts up a further obstacle to be negotiated by the desert conservationists.

'Mainstream' environmentalist organizations such as the national leadership of the Sierra Club sought to downplay the language of opposition and conflict in negotiating this terrain. For such groups, the solar industry was found to be an occasional target of some criticism, but also a potential ally. The more radical local groups, in contrast, were more intent on sharpening the notion that there exist fundamentally opposing interests between 'sides' in the politics of solar development in the Mojave. Talk of opposition and conflict was expressed in interviews and abundant in advocacy documents. In contrast to the proponent discourse with its themes of technological progress, advancement, and environmental benefit, desert conservationists use metaphors and imagery of unbridled greed, violence, power, and environmental abuse. Referring not only to the barrage of site applications to BLM for solar plants (many of them speculative) and associated plans for transmission line development. but also the many other activities that threaten Mojave land, Argandoña states:

> It's a land grab [...] my guess is that there's not going to be much left of the California desert in ten years that isn't designated for something [...] whether it

be military expansion, whether it be energy corridors, off-road places, wilderness, development. There'll be something. It's a land-grab and everyone wants their piece. Solar and wind is just one piece of it. (Argandoña, personal interview)

The notion of a solar 'land grab' across the Southwest, or 'the desert area of California' being 'up for grabs' (Jim Harvey of the Alliance for Responsible Energy Policy quoted in Debra Kahn 2008) appears time and again in the conservationist discourse.

Related tropes, used with comparable frequency, draw upon the cultural memory of greed, sudden human overrunning of wild land in the American West and of anarchic free-for-alls after the discovery of an exploitable natural resource. Jim Harvey, in the same article, contends: 'There's a gold rush to exploit it, particularly the Mojave' (Debra Kahn 2008). Similarly, Michael Cipra, desert program manager for the National Parks Conservation Association, calls the solar siting speculation 'like a gold rush' (Marquis 2009). 'Solar boom' (Marquis 2009) recalls the silver and gold boomtowns that sprung up all over California and Nevada in era of the '49ers. A piece written by April Sall of the Wildlands Conservancy for *The Desert Report* entitled 'A Feeding Frenzy in the Desert: The New California Gold Rush' adds a reference to violent predation (Sall 2008).

Indeed, the theme of violence, often as perpetrated against a 'fragile' and already 'dwindling' desert ecosystem (as well as its inhabitants) is a common one, especially among the local and more radical organizations. A press release from the California Wilderness Coalition decries the coordinated, 'full-scale assault' by developers and policy-makers against 'some of the last wild places owned by the American public' (California Wilderness Coalition 2005). Then there are the evocative verbs used by environmental advocates to describe the building of large-scale solar plants: 'scrape the desert' (Hogue, personal interview), 'bulldoze', 'pave over' (to be fair, the first two could also refer to technical construction processes, but they are also deployed for emotional effect), '... blitz these animals and their habitats on private lands, and the conservation would all take place on public lands' (Anderson, personal interview).

For some environmental organizations, 'violence' of this sort presents not a call for resistance but an opportunity to engage in conflict resolution. The Sierra Club represents the far end of the spectrum in terms of working with the state and with the solar industry. As Carl Zichella, Sierra Club's transmission and renewable energy siting director for the Western United States, explains in a video produced by the Center for Energy Efficiency and Renewable Technology:

> We know right now, sitting here, that there are going to be compromises that have to be made. When you look at the bigger picture, and the effects of global warming and climate change on these ecosystems, we have little choice. We want to see Joshua trees in Joshua Tree National Park. We need to do something about global warming and climate change, and we are running out of time. [...]

We need to do the same thing we're doing in California in other states. Big Solar is a very important part of that.[3]

Local activist groups, such as the Alliance for Responsible Energy Policy and the Desert Protective Council, and a few state and national environmental organizations are much less willing to engage 'Big Solar' along these lines.

Conclusion

As we have shown, a firm belief in technological progress as the source of ecological salvation suffuses the desert solar development discourse. When this sort of techno-optimism meets the desert, it cannot help to seek to transform it. Pro-solar government reports, media stories, and industry brochures typically features at least one photograph of gleaming solar reflectors (usually parabolic troughs). When shot as a group and angled steeply downwards or upwards against the clear blue sky, the image of these highly reflective mirrors evokes a gleaming pond or series of channels of water: a desert oasis. Thus the imagery associated with public information on solar energy in the Mojave Desert serves to promote certain ways of thinking about the sites of these power plants. First, vegetation has already been cleared from around the reflectors, reinforcing the notion that the desert is indeed wholly barren. Second, solar power plants bring a symbolic 'oasis' to the desert wasteland – an oasis of human usefulness, created by the rational transformation of the 'inhospitable' or 'challenging' desert.

The cultural dominance of this narrative, we have argued, has complicated the efforts of desert conservationists who question the wisdom of the present run to cash in on the Mojave Desert's solar resources. The State of California's reliance on this same narrative to bolster its status as an environmental policy leader has arguably been more successful. Efforts at the national level, led by Senator Dianne Feinstein (D-CA), to protect what are described as 'core areas' of the Mojave Desert's wilderness bordering both Joshua Tree and the Mojave National Park from solar development may go some way toward meeting the desert conservationists' aims, but they do not amount a to a wholesale shift away from the ideas enshrined in the Solar Grand Plan. However disappointing or successful any one group of environmentalists may judge the gains in land protection implied by Senator Feinstein's California Desert Protection Act (CDPA), the law is unlikely to pass in the post-2010 Congress.

The solar advocates, such as the US Secretary of Energy Steven Chu, the Solar Energy Industries Association (SEIA) and solar energy companies continue to argue that the Mojave Desert is the most logical area to build large-scale solar projects (Chu 2010, SEIA 2010). Advocates for solar energy believe the bill does not offer enough incentives for solar energy development, and that the CDPA would set aside too much desert land when solar energy development should be given a higher priority. Ultimately, these advocates argue that the Mojave Desert 'is arguably the best solar land in the world, and Sen. Feinstein shouldn't be allowed to take this land off the table without a proper and scientific environmental review' (Kennedy cited in Woody 2009). A much weakened version of the CDPA introduced by Senator Feinstein in 2011 has dropped the provisions related to solar energy and seeks only to expand the two national parks in question.

Given widely held cultural views of the desert as a barren wasteland, it remains unclear how much headway to expect from desert conservationists' efforts to protect such habitats from solar energy development. Like other relatively unpopulated areas of the world – the Polar regions come to mind – deserts are at first glance promising candidates for the conservationist case to protect nature for nature's sake. But in a predominantly capitalist society ecocentric arguments for habitat conservation are a hard sell under the best of circumstances, and building a statewide let alone national audience receptive to such pure ecological appeals on behalf of relatively undisturbed desert habitat has proved exceedingly difficult. It may be that small rodents and rare tortoises are inherently less attractive than are polar bears and emperor penguins in terms of aiding conservationists in making the case for protecting the Polar regions from industrial development (and *that* case is now coming under attack from interests seeking to increase exploitation of the Arctic's mineral resources).

Efforts to protect the Mojave Desert and other southwestern deserts areas from solar development based on anthropocentric appeals may not have a much brighter future. Unlike the locally cherished landscapes that have fueled political contention around proposed wind farms, the desert is *not* a place where a great many people live or indeed want to live. Many of the southwestern deserts' human residents – Native Americans, low-income retirees attracted by low or non-existent property taxes, or just folks with a preference for 'living off the grid' – are politically marginalized. Desert communities typically do not have the resources to stage the sort of high-profile showdown that unfolded, for example, between an offshore windfarm developer and wealthy Cape Cod residents in the first decade of the twenty-first century (Phadke 2010) – many such communities might in fact welcome the financial windfall associated with solar development. Building large-scale solar energy facilities in the desert, then, is effectively to place them 'out of sight, out of mind' of most of the residents of metropolitan Los Angeles or San Diego. The proposition to exchange 'barren' land for a source of electricity that is less dependent on fossil fuels than conventional sources will probably continue to look like a 'no-brainer' to a majority of Americans.

Notes
1. We have borrowed the term 'solar grand plan' from the title of Zweibel *et al.* (2007).
2. To his credit, the governor envisioned solar power installations would sprout on every conceivable surface in his state. Speaking at the Solar Power International conference in October 2008, he said: 'I can envision going with the helicopter up and down California and seeing no more warehouses without solar panels. No matter where you look, there's solar involved. It's everywhere' (quoted in Kho 2008).
3. Available from: http://cleanpower.org/Ceert_Video/CEERT_4%20MINUTE%20v5.wmv

References

Anton, M., 2008. Team of lone rangers scours the new Wild West. *Los Angeles Times*, 25 September. Available from: http://articles.latimes.com/2008/sep/25/local/me-ranger25 [Accessed 11 March 2009].
Barry, J., Ellis, C. and Robinson, C., 2008. Cool rationalities and hot air: a rhetorical approach to understanding debates on renewable energy. *Global Environmental Politics*, 8 (2), 67–98.
Beck, J., 2001. Without form and void: the American desert as trope and terrain. *Nepantla: Views from South*, 2 (1), 63–83.
Becker, B., 2008. The subsidy tease, part II. Available from: http://gristmill.grist.org/story/2008/2/14/111544/211 [Accessed 24 February 2008].
Bureau of Land Management, 2007. *Solar energy development policy*. Washington, DC: Bureau of Land Management.
California Energy Commission, 2008. Large solar energy projects. Available from: http://www.energy.ca.gov/siting/solar/index.html [Accessed 1 June 2008].
California Wilderness Coalition, 2005. No more wilderness: the Interior Department's Attack on wilderness protection. Available from: http://www.calwild.org/campaigns/nowild.php [Accessed 1 June 2008].
Chu, S., 2010. Energy efficiency: achieving the potential. Available from: http://www.energy.gov/news/8764.htm [Accessed 18 March 2009].
Debra Kahn, J.J.F., 2008. *A solar-motivated land rush hits the southwestern deserts. Climatewire*. San Francisco: Earth News.
Dryzek, J.S., 2005. *The politics of the earth: environmental discourses*. Oxford: Oxford University Press.
Environment News Service, 2004. Bush administration backs solar development on public lands. Available from: http://www.ens-newswire.com/ens/oct2004/2004-10-25-03.html [Accessed 24 February 2008].
James Jr, W.L., 1994. *Challenging the desert: the making of the American landscape*. Ed. M.P. Conzen. New York: Routledge.
Jessup, B., 2010. Plural and hybrid environmental values: a discourse analysis of the wind energy conflict in Australia and the United Kingdom. *Environmental Politics*, 19 (1), 21–44.
Kho, J., 2008. Schwarzenegger: solar can't be stopped. *Greentechmedia.com*, October 14. Available from: http://www.greentechmedia.com/articles/schwarzenegger-solar-cant-be-stopped-1577.html [Accessed 11 March 2009].
Kroeger, T. and Manalo, P., 2007. *Economic benefits provided by natural lands: case study of California's Mojave Desert*. Washington, DC: Defenders of Wildlife. Available from: http://www.defenders.org/programs_and_policy/science_and_economics/conservation_economics/valuation/economic_value_of_the_mojave_desert.php [Accessed 11 March 2009].
Kuletz, V., 1998. *The tainted desert: environmental ruin in the American West*. New York: Routledge.
Leitner, A., 2002. *Fuel from the sky: solar power's potential for western energy supply*. Golden, CO: National Renewable Energy Laboratory.
Leitner, P., 2008. Siting issues for desert solar projects. Letter to Rick York, California Energy Commission.
Marquis, A.L., 2009. Solar rush: California's solar boom threatens the very places it's meant to protect. *National Parks*, 83 (1), 16–18.
Mieszkowski, K., 2009. The tortoise and the sun: it's a showdown among environmentalists out West, where proposed solar-energy plants threaten the desert ecosystem. *Salon.com*, 22 January. Available from: http://www.salon.com/env/feature/2009/01/22/desert_tortoises/index.html [Accessed 11 March 2009].

Nanosonic and Department of Energy, n.d. DOE awards abstracts: high preformance, low-cost nanostructured mirror surfaces. Available from: http://www.science.doe.gov/sbir/awards_abstracts/sbirsttr/cycle24/phase2/075.htm [Accessed 11 March 2009].

Padke, R., 2010. Steel forests or smoke stacks: the politics of visualisation in the cape wind controversy. *Environmental Politics*, 19 (1), 1–20.

Sall, A., 2008. A feeding frenzy in the desert: the New California goldrush. The Desert Report, Sierra Club California/Nevada Desert Committee.

SB 107, 2006. *Public interest energy research, demonstration, and development program.* Sacramento, CA: California State Assembly.

Schlosberg, D. and Rinfret, S., 2008. Ecological modernisation, American style. *Environmental Politics*, 17 (2), 254–275.

Schwarzenegger, A., 2008. Keynote address at Yale Climate Change Conference. Available from: http://gov.ca.gov/speech/9360/ [Accessed 11 March 2009].

Solar Energy Industries Association, 2010. Poll: 3 out of 4 Americans approve of solar energy development on public lands. Available from: http://www.seia.org/ [Accessed 18 March 2009].

Solar Power and Sun Lab, n.d. Concentrating solar power technologies overview. Available from: http://www.energylan.sandia.gov/sunlab/overview.htm [Accessed 11 March 2009].

Solar Task Force, 2006. *Solar task force report.* Denver, CO: Western Governors' Association.

Talamo, D., 2008. A place of quiet in a frantic world. *Desert Report*, June, 17.

Taylor, J., 2008. 'Big solar' – solution or threat? *Desert Report*, March, 2, 5.

Wehr, K., 2004. *America's fight over water: the environmental and political effects of large-scale water systems.* New York: Routledge.

Woody, T., 2009. Desert vistas vs. solar power. *New York Times*, 21 December. Available from: http://www.nytimes.com/2009/12/22/business/energy-environment/22solar.html?_r=1 [Accessed 18 March 2009].

Zweibel, K., Mason, J. and Fthenakis, V., 2007. Solar Grand Plan. *Scientific American*, 298 (1), 64–73.

A middle range theorization of energy politics: the struggle for energy efficient appliances

Rachael L. Shwom

> Treadmill of production (TOP) theory and ecological modernization theory (EMT) are adapted to a middle-range theorization of energy politics, specifying the conditions that each theory would best apply to struggles over the energy system. It is hypothesized that EMT will prevail when there are high levels of public awareness of an issue, a record of past regulation, a threat of future regulation, and disunity of the business class; and that TOP power relations are more likely to prevail are low public consciousness, absence of past regulation, low threat of future regulation, and high levels of business unity. The usefulness of this contextualized approach is explored using a historical qualitative case study of the struggle in the United States to implement national mandatory and voluntary definitions of energy efficiency for home appliances. The implications of the findings are discussed in light of efforts to transform energy systems.

Introduction

While much of the climate change discourse has focused on how individuals can change daily behaviors to reduce their individual contributions to climate change via decreases in energy use, structural changes in our production systems are needed to enable citizen behavioral changes. For example, media campaigns encourage consumers to purchase compact fluorescent light bulbs and energy-efficient appliances. This individualistic discourse of consumer consumption is dependent on a market rationale that consumer demand for green goods will be met by supply. However, in the case of many energy-efficient and green products these 'perfect market conditions' are never met (Goldstein 2006). In the case of energy-efficient appliances, the simple story of consumers demanding energy-efficient appliances and manufacturers meeting this demand ignores a three-decade political battle to bring these 'green' products to the market for purchase. In fact, the apparent challenges in moving 'market-ready' and available technologies into the market without major policy changes has led Robert Socolow to fear that his well-cited paper on technological 'wedges' that could be used to stabilize greenhouse gas emissions (Pacala and Socolow 2004) may have made it seem too easy to address climate change (Struck 2011).

Insights from economic, political and environmental sociology provide healthy critiques of this dependency on the 'invisible hand'. One thread of this critique leads us to question the social relations that lead to market production and consumption patterns. There is much to be gained from focusing on the politics of production that determine the availability of 'green' or 'climate-friendly' options for consumption. Gould *et al.* (2004, p. 297) argue that 'consumer choice devolves from: the constraints of specific prior production decisions; specific prior economic distribution decisions; and a specific distribution of policy and decision-making power. To place consumption decisions first in our analyses would obscure the power relations embedded'. As the social struggle to mitigate and adapt to climate change takes center-stage (Giddens 2009), this paper seeks to enhance our understanding of the politics of getting 'greener' choices to consumers in the struggle to transform our energy systems.

Environmental sociologists have often used two major theoretical lenses to make sense of US environmental politics: treadmill of production (TOP) theory and ecological modernization theory (EMT). TOP theory emphasizes the structure of capitalism and its intrinsic acceleration of resource use and misuse, while EMT focuses on the potential for modern capitalist societies to transform industrial structure and production to improve resource use. Both perspectives have been able to point to cases that support their theoretical argument (Pellow *et al.* 2000, Scheinberg 2003). Almost all have agreed that each theory can account for the experiences of specific nations or industries at certain times, indicating that the underlying institutional contexts may be able to account for the differing outcomes predicted in each theory (Buttel and Gijswijt 2000, Mol and Spaargaren 2000).

The middle-range focus used here to explore these political economic theories of the environment is inspired by Hooks' (1993) approach to investigating competing theories of the state in political sociology. Heeding Merton's (1968) call for middle-range theory, Hooks (1993, p. 75) argued that the strong versions of theories of the state made 'a priori commitments that only the converted would endorse'. Acknowledging the limits of the various theories, weaker variants put forth relaxed the strong assumptions and used pieces of each theory to explain phenomena in an *ad hoc* fashion. This allowed the weakened theoretical formulations to account for more of the complexities of history, but also caused them to become less theoretically distinctive. Indeed, this is the very situation that environmental sociologists face today in theorizing the political economic forces of environmental degradation and reform. Here I specify the institutional contexts that account for the environmental degradation predicted by TOP and improvement or 'greening' predicted by EMT. This middle-range political economic theorization is then applied to examining the evolving institutional relationships among the state, businesses and social movements and their outcomes around the definition and promotion of energy efficient residential appliances.

The state of green energy politics in current political economic theory of the environment

There has been a great deal written about the power of markets to bring about changes in the environmental impacts and human safety of products, but the political economy of consumer products and market failures must be understood. The political economy of green products that I develop builds on competing established theories of environmental impacts resulting from production. These theories to date have been used to explain resource use by producers in making a product rather than the environmental attributes of the end product itself. In the case of energy-efficient appliances, the targeted change is to get manufacturers to produce an energy-efficient product for consumers, not to make their production practices more efficient. I argue that the power relations between societal sectors that EMT and TOP predict are well suited to apply to any case where there is a conflict between users' interests and the producer's interest in a product as well.

Ecological modernization is often described as the process of 'economizing the ecological' and 'ecologizing the economic' (Mol 1995). This means that ecological modernization is the process by which the market comes to value natural resources and ecosystem services and account for their value in prices. If market signals are clear and account for environmental costs, 'economizing the ecology', then production processes will automatically become more resource efficient and end-users will demand more efficient, green, safe products (Mol 1995, Mol and Spaargaren 2000). However, market failures are commonplace in natural resource management, particularly in energy efficiency (for a detailed account of market failure, see Goldstein 2006), and the middle-range theory I propose is focused on the predicted power relations in EMT and TOP that determine what ecology gets economized and what economy gets ecologized and how that happens. That is, what is internalized and externalized is a result of the exercise of power.

The strong variants of EMT and TOP are broad macro-level theories of the state, business, and social movements that explain the extent of environmental degradation or improvement in modern capitalist societies. As is, these theories are difficult to support or disprove, and efforts to evaluate them have consisted mainly of a single nation or industry leading to problems of case selection.[1] In addition, even empirical work on the same industry, urban recycling, has led different researchers to different conclusions about the meaning of events and the ecological outcomes (Pellow et al. 2000b, Scheinberg 2003). Despite advocacy for more well-constructed empirical research to shed light on this debate, work that contextualizes these theories and views them as ongoing processes in time and space continues to be lacking (York et al. 2010). Here I will develop a middle-range theorization of energy politics that integrates both theories through a longitudinal case study of the dynamic power relations of US energy efficiency policy.

The strong variant of ecological modernization states that the objectives of business, the state, and civil society align to account for both economic and ecological values in decision-making. Environmental problems are a result of the failure of capitalism and accompanying political institutions to modernize enough to bring about the technological solutions that result from a merging of ecological and economic objectives. In EMT, public pressure and market regulation are strong enough forces to lead corporate actors to incorporate ecological rationales into their decision-making, effectively greening production. As this process occurs, EMT predicts that businesses participate in leading this ecological restructuring by taking pro-environmental actions beyond those required by regulation. State agencies focus on facilitating business leadership through a shift away from command-and-control regulation and toward more inclusive negotiated rule-makings and flexible approaches. Environmental social movement organizations adopt new tactics in moving these goals forward by engaging in direct cooperative partnerships with businesses (Mol 1995). Intensifying relationships among these groups are indicative of the shared logics of 'greening' the economy and development of cooperative working relationships to reach these goals.

This early strong formulation of ecological modernization has come under a number of criticisms. The most strident is the critique that the capitalist logic of profit has not been and cannot be ecologized and any appearance as such is window-dressing (Pellow et al. 2000). York and Rosa (2003) put forth a call for empirical support for the suppositions of EMT. Specifically, they seek evidence that: the modernization of institutions yields real ecological improvements; superindustrialization resulting in green production and consumption is a common occurrence; overall impacts from industries and firms are being reduced and not simply shifted geographically or from one kind of impact to another; and the pace of increases in resource efficiencies are outstripping the pace of increases in overall production (Clark and York 2005, York 2006). This line of criticism claims that increasing ties among business, environmental movement organizations, and the state are not a reflection of converging interests, but a tool to subordinate social movements' goals to the profit motive of business (Pellow et al. 2000). Buttel (2000) critiques EMT's failure to clarify and ground itself in broader sociological theories of state-society.

In response to these critiques, several tenets of the strong formulation of EMT have been weakened. The first is an acknowledgement that the pathway of development toward an ecological economy and the content of modernity is contingent upon many factors. The integration of ecological concerns is not inevitably a product of superindustrialization, but instead a product of a political process where the pathway is dependent on contestation among state, private firms and civil society groups. It is a 'purposive change due to political decision making and institutional restructuring' that allows for heterogeneity in patterns of development (Perz 2007, p. 422). Similarly, EMT has moved away from the stringent assumptions regarding the environmental outcomes of capitalism (Perz 2007). This weaker variant leaves space for contextualizing the power relationships among states, environmental social movement organizations (ESMOs) and businesses, but fails to take the opportunity to specify the institutional conditions that lead to these relative power relations and their corresponding environmental outcomes.

Contrary to EMT, TOP argues that there is a fundamental conflict between the environment and capitalist economic production. Schnaiberg (1980) theorizes that the institutional arrangements under monopoly capitalism result in the competition and concentration of capital that leads to increases in capital investment and technological production efficiencies. This increase in productive physical capital requires even more ecosystem resources and results in the increasing rates of withdrawals of material resources from the earth and additions of these material resources transformed into waste and deposited into the environment. This cycle is referred to as the 'treadmill of production'. It generally predicts a worsening of the health of the environment through an accelerating treadmill. 'Environmental improvement' is understood as a substantial slowing or dismantling of the treadmill. Producers will not account for ecological harms in their decision-making unless forced to do so because it would reduce profits. The state is dependent on expanding capital production and consumption for increasing tax revenue. Workers are dependent on it for jobs. Any efforts to slow the treadmill of production are tempered by a belief by all actors that some form of economic expansion is needed to meet their material needs (Schnaiberg 1994). In TOP, civil society and business are fighting for scarce resources and the state is a mediator that tends to favor business, but will negotiate between the two in a 'managed scarcity' approach when there is a resource crisis that becomes apparent to the public. Increasingly close relationships among these groups are generally viewed as a process of cooptation by business of state and civil society interests, rather than a shared logic of ecology.

TOP theory has faced its challenges over the past quarter-century. Broadly, there has been a general demise in the political and academic popularity of Marxian analyses or critiques of capitalism in sociology. Hannigan (1995, p. 22) argues that the whole model relies 'exclusively on the logic of the capitalist system' and a resulting economic determinism, although Buttel (2000) defends TOP against this assertion. The initial formulation of TOP was an analysis of the US political economy of resource use. The majority of recent critiques are based on globalization and its impacts on the political economy theorized by TOP scholars. The expansion of neoliberal capitalism globally is theorized to have increased the power of businesses to act as they wish while diminishing the autonomy of the state to control flows of money and resources across national borders. This has challenged TOP's theorization of the nation-state as a negotiator between business and civil society's resource needs. In addition, there is an emergence of transnational environmental movement organizations seeking to counter the rise of transnational corporate power (Gould *et al.* 2004).

Treadmill theorists have accommodated these critiques in a few ways though the thrust of their argument regarding the treadmill has remained the same. One response has been to de-emphasize the role that monopoly capital plays in the model. Gould *et al.* (2004) highlight instead how the global north's industrial treadmill is predicated on southern natural resource pools, labor pools, markets, and waste sinks. They also focus on the increasing ability of transnational corporations to shift production internationally. The authors argue that the reorganization of global capital has forced localities (nations, states, and so forth) to compete with others, undermining their ability to protect the environment through political action (Gould *et al.* 1994). In addition, they recognize that the forces of the treadmill are decreasingly tied to the US state (Gould *et al.* 2004). TOP advocates argue that there are new or renewed forms of political coalitions that seek to oppose the transnational treadmill such as new environmental–labor alliances and the anticorporate globalization movement, but they maintain these coalitions are greatly diminished by local and global treadmills and commodification (Buttel 2004).

Toward a middle-range adaptation of ecological modernization and treadmill of production

I argue that the debate on TOP and EMT has lingered for two reasons: it is easy to observe instances that appear to resemble each theory's characterization of relationships between state, social movement, and business actors – cooperative and combative; and it is difficult to assess the negative or positive environmental outcomes from these relationships. A middle-range theorization of these broad theories seeks to scope the conditions under which the dynamics predicted would emerge, illustrating how they may be complementary views of environmental politics. I do not address the negative or positive environmental outcomes in this study, although certainly advocate for research that tries to do so. In EMT and TOP, there are assumptions about the power relations among state, social movements and business and how each sector behaves. Rather than assume power relations are one way or another, it is better to specify the conditions under which the power relations predicted arise.

When recast as a middle-range theory, the relationships anticipated by EMT are likely to emerge when:

- environmental movement strength is high. This would be constituted by high levels of unity within and across movements (i.e. labor/environment

coalitions), high levels of public consciousness and support around an issue, and/or levels of capability for collective action. A strong social movement increases the societal pressures for business to adopt an ecological rationality;
- the state is open to public pressure to regulate industry, heightening the threat of future regulation via increased political opportunity structure for the public to actualize their objectives via regulation (McAdam *et al.* 1996);
- the industry has already been regulated on the issue, and thus has developed ways of incorporating regulatory costs that reduce further resistance (Fineman and Clarke 1996, Parson 2003); and
- business interests are fragmented, weakening business's ability to oppose regulation and pursue a single interest (Mizruchi and Bey 2005).

When recast as a middle-range theory, the relationships anticipated by TOP are likely to emerge when:

- there are high levels of counter-movement strength that organize public opposition to environmental movement efforts to influence the state (Gale 1986, Meyer and Staggenborg 1996);
- there are high levels of business unity to oppose social movement influence on the state to force business to be responsible for environmental costs of their activities, this condition being dependent upon either a monopolistic or oligarchic industry structure with low competitive pressures and/or a strong trade industry association that facilitates industry unity (Mizruchi and Bey 2005); and
- there is low threat of regulation and little previous regulation of an industry. Overall, there is little threat in times of economic crisis when state autonomy is decreased and it becomes more dependent on business decreasing receptivity to civil society concerns. The state is differentiated and thus the threat of legislation/regulation also depends on the relative strength of the governmental branch (that is, congress) or agency responsible for the action or being targeted by the social movements.

The case of energy-efficient appliances

The 1973 oil shock shook American's sensibilities about energy use. Until that point, policy-makers and economists assumed that if there were a demand by household consumers for an energy-efficient appliance, companies would respond by developing efficient appliance technologies for the market. The 'invisible hand' of the market would work so that supply met the emerging demand and there was no need for public policy actions. Facing rising input fuel costs and increased opposition to and regulation of new electricity plants, electric utilities managers and public policy-makers realized that increasing the supply of electricity would become more expensive. However, continuing low electricity prices for consumers through government regulation provided no market incentive for household consumers to want efficient products. One environmentally-friendly way to meet increasing US energy needs was to improve the efficiency of residential appliances.

This case focuses on the societal struggle to empower residential energy consumers to save energy and money by improving the efficiency of residential appliances for consumers. I find that a high threat of regulation of manufacturers is a major driver of business's willingness to cooperate with energy and environmental advocates. High threat of regulation occurs under conditions where the state is open to environmental movement influence, the presence of environmental crisis, and high levels of environmental movement organization and support. The conditions that result in a low threat of regulation are strong anti-environmental movement, high business unity, economic crisis, and low levels of political opportunity for environmental movement influence. Under conditions that lead to a low threat of regulation, the power relations described by TOP prevail and business interests dominate environmental issues. Under conditions that result in a high threat of regulation, the power relations and subsequent environmental reform described by EMT prevail. Standing alone, neither can explain the variations in the relationships among state, business and social movements and environmental outcomes. However, brought together by specifying the conditions under which each prevails, a middle-range theorization can explain efforts to green consumer products.

The shifting political economy of US appliance efficiency

In the early 1970s, the idea of an unending supply of cheap electricity was threatened by an increasing realization of US vulnerability to foreign oil producers and rising prices of inputs for electric and gas utilities. In addition, energy utilities were encountering technological limitations of a centralized energy system with a slowing rate of increases of efficiencies from economies of scale in electricity production. Finally, energy utilities were finding it more difficult and costly to site new plants, including nuclear power plants. These conditions led to a substantial political interest in empowering US citizens to reduce their demand in energy for the first time in US history. However, despite a wide understanding that energy-efficiency was an obvious 'win–win' solution with its potential to save money and save the environment (Hayes 2000), market supply and demand for energy efficiency did not materialize evenly across the economy (California Energy Commission 2005). The residential sector seemed especially laggard. Academics and advocates interested in energy efficiency sought to understand the reasons for these market failures. They identified multiple barriers to market development for energy efficient lighting and appliances including distortion of energy prices by US energy policies, lack of consumer knowledge and understanding of long-term energy costs of purchases or behaviors, and split incentives where one party purchases a product and another pays the operating costs (California Energy Commission 2005). These market barriers created the need for specific policies or actions to be undertaken in order to increase energy efficient product availability and demand.

One of the first things state and federal policy-makers did to address the market barrier of lack of consumer knowledge was to develop test procedures for appliance energy use. The intent was to provide comparable measures of appliance energy use so that consumers could compare and choose. The development of these test procedures also provided a basis for defining efficient appliances through voluntary labeling programs or eliminating the worst energy-performing products through minimum efficiency standards. From the early 1970s, policy-makers discussed both voluntary and mandatory approaches for defining and promoting efficient products in the marketplace. States like California and New York led, while the federal government followed.

Defining a product as energy efficient or not efficient is a political process that leads to an environmental outcome. It is political because the decision is one where various parties have a stake in the outcome and power relations are enacted to decide 'who gets what, when and how' (Laswell 1936). Higher levels of efficiency for an appliance mean, all things being held constant, avoided need for energy supplies and reductions in greenhouse gas emissions and air pollutants from the avoidance of fossil fuels extraction and combustion. The development of appliance efficiency specifications has been a rocky road characterized by antagonistic relationships, lawsuits, cooperative coalitions, broken coalitions, and administrative interventions. The US national laboratories provide exhaustive analyses of the economic and technological options and impacts for mandatory rule-makings of efficiency standards. Efficiency advocates and manufacturers closely scrutinize the assumptions and meaning of what is technologically and economically feasible (Association for Home Appliance Manufacturers [AHAM] 1996). All sides lay claim to being experts and the national laboratory scientists must defend their objectivity and findings against claims of 'ineptitude and bias' (AHAM 1996). Manufacturers of the products being defined have an interest in ensuring that they are already producing items meeting the efficiency standard or that they can produce these products without high incremental investments. Depending on these relative competitive advantages that manufacturers have, they may vary in support for level of efficiency being specified in a standard. Often manufacturers producing products with the highest levels of efficiency are most opposed to an increase in mandatory minimum standards as it raises the floor, making it harder to differentiate their product from others. Energy efficiency, consumer, and environmental advocates have sought to set levels of efficiency higher ensuring maximum savings for consumers and reductions of impacts on the environment. Meanwhile the state's position in these debates has varied from objective negotiator to interested party with agencies facing off and all three branches of government intervening at various points. In this study, I utilize archival materials from debates defining energy efficiency as well as data on sociopolitical conditions to explore how changes in sociopolitical and economic conditions are correlated with changing power relations among state, environmental social movement, and business and outcomes for appliance efficiency. In this study, the state is instantiated as government agencies, business as for-profit organizations and industry associations, and social movements as non-profit organizations advocating for energy efficiency.

The process of defining energy-efficient residential appliances is a useful empirical case for this purpose for three reasons. First, efforts to improve energy efficiency have drawn attention from both EMT and TOP advocates (Schnaiberg 1994, Mol and Spargaaren 2000). Schnaiberg (1994) suggests that the politics of energy efficiency that have emerged is an example of the state and business's dedication to upholding the capitalist treadmill. In this case study on the political economy of energy policy-making he reminds us that two options emerged in response to the rising oil prices. The appropriate technology movement sought to 'dismantle the treadmill and substitute a more subsistence-like, stable, intermediate technology' (Schnaiberg 1994, p. 27; see also Schumacher 1973). Meanwhile, Amory Lovins put forth the less radical 'soft energy path' that focused on energy efficiency (Lovins and Thorndike 1978). Schnaiberg has characterized the focus on energy efficiency that has prevailed as a 'change in the forces of production associated with energy transformations with little change in business-labor class relations' as opposed to the appropriate technology movement which sought to alter production and class relations (Schnaiberg 1994, p. 28). He argues that in this way the treadmill of production and its relations were preserved by energy efficiency. Meanwhile, advances in energy efficiency through cooperative market-based approaches used to promote it have served as a prime example of ecological modernization (Melchert 2007). The second reason I focus on the case of residential energy efficiency is that past studies indicates that power relations among the sectors have influenced the development and adoption of energy efficiency policies and multiple approaches to efficiency have evolved over time (Varone and Aebischer 2001). Finally, the availability of historical notices, transcripts from meetings, and organizational comments in negotiations available from proceedings on mandatory and voluntary negotiations on appliance efficiency allow for a detailed analysis of organizational participation, relationships and stances on these issues.

The face of treadmill of production 1981–1986: Reaganism, pre-regulation, and resistance

In 1977, the energy crisis was back on the pages of the newspapers and in people's minds with 301 articles being run in the *New York Times*. During the 1973/74 OPEC embargo, the newspaper had run 929 articles with 'energy crisis' or a related term in its headlines or first paragraph, but this had fallen to a mere 31 articles in 1976. The general public's support for government doing more to protect the environment had fallen from its highs in the early 1970s but hovered around 50% (Dunlap and Scarce 1991, Dunlap 1992). Subsequent to the first wave of the energy crisis, the Republican Ford administration had taken a voluntary approach issuing a federal directive that suggested the energy efficiency of residential appliances attain voluntary 20% improvement targets (subsequently formalized in the Energy Policy and Conservation Act of 1975). In 1977, the Democratic Carter Administration came into power and proposed mandatory energy efficiency standards for residential products. The debate over making energy efficiency standards mandatory was contentious in the US Congress, generally falling along party lines. In the end, the National Energy Conservation and Policy Act of 1978 (ECPA) was adopted with mandatory energy efficiency standards. The DOE, under the Carter administration, formulated minimum energy efficiency standards and was near implementing them when a change of presidential party occurred once again (Nadel 1997).

As the United States approached the 1980 elections, it was clear that a new social agenda was emerging. The environmental movement had been successful at implementing its legislative agenda with broad support from the public across party lines. The conservative movement exercised its voting power to elect Reagan. While the conservative movement had not necessarily zeroed in on anti-environmental goals as it was still preoccupied with 'Cold War' objectives, its anti-regulatory free-market stance was well represented in Reagan's election (Jacques *et al.* 2008).

In 1981, Ronald Reagan became president and a new Republican administration began. Although Reagan's attack on environmental regulation spawned a backlash from the public that preserved environmental regulations (Kraft and Vig 1984), Reagan's assault on the Department of Energy and environmentally-friendly energy policy went largely unanswered. The Reagan administration 'marked a dramatic change in approach to energy policy' (Lovins *et al.* 1993, Miller 1995, p. 719). Reagan sought to abolish the DOE and saw little need for an energy policy beyond the strategic petroleum reserve and a strong military presence in the Middle East. His budget director, David Stockman, expressed the Reagan philosophy as 'strategic reserves and strategic forces' (Miller 1995, p. 719). Reagan appointees to the DOE were there to carry out this agenda of deregulation. Consistent with the anti-government intervention, free market philosophy of the administration, a notice of intent was promptly published in the Federal Register on 23 February to review the standards developed by the DOE under the Carter Administration for nine appliances. The notice of intent noted the administration's particular concerns about the 'economic justification' for the energy efficiency standards (CAS-RM-78-100 Comment 8).

The Reagan administration's review of the standards and general anti-regulatory stance signaled to industry a decreased probability that national appliance standards would be enacted. In addition, the public's concern for environmental and energy issues diminished as support for environmental regulation dropped to new lows and the 1979 energy crisis disappeared from the newspaper pages with falling oil prices. Meanwhile, the economy remained a focus of attention as the US economy plunged into a deep recession in 1981. Under these conditions we expect the power relations predicted by TOP to emerge where: the state, with decreasing autonomy due to economic crisis, favors business interests; civil society has little opportunity to influence the state to protect the environment; and competing business and civil society interests are mediated by the state. Inspecting newspaper articles from the *New York Times* and transcripts from the regulatory hearings (Docket CAS RM-79-113, Comment #3), there is no evidence of cooperative relationships between business and non-governmental organizations. The state's interest in not regulating the market, including energy efficiency, is aligned with appliance manufacturers' interests in not being regulated.

In October 981, left with no other opportunity to influence the state's adoption of mandatory standards, the Natural Resources Defense Council (NRDC) and Consumers Union of the United States filed suit against DOE to compel promulgation of appliance efficiency standards (NRDC, Inc. v. Edwards, Civ. No. 8102546). On 2 April 1982, the DOE published its findings on its review of the Carter administration's proposed standards. The DOE found that the previously proposed standards neither provided significant energy savings, nor were economically justified as required by Energy Policy and Conservation Act of 1975. The DOE's findings were based on drastic revisions of what 'significant' savings meant and re-calculations of the benefits and burdens of mandatory standards. Based on these findings, the DOE proposed that no standards were justifiable for any of the eight appliances that were to be covered under the ECPA (47 Fed.Reg. 14,424:1982). This came to be referred to by the energy efficiency advocacy community as the 'no standards standard'. As required by procedural law, the DOE provided opportunity for comment on the proposed rule.

The DOE's notice did not state when the DOE would make its final decision on appliance efficiency, so the NRDC and Consumers Union pressed forward with their litigation to force the DOE to implement standards. The DOE settled the suit by agreeing to establish efficiency standards no later than 29 October 1982, unless prevented by good cause (47 Fed.Reg. 57,198, 57,200:1982). The DOE failed to meet that deadline. On 22 December 1982, the DOE published its final rule determining that standards for kitchen ranges and ovens and for clothes dryers would not result in significant conservation of energy and in any event would not be economically justified. On 30 August 1983, the DOE announced its refusal to prescribe mandatory standards for the six remaining priority products (48 Fed.Reg. 39,376:1983). The DOE concluded that for seven of the eight appliances considered in the December 1982 and August 1983 rules, standards would not result in significant conservation and would not be economically justified. For the eighth, central air conditioners, the DOE concluded that a standard would result in significant conservation but would not be economically justified. These final rules ended federal consideration of standards for the eight appliances and pre-empted state efficiency regulation of those appliances. The DOE also decided that it was not required to prepare an environmental assessment or environmental impact statement for its 'no-standard standard' determinations.

These decisions by the DOE illustrate it pursuing the objectives that met its immediate needs for administration approval and business profit in the face of economic crisis. Its manipulation of the tests that determined the significance of savings and costs of energy efficiency clearly aligns its interests with the interests of targeted regulated manufacturers at the expense of public and environmental interests in energy conservation. In its determination of 'no-standard standards', the Republican executive branch clearly favored appliance industry interests that focused on avoiding the costs entailed in re-tooling manufacturing plants for energy efficiency. The NRDC, Consumers Union of the United States, Representative Richard Ottinger (Democrat from New York), the California State Energy Resources Conservation and Development Commission, the State of Minnesota, and the State of New York filed suit against the Department of Energy once again (NRDC v. Herrington, 768 F.2d 1355). The State of Texas Energy Office, the Northwest Power Planning Council, the Florida Department of Community Affairs (Energy Office), the Oregon Department of Energy, and the Iowa Commerce Commission provided support for the petitioners' claims. Various appliance manufacturers and the Association of Home Appliance Manufacturers intervened in support of the Secretary of Energy Herrington.

The court's findings from this lawsuit are instructive on how definitions can be influenced by powerful organizations to fit their agenda in appliance standards. The DOE had redefined what was technologically feasible to only those products currently available on the US market and would not consider any prototype technologies or technologies currently available in foreign markets. Economic justifiability was limited to a five-year payback from a technology's specific energy savings even though all appliances under consideration last between 12 and 23 years. The discount rate for consumer decisions was doubled from 5% to 10%.

The lack of opportunity for efficiency advocates to influence the DOE is exemplified in the court's findings that the DOE had violated section 336(a)(2) of the ECPA. That section provides that in prescribing the energy efficiency standard:

> the Secretary shall, by means of conferences or other informal procedures, afford any interested party an opportunity to question employees of the United States who have made written or oral presentations, with respect to disputed issues of material fact. Such opportunity shall be afforded to the extent the Secretary determines that the questioning pursuant to such procedures is likely to result in a more timely and effective resolution of such issues.

In a 1982 hearing, the NRDC had requested to ask questions in person and they were denied but told to submit questions in writing. The NRDC submitted six questions regarding the appliance rule-making and the DOE replied that the questions failed to demonstrate how their questioning would result in a more timely and effective resolution. The DOE wrote back to the NRDC that the NRDC needed to identify the disputed issues of fact and who they wanted to question for the DOE to reconsider. However, when the NRDC submitted these materials they were again denied the opportunity to question the DOE (Natural Resources Defense Council, Inc. v. Herrington, 768 F.2d 1355 D.C. Cir. 1985).

The 'no standards' standards were set aside by the courts in the NRDC v. Herrington and rule-making for standards ordered to start again. This ruling, along with the state-level energy standards already in place, made national mandatory appliance efficiency standards more likely. The major appliance manufacturer organizations began negotiations in early 1986 with the NRDC to develop national standards. An agreement was reached in July 1986, which was subsequently written as proposed legislation based on previously enacted state standards. This legislation was introduced in August 1986 in both houses of Congress (H.R. 5465, S. 2781). The legislation was largely viewed by manufacturers and states as a compromise – states gave up the right to develop their own standards providing manufacturers the 'non-patchwork' unified national market they needed and in return manufacturers acquiesced to national standards to be updated periodically. On 1 November 1986, despite industry support for it, President Reagan pocket vetoed the measure. He argued that appliance efficiency standards were not consonant with the administration's policy of minimal Federal regulatory involvement in the marketplace. The next year, however, Congress passed an essentially identical bill (S. 83, or the National Appliance Energy Conservation Act [NAECA]) on 3 March and President Reagan signed it on 17 March 1987, ending the nine-year struggle to implement the first mandatory appliance energy efficiency standards.

In the years 1980 to 1986, I find that the case of appliance energy efficiency supports my context-dependent theory of TOP and the expected political outcomes. The Reagan administration's *laissez-faire* market approach along with the 1981/82 recession that assured state dependence on business resulted in the threat of regulation being low. As a result, business was not inclined to cooperate with environmental groups and energy advocates to pursue efficiency goals. The lack of political opportunity to influence the state lead to the kinds of oppositional politics described by TOP where regional and state energy offices with energy efficiency advocates pursued their interests through the courts to enforce the statutory laws and required the DOE to carry out its regulatory functions. In the end, the courts upheld their role as an independent adjudicator of the law. This highlights the important role the judicial branch has played in enabling environmental policies, once in place, to have real impact despite shifts in political administration and public opinion. Although lawsuits are decried as expensive, time-consuming, and blamed for negative and combative relations among the societal sectors, they have often provided

ESMOs with their only opportunity to pursue their interests when the state and business interests are dominant. With the court's ruling, national mandatory standards became imminent. This increased threat of regulation, along with the growing state patchwork of appliance standards, provided the conditions where business capitulated and agreed to negotiate with efficiency advocates.

The face of ecological modernization 1992–2001: pre-negotiated standards and market transformation

Once the first mandatory standards were implemented, a transition of power relations occurred among ESMOs, government and industry. After a low of 49.7% in 1980, public support for environmental regulation resurged in 1990 to 69.8% of the general public supporting increased government involvement to protect the environment (Dunlap and Scarce 1991, Dunlap 1992). While the first Bush administration was a continuation of the Republican policies of Reagan, it was arguably not as ardent in its dedication to the free market. The Bush administration also faced the reality of foreign oil disruptions once again with the first Iraq War (Miller 1995). Recognizing the problem of a patchwork of state standards, the Bush administration did not block new national standards that had industry support. In 1988 and 1991, motivated by states establishing standards for products not covered by the NAECA, manufacturers and efficiency advocates negotiated new standards for a number of appliances. Ultimately these discussions led to passage of federal legislation in 1988 establishing efficiency standards for fluorescent lamp ballasts. In 1992, the Energy Policy Act expanded standards to include a variety of lamps, electric motors, and commercial heating, cooling, and plumbing products. By 1992, the AHAM and its manufacturers were negotiating standards with Natural Resources Defense Council, the American Council for an Energy-Efficient Economy (ACEEE) and a number of states (most prominently California, Massachusetts and New York) to bring to the DOE on a regular basis.

In 1993, the Democratic Clinton administration entered the White House after 12 years of Republican rule. While the Democrats' willingness to regulate industry was higher than that of the previous Republican administration, the Clinton administration had also adopted rhetoric consistent with the ideas of ecological modernization, espousing a willingness to provide more innovative approaches and work more cooperatively. Miller's (1995) analysis of the early energy policy under the Clinton administration documents a switch to market-based approaches as a substitute for more prescriptive regulatory mandates. Miller points to: the Clinton administration's support of 'market transforming' strategies emphasized in Climate Change Action Plan; the system of competitive bidding for new power plants that has evolved in response to Public Utility Regulatory Policies Act; the emissions trading system central to the acid rain program for coal burning power plants incorporated in the Clean Air Act Amendments of 1990; and the concept of 'joint implementation,' a variant of emissions trading included in the Framework Convention on

Climate Change. All of these programs provided regulated industry with greater latitude in choosing the means to achieve energy and environmental goals, while creating incentives for technological innovation. This reflects a changing role of the state around energy issues as it moved to become a 'market facilitator'.

In the meantime, environmental and energy groups identified and built new relationships with an unexpected 'big business' – electric power utilities. Utilities are in the business of selling energy – so why the interest in efficiency? Some electric utility companies facing strict regulations and public opposition to the building of new power plants and/or transmission infrastructure still needed to meet the increasing energy demands of industry and the public. Often these utilities have challenges meeting the highest times of public electricity use (called peak demand), which occur on the hottest days when customers all run air-conditioners at the same time. Utilities serving the metropolitan areas of California and the densely populated northeast corridor from Boston to New York City are the most affected by the problem of peak demand. Reduction in appliance energy use was a relatively inexpensive way to avoid expensive power plant construction for utilities. State regulators had been supporting this approach by using efficiency as part of the least cost planning process for utilities. In fact, many states collected a small surcharge on energy use called a systems benefit charge that was dedicated to run energy efficiency programs to decrease demands. Mandatory energy efficiency standards are essentially a way for electric utilities to shift costs from their industry to the appliance industry.

The recognition of these overlapping interests in energy efficiency led to innovations in industry and environmental movement partnerships that are characteristic of ecological modernization in the appliance efficiency field. For example, the 1993 Clinton/Gore Climate Change Action Plan cites the 1990 Super Efficient Refrigerator Program (SERP) as an example of a favored approach that emphasizes ESMO–industry cooperative efforts that have a minimal role for government (Gore 1993). The idea of the SERP was born in 1990 during discussions between Pacific Gas & Electric (PG&E), the nation's largest investor-owned utility, and the NRDC on how utilities could best leverage their money to gain the most energy saving. PG&E and the ACEEE proceeded to organize the SERP with 24 utilities from a range of states to pool $30 million to award the manufacturer that could build the most efficient CFC-free refrigerator at the lowest cost. The Environmental Protection Agency provided a minimal amount of money and had limited involvement. The SERP went on to be incorporated as the Consortium for Energy Efficiency, which develops voluntary specification for appliances for utilities running conservation programs.

Indeed these kinds of approaches became encompassed in an approach commonly referred to as 'market transformation'. Market transformation is a 'process whereby energy-efficiency innovations are introduced into the marketplace and over time penetrate a large portion of the eligible market'

(Geller and Nadel 1994, p. 302). The strategies are targeted at increasing technology diffusion and include research and development, demonstration and field tests, commercialization incentives, marketing and consumer education, grants, loans, and tax incentives, voluntary commitments, bulk purchases, building codes and appliance standards (Geller and Nadel 1994). In 1997, the American Council for an Energy Efficient Economy instituted an annual 'Market Transformation' Symposium in Washington, DC.

This is an example of an evolution of partnerships between utilities and other industries, on the one hand, and environmentalists, on the other, that allow for mutually beneficial outcomes, as opposed to litigation and regulatory confrontations that produce winners and losers. However, these approaches only work with the options to litigate and regulate still in play to encourage compromise and the search for common ground. An instructive example of this occurred in 1994 when there was a change in control of Congress and Newt Gingrich led renewed efforts to dismantle the DOE and reduce regulation.

In the 1990s efforts were underway to revise the first set of standards put into place in 1986. The revision of mandatory standards by the DOE involves conducting analyses, proposing standard levels, soliciting public comments, and then issuing final standards. While this type of process sometimes works successfully, this process has often led to bitter fights among competing interests and resulted in a standard that several parties were dissatisfied with. An alternative to this type of formal standard-setting process is for manufacturers, consumers, ESMOs, and government agencies to work together to negotiate on standard levels. This has often been done with limited government involvement where parties then bring the 'pre-negotiated' standard to the DOE to adopt.

On 11 November 1994, the Natural Resources Defense Council, Association of Home Appliance Manufacturers and American Council for an Energy Efficient Economy, along with the New York State Energy Office, the California Energy Commission, PG&E, and Southern California Edison, presented joint comments to the US Department of Energy describing a two-year negotiation process and a pre-negotiated standard for refrigerators, refrigerator-freezers, and freezers. All parties above expressed that rule-making procedures, even informal rule-makings such as those conducted under the NAECA, tend to cause participants to take relatively rigid, adversarial, and ideological positions. The manufacturers, advocates, and utilities that had participated in the negotiation process expressed hope that the informal pre-negotiations would facilitate the candid sharing of information and development of more innovative approaches. For manufacturers, the pre-negotiation of standards provided certainty about the products they would need to produce in the future. Negotiating the standards before the formal DOE rule-making also provided manufacturers extra lead time to re-tool for the new standards and to coordinate this re-tooling with CFC phase-outs. Non-industry participants were motivated to participate by improved access to manufacturer's technical and economic information. This enabled them to make more informed judgments as to the economic feasibility of different levels of energy efficiency along with avoiding the costs of participating in prolonged rulemakings.

All parties to the negotiations urged the DOE to act quickly to enable manufacturers to prepare for the upcoming implementation. However, the Republicans had become the majority in Congress. In 1995, allegedly at the prompting of AHAM (National Association of State Energy Offices 1995), a proposal for a moratorium on new appliance efficiency standards was inserted into the Interior and Related Agencies Appropriations Act for Fiscal 1996. On 20 July 1995 the DOE published the Notice of Proposed Rule that, for the most part, adopted the jointly proposed pre-negotiated standards as its proposed levels. In a letter dated 11 August 1995, the AHAM requested a postponement of the hearings and written comment deadline because of the legislative proposals before Congress to withhold appropriations for DOE appliance standards making, which would delay the adoption of the standards. In a hearing on 25 October 1995, the AHAM made oral comments backing away from the pre-negotiated standards by taking a 'no standing' on the proposed rule as the legislation had been passed by the House of Representatives and Senate. Whirlpool, an AHAM member, broke with the trade industry by voicing disapproval of AHAM's silence on the issue and continued support for the joint proposal and the DOE's proposed rule. Whirlpool acknowledged it had a good competitive position in relation to the standard with plenty of products that met the standard on the market, but also cited that it felt it had an 'ethical obligation' to stand by the standards it had agreed to (Whirlpool 1995). The ACEEE and NRDC also continued their support with the proviso that if the DOE re-opened the rule-making, the compromises they agreed to in the pre-negotiation phase would have to be revisited. On 12 August 1996 the DOE published a second Notice of Proposed Rule that re-opened negotiations for new refrigerator/freezer standards. In the end, the pre-negotiated standards that had been negotiated since 1992 became effective in 2001.

Discussion and conclusion

This study illustrates that recognizing the broader sociopolitical conditions that alter societal power relations provides insight into when TOP or EMT theories are applicable in to efforts to green our energy system. By using this context-sensitive approach, it is clear that TOP theory is instructive in explaining power relations among state, business and civil society during the early Reagan years of first trying to regulate energy efficiency in residential appliances. However, EMT proved similarly useful for explaining more cooperative direct business–ESMO efforts to improve energy efficiency of appliances during the Clinton presidency. In contrast to the Reagan years where the state strongly favored business interests, during the Clinton years there was a purposeful effort by business to directly engage with local and state government and environmental movement organizations with limited federal involvement. In addition, the Clinton government developed as a market facilitator, rather than command-and-control regulator, through such programs as the voluntary labeling programs meant to foster less mandatory regulation and more cooperative efforts to bring efficient appliances to market in adherence with EMT. This study highlights the sensitivity of these two theories to the strength of the state, the unity of the capitalist class, and the state's likelihood to pass regulations on behalf of public interests that are at odds with business interests.

In addition to the theoretical insights, this research has some important implications for US policy efforts to address climate change. Currently, greenhouse gas producing fossil fuels – coal, oil and natural gas – provide more than 85% of all household energy consumed in the United States (EPA 2009). Reducing the United States' use of these fuels is one of the major pathways to mitigating its contributions to climate change. Since this study is focused on the political economy of a consumer product, it makes a contribution to understanding the political economic context of consumer choices to reduce their energy consumption and carbon footprint. Although there is a strong body of social science research on energy consumption and behavior (Gardner and Stern 1995, Biggart and Lutzenhiser 2007, Owens and Driffill 2008, Dietz *et al.* 2009), this study aligns with one aspect of the treadmill model in that it focuses more on economic structure and political power as the context for consumer decisions (Gould *et al.* 2004). That is, while much of the research focuses on why consumers choose an efficient or inefficient appliance, this research highlights the political and economic reasons for why they have the choices they have. This is an important aspect to emphasize as discussions of the 'behavioral wedge' (Dietz *et al.* 2009, Vandenbergh *et al.* 2010), the idea that widespread changes in public behavior can reduce greenhouse gas emissions significantly, proceed. The widespread availability of affordable energy efficient products is an essential condition to empowering US citizens to reduce their climate change impact. If Reagan had not been elected, it is arguable that the standards developed under the Carter administration would have been implemented and consumers would have been making choices across a very different range of efficient appliances in 1983 than the ones they had to choose from under Reagan.

This study also informs us about some of the challenges for policies intended to make energy-efficient products more available. Energy efficiency is often pointed to as the most economically feasible way to reduce energy demand – the 'low hanging fruit' in addressing climate change (Pacala and Socolow 2004). Yet, a review of energy efficiency history in the United States reveals that the path to improving efficiency has not been particularly straightforward or smooth. Even when there are technologies on the shelf for making energy using products more efficient, both regulatory and non-regulatory approaches require a strong commitment of resources from the state, ESMOs and industry. All policies to reform the United States' contribution to climate change are challenging, but the perception that improving technological energy-efficiency is an easily negotiated 'win–win' policy is misleading if history predicts the future.

Regulation emerges as an important factor in the development of efforts characterized by ecological modernization. While many nations have moved ahead with binding greenhouse gas reduction goals, US climate change policy has historically been consistent in its rejection of any mandatory climate change regulations. It instead has focused on the voluntary market approaches described in ecological modernization. Some in industry, facing climate change regulations at the state level (that is, California) and international level, have surmised regulation is imminent and have taken a proactive stance of requesting that the United States should adopt a climate regulatory regime. The Bush Global Climate Change Policy Book of 2002, after setting voluntary emission reduction levels, stated:

> If, in 2012, we find that we are not on track toward meeting our goal, and sound science justifies further policy action, the United States will respond with additional measures that may include a broad, market-based program as well as additional incentives and voluntary measures designed to accelerate technology development and deployment. (National Oceanic and Atmospheric Administration 2002)

An understanding of the conditions that encourage dedication of industry resources towards an issue and cooperation with environmental organizations and the state suggests that a purely voluntary approach without regulation or the threat of regulation is unlikely to lead to action on climate change.

Acknowledgements

This work has benefitted from the helpful comments of Tom Dietz, Linda Kalof, and Aaron McCright. The research was funded by the National Science Foundation's Innovation, Organization, and Change Program, Grant # 0724905.

Note

1. For an exception see York *et al.* (2003).

References

Association for Home Appliance Manufacturers, Transcript of Rulemaking Hearing, Docket #EE-RM-93-801.
Biggart, N.W. and Lutzenhiser, L., 2007. Economic sociology and the social problem of energy inefficiency. *American Behavioral Scientist*, 50 (8), 1070.
Buttel, F.H., 2000. Ecological modernisation as a social theory. *Geoforum* 31 (1), 57–65.
Buttel, F.H., 2004. The treadmill of production: an appreciation, assessment, and agenda for research. *Organization & Environment*, 17 (3), 323.
Buttel, F.H. and Gijswijt, A., 2000. Emerging trends in environmental sociology. *In*: *Blackwell companion to sociology*. Oxford: Blackwell.
California Energy Commission, 2005. *Compliance options approval manual for the building energy efficiency standards*. CEC-400-2005-007. Sacramento: California Energy Commission.
Clark, B. and York, R., 2005. Carbon metabolism: global capitalism, climate change, and the biospheric rift. *Theory and Society*, 34 (4), 391–428.

Dietz, T., et al., 2009. Household actions can provide a behavioral wedge to rapidly reduce US carbon emissions. *Proceedings of the National Academy of Sciences*, 106 (44), 18452.

Dunlap, R.E., 1992. Trends in public opinion toward environmental issues: 1965–1990. *American Environmentalism: The US Environmental Movement*, 1970–1990, 111.

Dunlap, R.E. and Scarce, R., 1991. Poll trends: environmental problems and protection. *Public Opinion Quarterly*, 55 (4), 651–672.

EPA, 2009. Inventory of U.S. Greenhouse Gas Emissions and Sinks: 1990–2007. EPA #430-R-09-004.Washington, DC: US Environmental Protection Agency.

Fineman, S. and Clarke, K., 1996. Green stakeholers: industry interpretation and response. *Journal of Management Studies*, 33 (6), 715–730.

Gale, R.P., 1986. Social movements and the state: the environmental movement, countermovement, and government agencies. *Sociological Perspectives*, 29 (2), 202–240.

Gardner, G.T. and Stern, P.C., 1995. *Environmental problems and human behavior*. Boston: Allyn and Bacon.

Geller, H. and Nadel, S., 1994. Market transformation strategies to promote end-use efficiency. *Annual Reviews in Energy and the Environment*, 19 (1), 301–346.

Giddens, A., 2009. *The politics of climate change*. Cambridge: Polity Press.

Goldstein, D.B., 2006. *Saving energy, growing jobs: how environmental protection promotes economic growth, competition, profitability and innovation*. Point Richmond CA: Bay Tree Publishers.

Gore, A., 1993. The climate change action plan. Available from: http://www.gcrio.org/USCCAP/index.html [Accessed 10 October 2008].

Gould, K.A., et al., 2004. Interrogating the treadmill of production: everything you wanted to know about the treadmill but were afraid to ask. *Organization & Environment*, 17 (3), 296.

Hannigan, J.A., 1995. *Environmental sociology: a social constructionist perspective*. London: Routledge.

Hooks, G., 1993. The weakness of strong theories: the U. S. State's dominance of the World War II investment process. *American Sociological Review*, 58, 37–53.

Jacques, P.J., et al., 2008. The organisation of denial: conservative think tanks and environmental scepticism. *Environmental Politics*, 17 (3), 349–385.

Kraft, M.E. and Vig, N.J., 1984. Environmental policy in the Reagan presidency. *Political Science Quarterly*, 99 (3), 415–439.

Laswell, H., 1936. *Who gets what, when, and how*. New York: Whittlesey House.

Lovins, A.B. and Thorndike, E.H., 1978. Soft energy paths: toward a durable peace. *American Journal of Physics*, 46, 868.

Lovins, A.B., et al., 1993. The cost of energy efficiency. *Science*, 261 (5124), 969.

McAdam, D., et al., 1996. Introduction: opportunities, mobilizing structures, and framing processes – toward a synthetic, comparative perspective on social movements. *In: Comparative perspectives on social movements: political opportunities, mobilizing structures, and cultural framings*. New York: Cambridge University Press.

Melchert, L., 2007. The Dutch sustainable building policy: a model for developing countries?*Building and Environment*, 42 (2), 893–901.

Merton, R.K., 1968. On sociological theories of the middle range. *In: Social Theory and Social Structure*. New York: The Free Press.

Meyer, D.S and Staggenborg, S., 1996. Movements, countermovements, and the structure of political opportunity. *The American Journal of Sociology*, 101 (6), 1628–1660.

Miller, A.S., 1995. Energy policy from Nixon to Clinton: from grand provider to market facilitator. *Environmental Law*, 25, 715.

Mizruchi, M.S. and Bey, D.M., 2005. Corporate control, interfirm relations, and corporate power. *In*: *The handbook of political sociology: states, civil societies, and globalization*. New York: Cambridge University Press.
Mol, A.P.J., 1995. *The refinement of production: ecological modernization theory and the chemical industry*. Utrech: Van Arkel.
Mol, A.P.J. and Spaargaren, G., 2000. Ecological modernisation theory in debate: a review. *Environmental Politics*, 9 (1), 17–49.
Nadel, S., 1997. The future of standards. *Energy and Buildings*, 26 (1), 119.
National Association of State Energy Offices, 11/1/1995, Comment #218, Docket EE-RM-93-801.
National Oceanic and Atmospheric Administration, 2002 President announces clear skies initiative. Available from: http://www.whitehouse.gov/news/releases/2002/02/20020214-5.html [Accessed 12 January 2008].
Owens, S. and Driffill, L., 2008. How to change attitudes and behaviours in the context of energy. *Energy Policy*, 36 (12), 4412–4418.
Pacala, S. and Socolow, R., 2004. Stabilization wedges: solving the climate problem for the next 50 years with current technologies. *Science*, 305, 968–972.
Parson, E., 2003. *Protecting the ozone layer: science and strategy*. Oxford: Oxford University Press.
Pellow, D.N., et al., 2000. Putting the ecological modernisation thesis to the test: the promises and performances of urban recycling. *In*: T. Smith, D. Sonnenfeld and D.N. Pellow, eds. *Ecological modernisation around the world: perspectives and critical debates*. London: Frank Cass.
Perz, S.G., 2007. Reformulating modernization-based environmental social theories: challenges on the road to an interdisciplinary environmental science. *Society & Natural Resources*, 20 (5), 415–430.
Scheinberg, A., 2003. A change by any other name: re-examining the urban recycling experience in North America and its implications for ecological modernisation theory. *Environmental Politics*, 12 (4), 49–75.
Schnaiberg, A., 1980. *The environment: from surplus to scarcity*. New York: Oxford University Press.
Schnaiberg, A., 1994. The political economy of environmental problems and policies: consciousness, conflict, and control capacity. *Advances in Human Ecology*, 3, 23–64.
Schumacher, E.F., 1973. *Small is beautiful: a study of economics as if people mattered*. London: Abakus.
Struck, D., 2011. Climate scientists fears his 'wedges' made it seem too easy. *National Geographic. News Daily*. Available from: http://news.nationalgeographic.com/news/energy/2011/05/110517-global-warming-scientist-concern/ [Accessed 6 May 2011].
Vandenbergh, M.P.,P.C., et al., 2010. Implementing the behavioral wedge: designing and adopting effective carbon emissions reduction programs. *Environmental Law*, 40, 10547.
Varone, F. and Aebischer, B., 2001. Energy efficiency: the challenges of policy design. *Energy Policy*, 29 (8), 615–629.
Whirlpool Corporation, 11/2/1995, Comment #210, Docket EE-RM-93-801.
York, R., 2006. Ecological paradoxes: William Stanley Jevons and the paperless office. *Human Ecology Review*, 13 (2), 143.
York, R. and Rosa. E.A., 2003. Key challenges to ecological modernization theory. Organization & Environment, 16, 273–288.
York, R., et al., 2003. Footprints on the earth: the environmental consequences of modernity. *American Sociological Review*, 68 (2), 279–300.
York, R., Rosa, E.A. and Dietz, T., 2010. Ecological modernization theory: theoretical and empirical challenges. *In*: M.W. Redclift and G. Woodgate, eds. *The international handbook of environmental sociology*. Cheltenham: Edward Elgar.

Regional integration to support full renewable power deployment for Europe by 2050

Anthony Patt, Nadejda Komendantova, Antonella Battaglini and Johan Lilliestam

The European Union is currently working on a achieving a target of 20% renewable energy by 2020, and has a policy framework in place that relies primarily on individual Member States implementing their own policy instruments for renewable energy support, within a larger context of a tradable quota system. For 2050 the target is likely to be more stringent, given the goal of reducing European carbon dioxide emissions by 80% by then. Preliminary analysis has suggested that achieving the 2020 target through renewable power deployment will be far less expensive and far more reliable if a regional approach is taken, in order to balance intermittent supply, and to take advantage of high renewable potentials off the European mainland. Analysis based on modeling is combined with the results of stakeholder interviews to highlight the key options and governance challenges associated with developing such a regional approach.

Introduction

The development of renewable electricity in Europe is very different depending on where you look and in what perspective. Some countries, like Denmark, Spain and Germany, exhibit strong development. In the past 20 years, Denmark increased its share of renewable power by over 1000%, and Germany increased production by 73 TWh/a between 1990 and 2007. In other countries, like France and Austria, the situation is less positive, as they have experienced decreasing shares of renewables, due to increasing electricity demand. In a European Union (EU) perspective, average annual growth has been a very modest 3.2% in the same period of time (Eurostat 2010). When considered together, EU countries will collectively have failed to meet the Union's non-binding 2010 renewables target (21% of final electricity consumption) by a wide margin (European Commission 2009).

Several support and incentive schemes are in place across Europe. At the EU level, the Climate and Energy Package, finalized in 2009, sets a number of binding targets for the year 2020: a 20% reduction in carbon emissions; a 20% improvement in energy efficiency; and the obtaining of 20% of energy from renewable sources (European Commission 2009). The Emissions Trading Scheme supports this by setting a cap on total carbon emissions from the power sector. The Guarantee of Origin (GO) trading scheme, embedded in the Renewable Energy Directive, creates a legal framework for countries to meet their renewable energy targets through development undertaken elsewhere, either by purchasing excess renewable energy credits from other EU states or by importing electricity of guaranteed renewable origin from non-EU states (Mendonça 2007, Kemfert and Diekmann 2009, Nilsson *et al.* 2009, Couture and Gagnon 2010). On a national level, the different support schemes are the main tool for promoting renewable power, but there is also a plethora of different incentive schemes at national, regional and local levels. As all effective, and almost all ineffective, support schemes are presently national or smaller scale (res-legal.de 2010), the efficiency of the support can be questioned: by far the largest share of European growth in photovoltaic power (PV) has taken place in Germany, and not in much sunnier southern Europe; 40% of the growth in wind generation has also taken place in Germany, while there is paradoxically much less in much windier countries, like Ireland, the United Kingdom, Norway or France (Czisch 2005, Eurostat 2010).

Looking even further ahead to 2050, there are no official European targets for renewables, but there are indications of what the total greenhouse gas emissions reduction effort will be: 60–80%, in the preambles of the Carbon Capture and Storage and Emissions Trading Scheme Directives (European Parliament 2009a, 2009b); or 80–95%, as recommended by both the Intergovernmental Panel on Climate Change and the European Commission (2010). Emission reductions of 80% or more by 2050 require the power sector to become completely carbon-neutral by then, to compensate for difficulties of decarbonizing other sectors (Battaglini *et al.* 2010, European Climate Foundation [ECF] 2010).

As renewable electricity is capital intensive, the quality of the production site is the most important determinant of costs; the dependence between costs and site quality (expressed in full-load hours per year) is more or less linear. Supporting PV in the not-so-sunny Czech Republic and wind power in not-so-windy Bavaria may be acceptable if the support scheme is conceived as a market introduction tool with the aim of supporting technology development, not mainly targeted at electricity production as such. The implementation of feed-in tariffs in some European countries has achieved exactly this: renewable technologies, especially wind, PV and biomass, have been successfully and efficiently introduced in the European market (Foquet and Johansson 2008).

Achieving a 33% share of electricity generated from renewable sources by 2020, and 100% by 2050, is quite different from this. Such targets cannot be considered to be either market introduction or technology support systems. Such high shares aim at producing large amounts of electricity, and then efficiency is a critical component. Inefficiencies that are acceptable on a low penetration level will now be magnified by the scale, and may become unacceptable. Harmonizing support schemes and markets – which is not necessarily the same as merging and uniting these systems – so that all countries in the power system can access the best sites, regardless of national and administrative borders, and exploit these with the best suited technologies may reduce total costs considerably. Below, we will discuss why this is

Reaching the 2050 target in a reliable and economically sound way: a European–North African Supergrid

Depending on the precise geographical region, the potential supply of renewable electricity can be constraining or not, at least in terms of an integral over time. But electricity suppliers need to be certain that they have enough electricity at any given time at a given place. Hence, they must cope with both the intermittency of the production and the uneven geographical distribution of resources, which is more challenging as the share of renewable power increases relative to fossil fuel-based power. Essentially, this is a challenge of minimizing both the curtailment of generation and the usage of storage (such as with batteries), both of which are expensive (Leonhard 2008, SRU 2010), while guaranteeing an adequate and stable power system at all times. Doing so requires power system planners to think not only of new renewable power plants, but to alter their mindset to include a world of much larger, often international or even intercontinental power grids and markets.

In a recent study, the German Advisory Council on the Environment (SRU) quantified the costs for 100% renewable power in a number of different scenarios. A purely German power system without interconnections to other countries would have an average producer cost of 11.5 €c/kWh, much due to the extensive use of expensive biomass and biogas as dispatchable capacities to smooth the supply-controlled feed-in of wind and PV. In a pan-European, trans-Mediterranean scenario, however, the average cost would be 6.9 €c/kWh on average; fluctuations would be smoothed, and cheap pumped-storage capacities (using excess power to pump water uphill into mountain reservoirs, to generate almost as much power later) would be available in a broader geographical perspective. Against this back-drop, the SRU concluded that 'an efficient trans-European power grid is a particularly cheap, but politically extraordinarily demanding, option for a completely renewable electricity supply' (SRU 2010, p. 66; own translation).

This is the setting in which we operate: all further discussion will aim at achieving a 100% renewable power supply for Europe, while coordinating with North Africa. In recent years, the North African countries have defined renewable power targets too, of different levels of ambition. Morocco, for example, has a target of 42% renewable power by 2020 (today renewables account for 8% of final electricity consumption). Given the rapid demand increase in the country, this should be seen as a very ambitious target, and it remains to see whether it is actually realistic. At the other extreme is Algeria, with its target of 5% by 2017 and 10% by 2025 (today renewables account for only 0.6%). The current renewable share of final electricity consumption in North Africa as a whole is 9%, of which about 8.5% comes from the Aswan dam in Egypt (Schellekens *et al.* 2010).

Numerous studies on such a *Supergrid* power system, often spanning all of Europe and the North African countries on the southern shore of the Mediterranean, have been published in the past few years, all reaching similar conclusions. A European or European–North African Supergrid is technically possible, and one of the cheapest options available to completely decarbonize the power system (for example, Czisch 2005, DLR 2006, ECF 2010, SRU 2010, Zervos *et al.* 2010). Below, we will explain why such a system is feasible and then discuss some of the political challenges with creating and operating geographically very large power systems.

Demand smoothing

Constructing an efficient grid over vast distances will smooth much of both the high-frequent and the very low-frequent demand variability. The relevant measure is the peak/off-peak ratio, and whereas a small, national power system would have to deal with large peak/off-peak swings, a Supergrid would experience considerably smaller demand swings.

The variability over periods of a day or less is smoothed by the different usage patterns in different parts of the grid. This is partly due to cultural differences – Italians tend to have dinner later than Swedes – but also due to the east–west size of a Supergrid. If it spans several time zones, this will effectively mean a relative time shift of peaks – the 8-o'clock evening news will start at different times across the grid – which reduces the peak/off-peak ratio. In a University of Kassel model for the European Union and Middle East/North Africa, including Eastern Europe and the Urals power system, this demand swing reduction amounts to 11%, comprised of 4% peak reduction and 7% minimum load increase (Czisch 2005). A study commissioned by the ECF found effects of the same magnitude (ECF 2010). As North African demand is still much smaller than in Europe (180 compared with 3300 TWh/a), the demand smoothing effects of a European–North African grid are unclear (Schellekens *et al.* 2010).

The seasonal smoothing largely originates from different usage patterns on the north–south axis. Electricity consumption in the north is higher in winter, due to increased heating and lighting needs, whereas the demand in the south is higher in the summer, primarily due to extensive usage of cooling systems. In the University of Kassel model, this amounts to a smoothing of only 2% of the seasonal demand variability, whereas the ECF study showed considerably stronger smoothing effects. With increased standards of living in North Africa, an increased use of cooling can be expected, but it is not clear what the effects of this on total system demand smoothing will be.

Stochastic smoothing of supply

Interconnecting renewable power plants can lead to considerable smoothing of the cumulated supply of the single power plant fleets. Wind and solar power plants are dependent on wind and solar input – that is, the weather – and it can be expected that the supply variability decreases with distance, at least up to distances of the same size as a typical weather system. Numerous studies have addressed this issue for wind; for solar power there has been less quantified study, but similar effects can be expected.

Wind smoothing can be observed in reality already today, following the rule of thumb that larger geographical dispersion leads to a smoothing at lower frequencies. Dispersion over 2 km can lead to smoothing on very short time scales – that is, <5 minutes (Kempton et al. 2010) – whereas interconnection over 800 km can reduce one-hour variability by up to 95% (Katzenstein et al. 2010). The smoothing over larger areas, and longer frequencies, is more disputed. The University of Kassel researchers examined the area between Morocco and the Ural Mountains (5000 km across, or roughly the size of North America). It was found that wind smoothing can reduce seasonal fluctuation by 65%, mainly by increasing the minimum available wind capacity (Czisch 2006). This effect is partly due to the different climate zones – in Northern Europe the windiest months are in winter, while in North Africa they are in summer – meaning that connecting them smoothes much of the seasonal variability (Czisch 2005). In contrast, Kempton et al. (2010), who considered offshore wind power along the eastern United States coast line – that is, within one climate zone – found that the correlation between wind power plant output is indeed very low for distances of 800–1300 km, but there is no additional smoothing by adding more remote power plants.

Power mix smoothing

Whereas stochastic smoothing makes use of reduced correlation between geographically dispersed power plants of the same type, a diverse power mix can make use of low, or sometimes negative, correlations between different recurring weather and climate patterns. For example, the European summer is sunnier than the winter, and cloudy days are more often windy than are sunny days. Wind and sun are to some extent negatively correlated, so that the cumulated output of a wind-solar power plant fleet can be expected to have a more stable output than that of a one-technology fleet. A more diverse power mix will thus be less impacted by adverse weather. Still, extreme events like storms may effectively halt both solar (no sun) and wind (too much wind) power generation across a large area. In such cases, the power supply in affected areas has to rely on transmission from outside. This is another strong argument for grid expansion.

A European–North African Supergrid would make use of the seasonal anti-cyclic wind (winter maximum) and sun (summer maximum) supply patterns, for several reasons. First, the wind patters in Europe and North Africa show a negative correlation, such that when it is calm in one region it is typically windy in the other. Second, the seasonal pattern of European wind power is negatively correlated with solar production from Spain and North Africa. To illustrate, northern Europe and Spain can generate about 40% as much wind power in July as they can in January. However, solar production in Spain and North Africa is two and a half times higher – the inverse of 40% – in July compared with January (Czisch 2005). Through a sensible combination of wind and sun, a more efficient seasonal smoothing of supply can be achieved. This can be clearly seen in the ECF study, which examined an 80% renewables scenario for 2050. Although the peak wind power supply in winter is twice as high as the minimum supply in summer, the cumulated supply from solar and wind power is relatively constant over the year, at 35–40% of total electricity supply (ECF 2010).

Site access

Renewable electricity assets are capital intensive with very low variable costs. This makes the quality of the production site – the windiness, or the insolation – the most important variable for the siting decision. In theory, the yearly average potential may be sufficient for 100% renewable power in Europe, as the supply potential and the demand are of similar magnitude. In practice, however, Europe would need to utilize all sites, including the marginal, less windy or sunny sites, where the return on capital investment is lower. Including the vast potential of North Africa would not only increase the potential by two orders of magnitude, thus allowing cherry-picking of sites and a consequent lowering of total costs (Battaglini *et al.* 2009), it would also include much better solar sites than are available in Europe. For example, the global horizontal irradiance (the main variable for PV siting) is around two-thirds higher in North Africa than in Germany, the world leader in installed PV capacity. The average direct normal insolation (the main variable for CSP) is 15–25% higher in North Africa than in Spain, Italy and Greece, and has considerably less seasonal variability (DLR 2005, 2006). With all other factors constant, North African levelized PV costs will be roughly one-third of the cost in Germany, while the levelized CSP cost will be about 15–25% cheaper than in southern Europe. (It is not economically feasible to operate a CSP power plant in northern Europe, due to frequent cloud cover.)

Even more importantly, the possibility of CSP production in North Africa and, to a lesser but still significant extent in Southern Europe, adds another dispatchable renewable power source to the mix. Producers are beginning to equip CSP power plants with units to store heat; for example, as high-temperature molten salt. These fill with excess heat during daytime, and can then produce power overnight and during periods without sun. Accordingly, analysts increasingly view CSP as a 'baseload technology' (for example, Club of Rome 2008, Trieb *et al.* 2009), which can assume the critical role of balancing other intermittent power sources, thereby reducing the need for expensive electricity storage, and reducing the pressure on the hydro-electric dams in Scandinavia and the Alps to handle the system balancing.

In these technical matters, there remain a number of unknowns or points of dispute. Analysts do not know exactly how much storage will be needed, or what kind of storage is the most appropriate. They also do not know what role other load management approaches can or should play in the future. Such options include pricing power differently throughout the day, or by using 'virtual power plants', where a single power provider guarantees a flow of power into the grid, but that flow may come from a number of different generating options. There is a consensus emerging, however, that a Supergrid offers the possibility to manage large portions of the fluctuating supply in a very cost-effective way. The literature cited in this and the previous sections is congruent in that it clearly proposes a Supergrid as the cheapest way to handle intermittency. Still, unifying European electricity policies and markets, and triggering the necessary amount of investment, especially in North Africa, is a daunting task with caveats and obstacles of a magnitude that could potentially make the entire vision remain a vision. We move to discuss some of the more serious caveats and obstacles.

Perceptions, challenges, and risks of a Supergrid connecting Europe and North Africa

Moving from the technical to the political level, there are three fundamental types of concerns associated with a Supergrid connecting Europe and North Africa. The first of these concerns the benefits that North African countries and citizens can and will receive from it, and whether these are compatible with the benefits that Europeans hope to receive; this would form the backdrop for any political deal. The second is associated with building it, and overcoming the obstacles to securing the required amount of investment. The third is associated with maintaining it, and ensuring that it can supply power in a reliable way. We describe each in turn.

A deal with North Africa

Any future system of intercontinental renewable electricity trade requires clear and stable deals between European and North African countries and/or companies (Patt 2010). However attractive such deals seem from a technical perspective, there is a significant caveat. Today, there is no clear understanding of what North African countries – their governments, power companies, and citizens – expect, wish, or need from such a deal, or if they are willing to let Europe use North African land for its power supply. Some authors have assumed that what North Africa needs and wants is electricity to satisfy the rapidly increasing demand, and desalinated water to reduce pressure on fossil aquifers (DLR 2007, Club of Rome 2008). To our knowledge, however, no systematic analysis of this assumed demand has been performed.

A number of political (the Barcelona Process and the Mediterranean Solar Plan), private sector (the Desertec Industrial Initiative), and research-oriented studies (led by the International Institute for Applied Systems Analysis [IIASA] and the Potsdam Institute for Climate Impact Research [PIK], and by the University of Giessen) have since 2010 begun to organize workshops and stakeholder surveys, some involving high-level political actors, on this issue. These studies may begin to provide robust insights by 2011. Anecdotal evidence from them suggests that the most important expectation from North African countries is of large-scale job creation, mainly in manufacturing and operating the power stations on their soil. This is one of the largest problems in North Africa, which has one of the lowest employment-to-population ratios in the world: only 45% of the population of active age is employed, and of these 42% are working poor, earning less than $2 a day. The total North African unemployment rate increased by 25% between 1997 and 2007 and is now the second largest in the world (International Labor Organization 2009).

It is not clear whether expectations of large job creation are realistic. The estimates for the entire CSP sector go up to two million people employed globally by 2050 (DLR 2005, Richter *et al.* 2009). The European Solar Thermal Electricity Association (ESTELA) estimated that the deployment of 20 GW of CSP capacity by 2020 – the target of the Mediterranean Solar Plan – could lead to the creation of 235,000 job years. Of these, ESTELA estimated 40,000 to be in manufacturing of components, 120,000 in construction, and 35,000 in operation and management (ESTELA 2009). But the method by which ESTRELA generated these estimates is not transparent. Preliminary work at the IIASA, which modified an employment model generated by the United States National Renewable Energy Laboratory to take into account North African labor costs, showed much more modest job creation. In the IIASA work, the same 20 GW of capacity would generate up to 120,000 job years, and then only if all components were manufactured in the region (which is not likely to be realistic), and taking into account indirect employment effects. Given that the North African countries are home to 150 million people, and projections indicate an increase to 250 million by 2050 (DLR 2005), this level of job creation would be welcome, but would not, on its own, make an important contribution to the reduction of unemployment.

Attracting risk averse investors

Even with a stable international or bilateral deal, investment in CSP in North Africa may still not take place because investors perceive renewable energy projects in the region as too risky. Several studies have shown that such risk aversion plays an important role in energy markets by delaying a certain type of technology. For example, banks have in the past in many countries been unwilling to provide financing for renewable energy projects, which they regarded as being too risky (Arrow 1985, Coenraads et al. 2006). It has also been shown that attracting finance is much easier, and the conditions better, when market instruments to reduce risks connected with renewable energy projects, such as feed-in tariffs, have been available (Mendonça 2007, Couture and Gagnon 2010). Risk-averse behavior not only leads to a situation in which fewer projects and less capacity are realized; in cases where perceived risk is high, but acceptable, investors require higher risk premiums and thus higher returns on projects. Recent research at the IIASA and the PIK has addressed the perceptions of such financial risks of North African CSP investments both in a stakeholder interview and questionnaire process, and the cost impacts of it in a modeling approach.

The interviews identified complex and corrupt bureaucratic procedures as the main problem, both with regard to its high probability and its high impact. This creates a situation where investments do not happen at all, as lengthy and unpredictable permission processes make investments unattractive. Instead, investments happen in other areas and regions where conditions are better, or in other types of projects. The stability of political regimes was also seen as an important obstacle, adding to the uncertainty of renewable energy projects. Interestingly, and in contrast to what European media reports, only two interviewees saw *force majeure* (including terrorism) as a serious concern, but all agreed that such events are not very likely (Komendantova et al. in press). Other risk categories, such as environmental and general financial risks, were perceived as low-impact and low-probability. In general, the findings show strong agreement between the perceived likelihood to happen and seriousness of concern, reflecting a propensity to conflate likelihood and magnitude (Patt 2007).

The identified risks not only reduce the growth rates by deterring investors, but also make the realized projects more expensive. The increased risk premiums are reflected in increased rates of return, effectively making the same renewable energy project more expensive. Based on this, IIASA and PIK researchers modeled the impact, or the cost increase, of the perceived investment risks using the MARGE generation cost estimator framework. With this model, Williges et al. (2010) showed that the total subsidy costs for driving CSP through the learning curve and making it competitive with coal could cost European tax payers subsidies in the order of magnitude of €20–40 billion over 20 years, a conclusion consistent with other results (Ummel and Wheeler 2008, Williges et al. 2010). Changing the internal rate of return, thus simulating a change in perceived risk level and consequently risk premium, showed a dramatic effect. When the internal rate of return moved from 5% (a low-risk public–private partnership project) to 20% (a pioneer project that, in the absence of a track record, the bank perceives as high risk), the total amount of subsidies required to scale CSP up to be competitive with coal jumped from €15 billion to €329 billion.

Measures aimed at reducing perceived risk will thus reduce the total investment needed to make CSP competitive with conventional generation technologies. As investors see regulatory risks, including corruption and inefficient bureaucracies, as the most serious and risks, this is a task that falls entirely on policy-makers. It is possible to treat such kinds of risks, and this does not imply any significant government expenditures.

There are already different programs conducted by international organizations, non-governmental organizations and the European Commission like the Mediterranean partnerships programs, which are part of the Barcelona process, the Extractive Industries Transparency Initiative and other programs aiming to improve regulatory climate in North Africa conducted by the United Nations Development Programme. Succeeding in these programs will not only facilitate an expansion of renewable power in North Africa, but also decrease electricity costs for consumers by several cents per kWh, all in all, savings in the order of magnitude of hundreds of billions of Euros are possible without increasing government spending. In short: reducing risks is a win–win situation.

Security of supply

There is considerable suspicion among many European decision-makers about the reliability of the North African countries as electricity suppliers. One observer writes about Desertec – a private-sector initiative to link the European and North African markets – and asks 'Why create a new hostage to fortune?', concluding that 'the stage is set to recreate an uncomfortable parallel with western dependency on oil from Saudi Arabia, Iran and Iraq' (Pearce 2009). The former CEO of Vattenfall, Lars Josefsson, adds that 'Europe must source its power from Europe', otherwise its supply will be threatened by unstable and unreliable governments (Lubbadeh 2009, Zeller 2009). The question of security of supply is indeed of great importance: if the electricity supply is not secure, the Supergrid approach to decarbonizing the power sector will not work.

This concern can only be partially explained by the track record of European–North African energy trade. Algeria and Libya are important suppliers of gas and oil to Europe, and have been so for a long time. Algeria's supply to the EU has been constant and has not been seriously interrupted due to political conflicts during the past 30 years. During the second oil crisis in 1980, Algeria unilaterally increased the gas price to France and withheld parts of the supply for two years, until the crisis was settled and the gas price was linked to the oil price. At the time, Algeria's reliability as a supplier was questioned, but it was also concluded that 'Algeria's increasing reliance on gas exports [...] may engender greater caution in the manipulation of gas exports' (Adamson 1985, p. 20). Since then, Algerian exports to Europe have been stable. During the Libyan–Swiss political conflict about the arrest of Hannibal Ghaddaffi in 2008, Libyan oil exports to Switzerland were cancelled, but resumed after two days. In March 2010, Libya declared a 'holy war' and a total embargo against Switzerland, a move that led to much media attention, but not to any significant economic effects or to oil shortages in Switzerland (RIA Novosti 2008, Windfuhr and Zand 2010).

Assessing security of electricity supply in a Supergrid scenario is difficult. Today, there are no robust tools to assess the security of electricity supply in a holistic scenario approach. There are, however, studies that look at different aspects of energy security, also for a Supergrid scenario. The reasons for investigating a Supergrid in the first place are economic – it will be cheaper to use only the best production sites – but also based on a security argumentation: the large grid will reduce the risks of intermittency and increase system stability (see above). This leaves the political risks, which need to be somehow assessed. Most existing approaches to energy security focus on diversity in oil and gas supply (see Lefèvre 2010, Stirling 2010), which are inherently different from electricity, as they are storable, partially substitutable (with each other) and, in the case of oil, traded on a liquid world market. The idea behind this diversity approach is that 'a highly import-dependent system that is well diversified, need not necessarily be a risky one' (Bhattacharyya 2009, p, 2412), as the system can absorb the failure of the largest supplier. However, an import-dependent system that is only slightly diversified, but based on supply from reliable partners is not a risky one, whereas a diversified system in which the suppliers unexpectedly form a cartel may be much more insecure. Thus, a diversity approach is a frequently used, but rather blunt instrument to assess political risks of energy imports.

So far, two studies have investigated the issue of political risks to European power system stability in a Supergrid Europe/North Africa in depth. Both of these studies conclude that the concerns are largely unfounded and the risks are relatively small, although they exist.

In the first study, Lacher and Kumetat (2011) investigate both the risks of terrorism and of intentional supply cuts – the 'energy weapon' – in a Supergrid scenario. They conclude that terrorist attacks against the power system 'cannot be dismissed entirely', but that, if such attacks happen, the effects are likely to be very limited due to the interconnectedness of the system, the complexity of a large-scale attack, and the fact that any blackouts are likely to be short-lived (Lacher and Kumetat 2011, p. 10). They find that vulnerability to terrorism is not likely to be higher than the current vulnerability due to Europe's imports of gas and oil from the region. The track record of terrorism against power installations shows that the risks have been small in the past. The United States national counterterrorism center database registered 2212 terrorist events against energy installations worldwide – around 2% of all registered terrorist attacks – between January 2004 and March 2011. Of these 76 attacks – about

3% of the total – affected electricity installations. Four of these events impacting the electricity sector took place in Europe and two attacks took place in Algeria, whereas more than 70% of all attacks took place in Colombia, Iraq or Pakistan (WITS 2011). Most attacks against power systems – more than 60% – were aimed at transmission facilities, because these are the least protected parts and the effects of disabling them are likely to be higher than attacks against other parts of the system (Tranchita *et al.* 2009, Toft *et al.* 2010); similar data have been reported also for the period 1984–1999[1] (Greenberg *et al.* 2007). Toft *et al.* (2010, p. 4419) explain this low frequency of attacks upon power systems in terms of the limited incentives terrorists have to attack such facilities: 'threatening this type of target is not highly intimidating, it is rarely a strong messenger of ideological symbolism and [...] it requires some skill and knowledge to destroy them'.

Lacher and Kumetat (2011) also conclude that European fears of intentional disruptions to future electricity deliveries are based on false analogies to the trouble experienced with Russian gas, as renewable electricity trade with North Africa will have completely different technical and geopolitical characteristics. As electricity is a perishable, non-storable good whereas gas and oil are storable goods, the economic interdependence between Europe and North Africa will be stronger for electricity than for fossil fuels, and this interdependence will be a strong deterrent to any politically motivated disturbances. Similar conclusions are reached by Taylor and van Doren, who argue that this interdependence is also high in the oil import case: 'Catastrophic supply disruptions would harm producers more than consumers, which is why they are extremely unlikely' (Taylor and van Doren 2008, p. 7).

In the second study, Lilliestam and Ellenbeck (2011) investigate this argument quantitatively and in detail, and argue that most countries refrain from acts that may be considered aggressive, unless they are given a reason and the possibility to create a credible threat to force its will on a trading partner. As electricity cannot economically be stored on a large scale, all electricity that is not sold at one instant in time is lost and a supply disruption would cause a continuous loss of revenue in the exporter country. In the importer country, however, the costs of a large and sudden import disruption would be initially high (caused by blackouts) but then decrease to almost zero as system stability is restored by other, geographically dispersed backup capacity, which must be in place to maintain a high level of operation security in a renewable power system. Lilliestam and Ellenbeck show that, in the Desertec scenario, the export revenue losses are likely to be higher than the importer's blackout costs. Hence, they conclude that 'energy weapon' events are unlikely, as the exporters would be unable to produce a credible threat: they would have no leverage and thus very bleak chances of intimidating Europe. Hence, they are unlikely to try to extort Europe using future electricity deliveries. Europe will only be vulnerable to extortion in the case where all North African countries coordinate action and embargo Europe together, and even this vulnerability can be mitigated by either increasing European reserves or by importing less electricity than foreseen in the Desertec scenario (Lilliestam and Ellenbeck 2011). In a rough estimation, Schellekens *et al.* (2010) quantify these costs, for a three-week, 25 GW disruption of exports from North Africa to Europe, to 0.3% of current European GDP and the lost income to 50% of current Tunisian GDP, or 10% of current Egyptian GDP.

Other, non-quantifiable costs like reputational damage may be prohibitively high and apply highly asymmetrically: such costs only apply to the actor who breaks the deal – in this case, the exporter – which makes a sudden, one-sided supply cancellation even more unlikely. Europe will thus have little to fear in terms of politically motivated supply disruptions: a North African country would have nothing to gain and much to lose. In contrast to the prevailing view in the European media, these results show that Europe will not be dependent on North Africa, it will be the other way around. In fact, North Africa may become dependent on the income from the electricity exports to Europe, and they may want to consider whether this risk is acceptable to them or not.

Conclusions

There are significant benefits of connecting Europe into one single, fine-meshed and long-distance power grid, and even larger benefits may arise if North Africa is included in this system. The benefits originate from supply and demand smoothing effects that only arise in a very large power system, and from accessing the best production sites for renewable electricity generation. A Supergrid makes it technically easier, at lower cost, to achieve very high rates of renewable power penetration.

Creating such a European–North African Supergrid system is, however, a political challenge of high magnitude. Today, we do not know what the North African countries expect or wish from a deal with Europe – whether they would be comfortable with European-financed renewable energy developments on their territory – nor do we know what Europe expects from North Africa and what it is willing to give to be allowed to use North African land for its power supply. Recent research has shown that the perception of risks of investing in renewable power in North Africa is presently high; bureaucratic difficulties and corruption are perceived as particularly problematic. This not only deters investors from investing, it also makes the projects that are indeed realized more expensive. Reducing the investment risks may save hundreds of billions of Euros for consumers and government budgets.

The idea of a European–North African Supergrid often provokes concerns about European security of supply, particularly given the unpredictable behavior of Libya in recent years. No commonly accepted method of assessing security of electricity supply exists today, but novel assessment frameworks indicate that the European power supply is unlikely to be interrupted due to political reasons, as North Africans would have nothing to gain and much to lose by cutting exports. On the contrary: Europe would not be very vulnerable, but the North African exporters would be strongly dependent on the income from the electricity trade with Europe.

Note

1. The cited data concern the United States during 1984–1999: here, 3% of all electricity system disturbances were attributed to 'sabotage or vandalism'; 59% of these disturbances affected transmission lines and towers.

References

Adamson, D.M., 1985. Soviet gas and European security. *Energy Policy*, 13, 13–26.
Arrow, K., 1985. The potentials and limits of the market in resource allocation. In: G. Feiwel, ed. *Issues in contemporary microeconomics and welfare*. London: Macmillan, 107–124.
Battaglini, A., et al., 2009. Development of SuperSmart Grids for a more efficient utilisation of electricity from renewable sources. *Journal of Cleaner Production*, 17, 911–918.
Battaglini, A., Lilliestam, J. and Knies, G., 2010. The SuperSmart Grid – paving the way for a completely renewable power system. In: H.J. Schellnhuber, M. Molina, N. Stern, V. Huber and S. Kadner, eds. *Global sustainability – a nobel cause*. Cambridge: Cambridge University Press, 290–305.
Bhattacharyya, S.C., 2009. Fossil-fuel dependence and vulnerability of electricity generation: case of selected European countries. *Energy Policy*, 37, 2411–2420.
Club of Rome, 2008. *Clean power from deserts*. Hamburg: Club of Rome.
Coenraads, R., Voogt, M. and Morotz, A., 2006. *Analysis of barriers for the development of electricity generation from renewable energy sources in the EU-25*. Utrecht: ECOFYS.
Couture, T. and Gagnon, Y., 2010. An analysis of feed-in tariff remuneration models: implications for renewable energy investment. *Energy Policy*, 38, 955–965.
Czisch, G., 2005. *Szenarien zur zukünftigen Stromversorgung. Kostenoptimierte Variationen zur Versorgung Europas und seiner Nachbarn mit Strom aus erneuerbaren Energien*. Kassel: Universität Kassel.
Czisch, G., 2006. *Low cost but totally renewable electricity supply for a huge supply area*. Kassel: Institut für elektrische Energietechnik/Rationale Energiewandlung, Universität Kassel.
DLR, 2005. *Concentrating solar power for the Mediterranean region*. Stuttgart: German Aerospace Centre (DLR).
DLR, 2006. *Trans-Mediterranean interconnection for concentrating solar power*. Stuttgart: German Aerospace Centre (DLR).
DLR, 2007. *Concentrating power for seawater desalinisation*. Stuttgart: German Aerospace Centre (DLR).
European Climate Foundation, 2010. *Roadmap 2050*. Den Haag: ECF.
European Commission, 2009. *The renewable energy progress report*. Brussels: European Commission, COM(2009)192 final.
European Commission, 2010. *Analysis of options to move beyond 20 percent greenhouse gas emission reductions and assessing the risk of carbon leakage*. Brussels: European Commission, COM(2010)265.
European Parliament, 2009a. *Directive 2009/29/EC to improve and extend the greenhouse gas emission allowance trading scheme of the Community*. Brussels: European Commission.
European Parliament, 2009b. *Directive 2009/31/EC on the geological storage of carbon dioxide*. Brussels: European Commission.

European Solar Thermal Electricity Association, 2009. *Solar power from the sun belt. The solar thermal electricity industry's proposal for the Mediterranean Solar Plan.* Brussels: ESTELA.
Eurostat, 2010. *EU Energy in figures. Electricity generation from renewables. Extended time series.* Brussels: European Commission, Directorate-General for Energy and Transport, Eurostat.
Foquet, D. and Johansson, T.B., 2008. European renewable energy policy at crossroads – focus on electricity support mechanisms. *Energy Policy*, 36, 4079–4092.
Greenberg, M., et al., 2007. Short and intermediate economic impacts of a terrorist-initiated loss of electric power: case study of New Jersey. *Energy Policy*, 35, 722–733.
International Labor Organization, 2009. *Global employment trends report 2009.* Geneva: ILO.
Katzenstein, W., Fertig, E. and Apt, J., 2010. The variability of interconnected wind plants. *Energy Policy*, 38, 4400–4410.
Kemfert, C. and Diekmann, J., 2009. Förderung erneuerbarer Energien und Emissionshandel – wir brauchen beides. *Wochenbericht des DIW*, 11/2009, 169–175.
Kempton, W., et al., 2010. Electric power from offshore wind via synoptic-scale interconnection. *Proceedings of the National Academy of Sciences*, 107 (16), 7240–7245.
Komendantova, N., et al., in press. Perception of risks in renewable energy projects: the case of concentrated solar power in North Africa. *Energy Policy*, DOI: 10.1016/j.enpol.2009.12.008.
Lacher, W. and Kumetat, D., 2011. The security of energy infrastructure and supply in North Africa: hydrocarbons and renewable energies in comparative perspective. *Energy Policy*, 39, 4466–4478.
Lefèvre, N., 2010. Measuring the energy security implications of fossil fuel resource concentration. *Energy Policy*, 38, 1635–1644.
Leonhard, W., 2008. *Energiespeicher in Stromversorgungssystemen mit hohem Anteil erneuerbarer Energieträger.* Frankfurt: VDE.
Lilliestam, J. and Ellenbeck, S., 2011. Energy security and renewable electricity trade: will Desertec make Europe vulnerable to the 'energy weapon'? *Energy Policy*, 39, 3380–3391.
Lubbadeh, J., 2009. Can Saharan solar power save Europe? *Der Spiegel, Hamburg.* Available from: http://www.speigel.de/international/germany/0,1518,664842-7,00.html [Accessed 9 December 2009].
Mendonça, M., 2007. *Feed-in tariffs: accelerating the deployment of renewable energy.* London: Earthscan Publications.
Nilsson, M., Nilsson, L.J. and Ericsson, K., 2009. The rise and fall of GO trading in European renewable energy policy: the role of advocacy and policy framing. *Energy Policy*, 37, 4452–4462.
Patt, A., 2010. Effective regional energy governance – not global environmental governance – is what we need right now for climate change. *Global Environmental Change*, 20, 33.
Patt, A.G., 2007. Assessing model-based and conflict-based uncertainty. *Global Environmental Change*, 17, 37–46.
Pearce, F., 2009. Sunshine superpower. *New Scientist*, 43, 40–43.
res-legal.de, 2010. *Rechtsquellen Enerneuerbare Energien.* Berlin: Bundesministerium für Umwelt, Naturschutz und Reaktorsicherheit (BMU). Available from: http://www.res-legal.de [Accessed 9 June 2010].
RIA Novosti, 2008. *Libyen nimmt seine Öllieferungen an die Schweiz wieder auf.* Moscow: RIA Novosti. Available from: http://de.rian.ru/business/20080730/115252269.html [Accessed 10 June 2010].
Richter, C., Teske, S. and Short, R., 2009. *Concentrating solar power. Global outlook 09.* Brussels: Greenpeace, SolarPACES, ESTELA.

Schellekens, G., et al., 2010. *100 percent renewable electricity – a roadmap to 2050 for Europe and North Africa*. London: PriceWaterhouseCoopers.

SRU, 2010. *100 percent erneuerbare Stromversorgung bis 2050: klimaverträglich, sicher, bezahlbar*. Berlin: Sachverständigenrat für Umweltfragen (SRU).

Stirling, A., 2010. Multicriteria diversity analysis. A novel heuristic framework for appraising energy portfolios. *Energy Policy*, 38, 1622–1634.

Taylor, J. and van Doren, P., 2008. The energy security obsession. *The Georgetown Journal of Law & Public Policy*, 6 (2), 1–16.

Toft, P., Duero, A. and Bieliauskas, A., 2010. Terrorist targeting and energy security. *Energy Policy*, 38, 4411–4421.

Tranchita, C., Hadjsaid, N. and Torres, A., 2009. Security assessment of the electricity infrastructure under terrorism. *International Journal of Critical Infrastructures*, 5 (3), 245–264.

Trieb, F., et al., 2009. *Characterisation of solar electricity import corridors from MENA to Europe*. Stuttgart: German Aerospace Centre (DLR).

Ummel, K. and Wheeler, D., 2008. *Desert power: the economics of solar thermal electricity for Europe, North Africa, and the Middle East*. Washington, DC: Center for Global Development.

Williges, K., Lilliestam, J. and Patt, A., 2010. Making concentrated solar power competitive with coal: the costs of a European feed-in tariff. *Energy Policy*, 38, 3089–3097.

Windfuhr, V. and Zand, B., 2010. *Die Schweiz ist eine Mafia*. Hamburg: Der Spiegel. Available from: http://www.spiegel.de/spiegel/0,1518,692436,00.html [Accessed 10 June 2010].

WITS, 2011. *Worldwide incidents tracking system*. Washington, DC: National counter-terrorism center. Available from: https://wits.nctc.gov/ [Accessed 23 March 2011].

Zeller, T., 2009. Europe looks to Africa for solar power. *The New York Times*, New York. Available from: http://www.nytimes.com/2009/06/22/business/energy-environment/22iht-green22.html?_r=4&pagewanted=1&partner=rss&emc=rss [Accessed 13 July 2009].

Zervos, A., Lins, C. and Muth, J., 2010. *RE-thinking 2050. A 100 percent renewable energy vision for the European Union*. Brussels: European Renewable Energy Council (EREC).

Climate deadlocks: the environmental politics of energy systems
Karena Shaw

> After struggling for decades to get climate change mitigation onto the political agenda, environmentalists now not only find themselves enmeshed in internal conflict over how to proceed, but also find these conflicts themselves functioning to delay or forestall necessary action. Reframing climate change as an energy systems – rather than an emissions reduction – problem allows us to see why these conflicts have arisen and what is at stake in them. This argument is illustrated through an examination of climate and energy politics in the province of British Columbia, Canada. Taking an energy systems perspective reveals both the complexity and importance of the political terrain activated by climate change: how societies reshape energy systems in response to climate change will have profound implications not only for their ecological impact but also for their political and social character.

Introduction

Trying to keep up with climate politics can provoke a strange kind of motion sickness: on the one hand, contexts seem to shift so quickly that they invoke whiplash; on the other, there is a pervasive feeling of stagnation. While climate contexts continue to shift dramatically, efforts to mobilize towards addressing them remain mired not only in resistance, but confusion and conflict. No groups struggle more with this than environmental movements. After struggling for decades to get climate change mitigation onto the political agenda, environmentalists now not only frequently find themselves enmeshed in internal conflict over how to proceed, but also at times find these conflicts themselves functioning to delay or forestall necessary action. In what follows I argue that reframing climate change as an energy systems – rather than an emissions reduction – problem allows us to see why these conflicts have arisen and what is at stake in them. I illustrate this argument through an examination of climate and energy politics in the Canadian province of British Columbia (BC). Taking an energy systems perspective reveals both the complexity and importance of the political terrain activated by climate change: how societies reshape energy systems in response to climate change will have profound implications not only for their ecological impact but also for their political and social character.

Reframing climate change as an energy problem

Advocacy and policy around climate change have frequently framed it as an emissions reduction problem.[1] This is not surprising, given that there is a well-established environmental policy framework around pollution control, which provides a conceptual and practical structure for responding to such a complex problem. However, I argue that climate change is better understood as an energy problem. Although there is still debate on the precise distribution of greenhouse gas (GHG) emissions, it is clear that a majority of global emissions are generated through the production and consumption of energy. In Canada, for example, the current estimate is that 81% of emissions are energy related (Environment Canada 2008). This figure includes emissions produced from extraction, processing, and transport of energy as well as the emissions produced when we utilize energy. This includes everything from the obvious – the whole energy system activated by fueling a car, including exploration, extraction, transport, processing, and use of fossil fuels – to the less obvious: the embedded energy in the car (materials, transportation, production, assembly, disposal) and supporting infrastructure (construction and maintenance of roads, bridges, parking facilities). It includes the embedded energy in food (fertilizers, tilling and harvesting, transportation, processing and preparation), clothes, leisure goods, and so on. Emissions from energy, in other words, are generated by more than flipping a light switch, taking a shower, or filling a gas tank. This is a large category of emissions, one that includes industrial and personal energy use, encompassing almost every aspect of daily life in one way or another.

Importantly, however, even the emissions not captured under the 'energy' category can be understood as arising from human practices that are essentially energetic, such as deforestation, agriculture and waste treatment. These emissions are a consequence of how we[2] extract energy from and manipulate energy across ecosystems; in particular, from how we have come to situate ourselves energetically in our worlds: what we consume, what waste we produce.

So, climate change can be understood as an energy problem. Energy, of course, is a social and ecological problem (Smil 2006). Energy mediates human relationships, and most centrally mediates human–nature relationships. An indication of how energy mediates human relationships emerges from any effort to map energy use on to something like the United Nations' Human

Development Index (HDI), which measures life expectancy, literacy, education and standard of living. Those countries that rank low on the HDI invariably use very small amounts of energy per capita.[3] This alerts us to serious equity issues. Improving the quality of life in these places requires providing access to energy resources. These, of course, are also the people who will be most directly impacted by climate change, and they have the fewest resources to respond to it.

In a carbon-constrained world, where those of us ranking high on the HDI have emitted far more than our fair share, this puts us in a debt of sorts: our actions, past and present, are directly responsible for their situation in relation to climate change. This debt is extended by the systematic way that we have extracted energy from those societies, in terms of both human and natural resources. The energy use that is deeply embedded in the structure of our daily lives (the embedded energy in what we eat, wear, consume) links us materially to people around the world, to their possibilities for life. Our collective choices matter to others, and this is expressed in patterns and habits of energy use.

Energy is also the most crucial mediator of human–nature relationships. It is through our energy use that we interact with the ecosystems that support us, and how we manipulate energy within and across ecosystems determines the extent and character of life they can support. Anyone who has studied ecology knows this: what shapes ecosystems is how energy flows through them, who eats who. Every time we use energy – to eat, clothe, transport, and entertain ourselves – we activate an energy system that ties us directly to an ecosystem. Our choices not only of how much energy to use, but of how to extract it, are determining of the health of those ecosystems, of their capacity to support other forms of life.

This is true directly: the environmental degradation that is due to extraction of energy resources is enormous (hydroelectric dams, coal mining, oil drilling, pollution, climate change itself). This is even true with renewables: to extract energy from an ecosystem – the kinetic energy of tides or wind or rivers, thermal energy from the sun, or chemical energy stored in biomass – will alter the balance of that ecosystem. Not all alterations are equal in their impact – some are concentrated, devastating; others perhaps will be within the realm of adaptation for a resilient ecosystem – but all have impacts.

This dynamic of impact is also true of other ways that we extract energy from ecosystems: agricultural practices, for example. Industrial agriculture – the production of food to meet our energetic needs and desires – systematically destroys biodiverse ecosystems in order to replace them with monocultures. This can only be supported and sustained through intensive energy inputs – fertilizers, also fuels and equipment to plow, and so forth. So how we eat directly impacts some ecosystems – those turned into farms – and indirectly impacts others – those manipulated to provide the energy and resources necessary to support these farms.

We can extend this to all of the other ways that energy is embedded in our lives. All can be traced back to ecosystem impacts: how we use energy determines the capacity of particular ecosystems, in particular places, to support life, in its diversity of forms. Climate change is just one indication of how out of balance we are in this regard, but there are plenty of others (Rockström *et al.* 2009). One useful way to evaluate the scale and impact of our energy use in relation to natural processes is through the concept of net primary productivity. Net primary productivity refers to the total biomass produced on the earth in a year, through converting solar energy (via photosynthesis) and chemical energy (via chemosynthesis) into plant mass. It is in a sense the earth's annual budget: what it has produced and is available to be reinvested in further productive activity. Prior to the industrial revolution, human societies – still primarily agricultural – were only able to harness around 5% of the global terrestrial net primary productivity. However, the advent of industrialism and Fordism, with their increased reliance on the exploitation of stored and transportable energy such as fossil fuels, and dramatic increase in production and consumption of material goods, changed all of that. More recently, human appropriation of net primary productivity has increased dramatically, to the point where today humans harness roughly 30% of the global terrestrial net primary productivity. By 2050 this is likely to surpass 50% (Haberl 2006). This is a massive interruption of natural flows: when we direct 30% away from ecosystem regeneration, we dramatically reduce the productivity and thus resilience of those ecosystems.

So, climate change is an energy problem, and energy is a social and ecological problem. Energy links us with each other and with our environment. We are out of balance in both regards. Energy is also, of course, a political and economic problem: we have inherited economies and political institutions that are addicted to energy use: the products and processes through which energy is embedded in our lives feed economic systems, and in turn political systems. Evidence of this is present if we examine, for example, the relationship between energy use and economic growth. Although the historical trajectory is towards a reduction in the *energy intensity*[4] of our economies, the fact remains that continued economic growth requires ever-increasing inputs of energy. High energy prices tend to stifle economic growth; a restriction in the availability of energy inputs would cripple an economy, and currently does so in many 'developing' countries. Meanwhile our governments remain essentially addicted to economic growth in order to sustain their own legitimacy, as evidenced by the intense political attentiveness to rates of economic growth and the near panic when they decline.[5]

The implications of this are probably clear: given that in 2008, 81.3% of total world energy use was fossil fuel-based (International Energy Agency 2010, p. 6), emissions reductions on the scale we need to aim for will require fundamentally reshaping energy systems, and this in turn will fundamentally reshape our societies as well as the ecosystems that sustain them. Addressing climate change, in other words, requires reshaping society.

However, *how* it will do so – both in terms of process and outcomes – remains up in the air. This is something yet to be determined, that will hinge in part on social response. This is the crucial linkage between energy systems and social change. Reducing emissions on the scale necessary will reshape society, and not just individual behavior. As the examples above suggest, although some of the key decisions about energy use are individual, the most important ones are collective. Our individual options are shaped by physical infrastructure, policies, social pressures and conventions. These are produced collectively, or at least reflect decisions made on behalf of the collective.

Much effort is going into finding technical solutions that can be implemented with minimum disruption to societies. There are good reasons for this: it is much easier to invent new technologies than to change societies. There is also a lot of debate about how far we can get taking this route, with consensus growing that it is unlikely we can achieve the scale of reductions we need through technology alone (Hoffert *et al.* 2002, Pacala and Socolow 2004, Green *et al.* 2007). What is clear, however, is that if we are willing to reshape societies in particular directions, the range of possible technical options increases. The scale and character of demand for energy services shapes what technological options are viable.

Understanding climate change as an energy problem thus activates a significantly different terrain of engagement than understanding it as an emissions reduction problem, which permits a fairly narrow focus on reducing GHG emissions.[6] In particular, engaging climate change through the imperative of making energy systems robustly sustainable puts social and ecological, as well as economic, concerns at the centre of decision-making. Although this may make the problem seem more complex, it also expands the range and diversity of ways the problem can and must be engaged. Decisions made about energy use, both direct (what kinds of generation facilities to build, how to price energy) and indirect (infrastructure, trade, work patterns, consumption), either by or on behalf of collectivities, will determine not only the scope and impacts of climate change, but also the character of societies more generally. Putting that consideration at the centre of decision-making about climate policy increases the potential not only for climate mitigation, but for this mitigation to proceed in a way that increases the sustainability of society.

Perhaps the most crucial thing that the energy systems perspective reveals, in other words, is a looming danger faced by humanity if we proceed with an exclusive focus on emissions reduction. It is entirely possible that we could reduce emissions, and simultaneously increase or worsen the environmental and social impact of our energy systems. Emissions reductions, challenging though they will be, simply cannot be the only criteria we pursue as we respond to climate change. I turn next to an illustration of this, one that foreshadows the case study that provides the focus for the latter part of the article.

Energy and sustainability: the ambiguity of renewables

As I have argued above, reshaping energy flows and systems has enormous implications for sustainability. However, figuring out how to restructure energy systems and relationships to increase sustainability, or ecosystem resilience, is not straightforward. To illustrate this point, it is worth taking a brief detour through some of the characteristics of renewable energies. I focus here because renewable energies appear to be a shoal upon which not only environmental movements, but mitigation efforts themselves, may founder. Environmentalist enthusiasm for renewables as an (at times even *the*) answer to climate change is understandable: for years the potentials of renewable energies have been quashed by the political economy of fossil fuels. However, this enthusiasm has often led to uncritical advocacy, and – given the characteristics of renewables I discuss below – this lack of critique is dangerous. The capacity of renewables to address the challenges posed by climate change depends much less on the sources themselves or the technologies involved than on the nature of the energy system and society they are integrated into. As such they provide a rich illustration of the importance of integrating an understanding of energy systems and sustainability into processes of collective decision-making for social change. In what follows I review three characteristics of renewable energy flows and consider their significance for energy system design.

Most renewable energy – except conventional hydroelectric,[7] geothermal and biomass – is intermittent. Solar and tidal are relatively predictably so; wind and wave are less so. Without adding storage capacity to electrical grids, this means that renewable energies must always be backed up by other energy sources. Depending on the nature of the energy system, this can be unproblematic (as if the rest of the system includes extensive hydroelectric power, which can be turned off and on at short notice with no negative impacts on the equipment) or deeply problematic. If the balance of power is provided by coal-fired thermal plants, for example, this poses a range of challenges, two most centrally: first, the intermittent nature of the renewable source might mean that total capacity for the system cannot be reduced, since at any given time the non-renewable plant might have to meet peak demand alone; second, the increased stopping and starting of thermal plants necessary to adapt to intermittency can result in both increased emissions and wear and tear on the plant that significantly reduces both its efficiency and lifespan (ESB National Grid 2004, Pitt *et al.* 2005). There is lively debate about the severity of this problem – how much intermittency can be integrated into existing energy systems without triggering it – but an emerging consensus that it is a problem that must be engaged seriously (Boyle 2007, International Energy Agency 2011). Care must be taken in how renewables are developed: should a society bet on massive expansion of renewables without addressing intermittency, it might fail to significantly decrease its emissions profile. This, combined with the environmental effects of renewable expansion (discussed below), could increase the overall environmental impact of the energy system.

The second relevant characteristic of renewables was mentioned above: tapping into most renewable energy sources – hydro (including river, wave and tidal), wind, solar, and biomass – involves interrupting an energy flow that performs ecosystem services. The direct impacts of tapping into those flows will vary dramatically. That the interruption of an energy flow can have dramatic impacts on an ecosystem should not surprise us: the ecological impacts of hydroelectric dams, for example, are well known (Smil 2003, pp. 246–249, World Commission on Dams 2000). Hydroelectric power causes enormous disruptions and alterations to the local environment during the construction phase, during which huge tracts of land are flooded, displacing people and wildlife. GHGs (primarily methane) are also produced during this phase, as the flooded organic material decomposes. Once the facility is in place, continuing effects include the disruption of fish migration rates, fish mortality, and increased stream turbidity (Cuddihy et al. 2005). Similar impacts characterize other renewable sources. The construction of transmission lines, wind farms, solar arrays, and tidal dams or turbines frequently degrades and fragments habitat, potentially compromising ecosystem function. No energy source is impact-free, of course. The key is that these impacts must be taken into account by those promoting massive expansion of renewables. Without careful attention to mitigating impacts, development of renewables could result in increasing stress on the ecosystems that sustain us precisely at the moments when they are under strain from climate change itself.

These potential impacts are exacerbated when we consider the third relevant characteristic of renewables: in comparison with the energy sources that have shaped the character of our societies (infrastructure, lifestyles, energy demands and expectations of quality of services), the *energy densities*[8] of renewables are very low, up to four orders of magnitude lower than those of fossil fuels. What this means in practice is that a society that depended on the harvesting of renewable flows to meet current levels of energy demand would have to harvest these flows over a much larger land area than is the case for fossil fuels. Much more land would have to be devoted to the harvesting and conversion of energy flows; more extensive transmission systems would have to be built, and there would be much less flexibility about where power conversion facilities could be located. The land-use implications alone of such a scale-up would be significant. As a crude illustration: the reservoirs of hydroelectric dams perform the function of concentrating energy flows adequately for relatively efficient power conversion. During the twentieth century, construction of large dams displaced between 40 and 80 million people; during the early 1990s the annual total was four million people (World Commission on Dams 2000). The social, economic, and political implications of this scale of disruption are at least as profound as the environmental ones, yet by 2000 hydroelectricity was still providing only 2.2% of the total global energy supply (International Energy Agency 2010, p. 6). Obviously, harvesting different kinds of energy flows – solar and wind, for example – would have different impacts, but as we can see from emerging controversies over the siting of wind farms as well as resistance to the building of new hydroelectric facilities, we would be foolish to believe that changes to land use on this scale would be either socially and politically straightforward or environmentally benign. That said, we can also see from the considerable benefits that large-scale hydroelectric power has brought that under the right conditions such changes might be desirable.

Of course, we interfere with energy flows in ecosystems all the time: we cannot live without impacting the ecosystems that support us. What is crucial is the scale and character of these impacts. All three of these characteristics of renewables only become problematic at certain scales. Scale is perhaps the most vital issue as we consider environmental impacts of each potential energy source and system, as the long-term impact on ecological resilience is perhaps more closely associated with the scale rather than kind of disruption. The environmental impacts of those energy sources we rely on heavily now – fossil fuels, hydroelectric, biomass – are relatively well known. As we seek to introduce and scale-up new sources, a consideration of environmental impacts is particularly important. A consideration of how to focus, mediate, and direct these impacts would be vital even if we were not facing the challenge of climate change: clearly in the past we have not been attentive enough to the close links between energy systems, ecological and biophysical systems. Climate change – itself a consequence of the human interruption of the biophysical system of carbon cycling – is the most obvious current indication of this, but as we can see from the above it is by no means the only one.

I emphasize these characteristics of renewables not to discourage engagement with them, but to draw attention to the dangers of any approach to mitigating climate change that fails to consider the wider sustainability of energy systems. The assumption that scaling up renewables (as emissions-free energy sources) will lead to climate change mitigation runs very real risks: because of the character of some energy systems, it might not lead to a reduction of emissions (especially if not combined with demand-reduction initiatives) while simultaneously impacting ecosystems in ways that compromise their resilience. For renewables to deliver on their potential they must be carefully developed and integrated into existing energy systems. This requires an approach that focuses on more than emissions reduction, one that takes ecological and social impacts into account.[9] As we seek to respond to climate change, it is vital to understand not only the dynamics of climate change, but of the wider energy systems we seek to modify, the societies that they sustain, and the ecosystems that we all rely upon.

More widely, the purpose of the above has been to sketch an understanding of climate change that foregrounds the ecological and social implications of our choices of how to respond to it, and thus the scope of political terrain that needs to be activated in our responses. The next section will explore debates over these issues currently raging in BC, by way of illustrating both the challenge and necessity of mapping this context onto political analysis and engagement.

Before moving on, however, just to emphasize what is most important about the context sketched above: this is truly a moment of opportunity as well as crisis. To the extent we are able to ground our decision-making in an understanding of and commitment to improving the resilience of the social and ecological systems we reside in, we will have an enormous payout: a dramatic increase in the sustainability of our societies. However, we should have no illusions about the difficulty of getting these issues at the heart of political engagement, or even of stimulating the kind of public engagement with these decisions that they deserve.

The politics of green: energy, power and sustainability

Over the past few years, BC has emerged as one of North America's 'poster children' for climate change policy. Since 2001, when they swept to power by winning all but two seats in the provincial legislature, the governing party in BC has been the Liberals, a party deeply committed to an essentially neoliberal policy program. However, in a case that echoes Governor Schwarzenegger in California, a couple of years ago the Premier of BC, Gordon Campbell, revealed a well-concealed green streak when he made climate change a policy priority. Following Schwarzenegger's lead, Campbell sought to create an ambitious climate change policy agenda, which included the first carbon tax in Canada, mandated cuts in GHG emissions by 2020 with further targets for 2050, a proposed cap and trade system to be developed with other western states and provinces, low carbon fuel standards, and a range of other policy initiatives (Province of British Columbia 2007).

Campbell's climate initiatives left the environmental movement – accustomed to struggling mightily against the Liberal government for the smallest gain in environmental policy – gasping, especially as it became increasingly clear that it was resulting in real policy changes, and that he had the leverage to ensure party support.[10] The situation became even more confusing when the New Democratic Party, traditionally laying claim to the left end of the political spectrum and generally more supportive of environmental initiatives, came out in opposition to the carbon tax.

With the political spectrum – particularly the environmental sector of it – thus destabilized, campaigning began for a provincial election in May 2009. The defining issue for the first week of the campaign caught many people by surprise. On the first day of the campaign, a prominent story in Canada's national newspaper focused on an apparent endorsement of the Liberal platform by a few prominent environmental groups in BC, based on the strong climate change action taken by the government (Hunter 2006, p. A4).[11] This unleashed a huge backlash from within the environmental movement, exposing a significant rift in the movement (Burrows 2009, Kimmett 2009, Littlemore 2009, Tieleman 2009).

Understanding the source and implications of this rift requires some backtracking into the history of energy policy in BC. The energy situation in BC is in some senses an enviable one: over 90% of BC's electricity comes from hydroelectric plants, and – as the system is primarily publicly owned – for decades oversupply and the capacity to sell to other jurisdictions has meant a steady flow of income to Provincial coffers (Hoberg and Sopinka 2011, p. 6).

However, more recently the trend is towards a net energy deficit, and based on BC's rapidly increasing population, the expectation is that it will increase.[12] Partly in response to this, and long before Campbell's climate initiatives, the Liberal government initiated a significant shift in provincial energy policy. Its 2002 Energy Plan required BC Hydro to start moving back towards 'electricity self-sufficiency', but to do so using exclusively privately owned power developments, in a significant departure from the past (Hoberg 2010).

Thus was initiated a rush of private power development in BC, particularly in the form of run of river hydroelectric development.[13] Within a few years, developers had snapped up water licenses on just about every stream with the least bit of potential in the province – and it is a wet, mountainous province. As of 19 March 2010 there were 145 current water licenses, and 628 applications pending.[14] Crucially, all watercourses are open to potential development; however, there is no systematic planning process for how this development might proceed: BC Hydro holds 'Clean Power Calls' during which they assess development proposals received and reward some with long-term power-purchasing contracts, a precondition for proceeding with development. However, although any given project has to pass through a range of permitting processes at different levels of government, there is no systematic oversight process through which system-level planning can take place, let alone landscape-scale or cumulative environmental impact assessment. In fact, if a project is less than 50 megawatts in size, there is no systematic (that is, project-wide) environmental assessment, and thus no forum for public engagement with or input into the project (Calvert 2007).

As might be expected, alarm bells quickly began ringing in the environmental movement. A primary area of concern was the enclosure of public resources for private gain. Given the long legacy of public ownership of energy resources in BC, and indeed the significant role they played in building the province's economy, the shift to mandated private ownership seemed perverse to many. BC also, of course, has a long history of essentially giving away public resources for private gain (witness its forest industry), but in these cases at the very least the industries provided employment that sustained local communities. After the construction phase, most run of river installations require at most one or two employees. So rural communities – many facing very severe economic times, as the forest and fishing industries are both in virtual collapse – faced the prospect of seeing 'their' local streams and rivers dammed, with implications for tourism, fishing, kayaking, recreation, and so on, while receiving absolutely no revenue from the venture.

Other concerns were more specifically environmental. Although touted as 'green' power, run of river facilities do have considerable environmental impacts. These stem from the diversion of river flow and the generating plant themselves, but also impacts from the construction process, development of road access, transmission lines, and so on. As some of these projects started to move to the construction phase, the scale of impact caught many 'green power' proponents by surprise. This turned to alarm when the lack of any systematic, cumulative environmental impact assessment and/or landscape level planning exercise, combined with the number of water licenses and thus potential projects, raised the prospect of a willy-nilly industrialization of the landscape (Caldicott 2007, Kimmett 2008). Existing environmental organizations in the province, such as the Western Canada Wilderness Committee, started campaigns in opposition to private energy projects; associations such as the Whitewater Kayaking Association of British Columbia and the Canadian Office and Professional Employees Union became involved, and new advocacy groups specifically focused on the issue emerged, including Save Our Rivers, BC Citizens for Public Power, BC Creek Protection Society, BC Guardians, and IPP Watch.

These concerns came to a head in conflict over a proposed run of river plant on the Ashlu River near Squamish, which the Squamish–Lillooet Regional District – concerned about the pace and scale of run of river development – blocked by denying a necessary rezoning request (Calvert 2007, pp. 165–180). Although their decision was supported by an extensive investigation and significant public consultation (Squamish–Lillooet Regional District 2003, 2006), the provincial government's response was unequivocal: they rushed through passage of a new bill – Bill 30: The Miscellaneous Statues Amendment Act – granting 'utility' status to Independent Power Projects (IPPs), and thus removing them from oversight other than that of the British Columbia Utilities Commission (BCUC), an independent regulatory agency of the provincial government primarily focused on monitoring the impact of power projects on ratepayers. Given its absence of expertise on community scale planning or environmental assessment, the BCUC had no real basis upon which to consider the kinds of concerns raised in the Ashlu case. In one fell swoop, the government thus removed the right of any municipality or regional authority to assert any control over IPP development within their jurisdiction (Calvert 2007, pp. 177–178). For those who had been observing the government's commitment to a private power agenda, this move was not a real surprise. For all communities across the province who were beginning to be concerned about run of river developments, it was a body blow. A storm of protest resulted, including a motion from the Union of BC Municipalities demanding the repeal of Bill 30 (Union of BC Municipalities 2006). The government, however, refused to back down. Construction on the Ashlu project started in 2006 and it is now operational.

The consequence of these conflicts over the development of IPPs was an increasingly wide-ranging coalition opposing the government's energy policy. Comprised of environmental groups and recreational backcountry users concerned about the impact of these projects, unions concerned about the social implications of private energy development, and municipalities and local activists concerned about the attack on municipal authority, they were prepared to mount a systematic campaign against the Liberal Party in the BC elections in 2009. When ForestEthics, the David Suzuki Foundation and the Pembina Institute launched their campaign efforts by providing the Liberal

Party with an apparent environmental endorsement, these groups were understandably infuriated. Thus began a vitriolic public confrontation over what should count as a properly 'green' stance in the province. Although it is difficult to assess what impact the conflict had on the election itself – the outcome was a return of the Liberal Party to power with a fairly limited shift in the distribution of seats – the conflict does reveal the stakes of the question of how to frame the problem of climate change.

On the one hand were those groups who framed climate change as their primary, if not exclusive, focus. They operated on the explicit assumption that mitigation of GHG emissions was an overriding priority, and – in their most extreme articulation – that it should trump other considerations.[15] Rapid development of renewable energies was in their view a crucial element of this, and the government was to be supported for its efforts in this regard. On the other hand was a diverse range of groups who argued that the overall trajectory of energy policy in the province was too problematic to endorse for a variety of different reasons: environmental impact, democratic process, social and equity implications, and indeed capacity to mitigate climate change.[16] On this telling, the source of the rift appears to be the priority given to climate change: should climate change in general, and efforts to bring non GHG-emitting sources of energy online more specifically, be the priority for policy-making? However, if we understand climate change as an energy problem in the way proposed above, the conflict looks rather different. In particular, it is not at all clear that those groups explicitly prioritizing climate change actually have an approach to mitigating it that will address its underlying sources, still less that they will do so in a way that enhances sustainability more generally. On the contrary, many of the concerns raised by the other groups – the long-term environmental and social impact of energy systems, in particular, as well as the question of the best scale at which energy systems decisions might be made – may provide a better foundation from which to address climate concerns. These groups did not situate their concerns within a wider context that systematically included climate change, however, and at times their rejection of the Liberal approaches to climate change seemed to imply their rejection of the urgency of the problem more generally.

What is at stake in the conflict is thus only partly the primacy that should be given to climate change; at least at much at stake is how to understand the problem of climate change itself. It is in this context that framing climate change as an energy problem, and understanding the energy problem as one situated within a social and political, as well as ecological, context, potentially provides a meeting point for the parties. The objections to the rapid development of run of river power raised by the diverse groups echo and extend some of the concerns about renewables developed above. They echo the concern about the usefulness of an intermittent source (run-of-river hydro-electric) that might duplicate existing resources in the energy system, as well as the concern about the impact the scale of development of the resource might have in terms of ecological resilience (especially habitat fragmentation). They extend these further when they raise questions about social justice (who should benefit – and bear impacts – from the development of energy resources). Crucially, by raising these points they – intentionally or not – laid groundwork for climate change to be addressed as an energy – not emissions – problem, and to be addressed in a way that would be responsive to sustainability concerns more generally. Intentionally or not, they forced politics back into the conversation, by situating energy policy within a wider context of environmental and social justice struggles rather than allowing a 'crisis' of climate change to overrun these concerns.

Subsequent to the election, this trajectory has been enriched and further developed as some of the environmental groups involved reached out in an effort to establish a consensus around energy policy that might allow for a more coherent environmental voice to emerge. This took the form of working together to establish a common set of recommendations to guide energy policy in the province. The outcome of this effort was a report entitled 'Recommendations for Responsible Clean Electricity' (David Suzuki Foundation et al. 2009). The process was organized by the David Suzuki Foundation, Pembina Institute, Watershed Watch Salmon Society and West Coast Environmental Law, and the report was endorsed by 21 additional environmental organizations. To some degree, the Recommendations represent a healing of the fracture lines that had developed in the environmental movement over renewable energy development. The environmental groups who endorsed the Recommendations hold a variety of perspectives with respect to environmental sustainability versus climate change imperatives and the legitimacy of private versus public energy infrastructure ownership.[17] Recommendations reconcile these differences by, among other things, proposing that in order to garner the social license to push an ambitious renewable power development agenda forward, a long-term land-use framework and related planning process should be developed. The framework should identify the best and worst areas in BC for renewable energy development, taking into account cumulative impact, and plan the pattern of development accordingly. Additionally, the Recommendations propose that community and First Nations-owned renewable power projects be given water license priority and that the latter have meaningful opportunities to affect project plans, and to appeal licensing and leasing decisions. In this way the Recommendations seek to situate energy policy within an ecological, social and political context – pushing sustainability to the centre of energy policy planning, rather than allowing this to be overridden by the urgency of emissions reduction (David Suzuki Foundation et al. 2009).

While these proposals were being developed, however, energy policy and politics in the province did not stand still.[18] During the election campaign, the Liberal government had assessed that the level of public discontent – expressed in the conflict within the environmental movement, but also more widely – about its plan for energy development was such that some damage control was necessary. To that end, in the fall of 2009, the government formed a 'Green

Energy Advisory Task Force' to ostensibly seek stakeholder input and provide an opportunity to clarify and build social license around its clean energy strategy. The Task Force consisted of four working groups dealing with: carbon pricing, trading and export market development; procurement and regulatory reform; resource development; and community engagement and First Nations partnerships. Notably, the Recommendations for Responsible Clean Electricity were submitted to the Task Force, and representatives from PowerUp, the Pembina Institute and David Suzuki Foundation sat on two of the working groups.

The Green Energy Task Force Report made public in April 2010 echoed a number of the proposals advanced by the Recommendations for Responsible Clean Electricity report (Green Energy Advisory Task Force 2010). The emphasis of the Task Force Report, however, was to explicitly articulate and legitimize the notion that BC should look beyond self-sufficiency to develop its export platform – establishing itself as a so-called 'Clean Energy Powerhouse'. In broadening the scope of the BC energy system to prepare for export opportunities, the Task Force recommendations called for accelerated development of renewable energy resources and streamlined procurement processes. Accordingly, the Task Force report recommended undertaking regional planning in areas that are appropriate for more intensive development in conjunction with cumulative impact assessment. The more controversial recommendation made by the Task Force was that electricity procurement, generation operations, and export be moved outside BCUC regulation, which would remove the last site of independent assessment of the public value of energy development. The implications are that in order for private renewable energy development to remain competitive and meet the growing domestic demand and export opportunities in the future, the government must remove as many regulatory obstacles as possible.

Shortly after the Green Energy Task Force Report was released, the BC Government introduced The Clean Energy Act (Province of British Columbia 2010). As expected, in a bid to expedite its renewable energy agenda, the Act exempts most of the government's major energy initiatives from independent regulatory oversight via the BCUC. The Act requires that BC Hydro now submit long-term Integrated Resource Plans to the government for approval instead of the BCUC. The Act does not include any explicit language on new planning processes for cumulative environmental impact or support for community owned renewable energy projects beyond First Nations communities.

This outcome suggests that efforts by the environmental movement to regroup and articulate a new message – that long-term, politically inclusive and environmentally cumulative planning will be more effective in generating enduring and sustainable solutions to climate change than emergency solutions – appears ultimately to have been for naught. While the Green Energy Task Force appeared to be an occasion for public input, it functioned more as a public outlet, in so far as it led to strengthening of the existing trajectory of energy policy in the province rather than engagement with public concerns about it. It was followed by a shift in the very terms of the debate over energy policy, from electricity self-sufficiency to the imperative of rapidly developing new renewable energy resources to address climate change, a prospect characterized as an economic opportunity requiring unobstructed development. In light of the ongoing recession, it is hard to argue against economic opportunities, particularly in the post-resource extraction small communities of BC. To be clear, there is nothing wrong with economic opportunities that are environmental and socially sustainable. However, rather than empower many of these local communities to take ownership of renewable energy projects either through direct ownership or regional planning processes, and thus to potentially see greater economic benefits, the government further consolidated its authority over energy planning. Certainly offering incentives to First Nations communities to develop IPPs is a start, and to the credit of the Campbell government there are many unnoted progressive policies in the Clean Energy Act dealing with demand-side management and feed-in tariffs for smaller distributed generation. However, beyond those progressive elements, it is worth recalling that oversight over renewable energy projects has shifted twice over the course of the Campbell administration: the first time with Bill 30 giving IPPs utility status and thus removing them from local government oversight, and the second time, with the Clean Energy Act removing them from the independent regulatory oversight of the BCUC. The consequences of this shift for a democratic and sustainable response to climate change are problematic to say the least.

Several threads are worth emphasizing from this brief foray into the climate change politics of BC; I proceed below with the two that are most compelling. The first concerns the importance of situating climate and energy policy within a wider social, ecological and political context. The second concerns the challenges posed by doing so.

Keeping an eye on the ball

Unpacking what is at stake in the conflicts over climate and energy policy in BC is a struggle, not least as so many different things are at stake.[19] What I seek to resist here is what I argue was the source of the conflict amongst environmentalists described above: the reduction of climate change policy to an emissions-reduction agenda. Reducing the problem in this way – although it does make it more tractable as a policy issue – runs a range of very real risks.[20] Most centrally, it runs the risk of decreasing the sustainability of our societies precisely as we seek to address climate change, through increasing the environmental impact and social inequality produced by our energy systems. Although the impact within BC of the kind of large-scale renewable energy development promoted by the Liberal government will depend largely on the policy framework through which it is enacted, there are few indications that this framework will include attentiveness to values of ecological resilience and social equity – quite the opposite.[21] Further, it is unclear that developing renewable energy for export will actually have much impact in reducing GHG emissions. There is no clear policy framework to ensure that exported energy will displace GHG-producing sources,[22] and even if maximized BC's export capacity will be a drop in the bucket of demand from its southern neighbors. The most concrete impact is likely to be economic, but private ownership of the plants minimizes some of this benefit to British Columbians, even as it also distributes some of the risk.[23] So the current approach runs some serious risks – to biodiversity, equity, and climate change mitigation itself – for some fairly tenuous benefits.

All of this is not to say that the Liberal climate policy is for naught: it contains many important elements, and may well result in a reduction of domestic GHG emissions. It may also do so in a way that is economically beneficial to the province. However, the energy policy element of it also runs the risk of worsening the longer term sustainability profile of the province. Most worrisome in this regard is the further exclusion of the public from any engagement with energy policy itself. Decisions are being made at a range of scales that will determine the character of BC for the foreseeable future – its economic structure, large-scale infrastructure, environmental impact (both generalized and specific), capacities for mitigating and adapting to climate change – without the explicit engagement of the citizens of the province. And the trend is towards reducing their capacity to participate in such decision-making: with the passage of the Clean Energy Act, all major energy decisions in the province will be removed from any independent oversight. These are decisions with direct ramifications for climate change: whether to build a large transmission line to northwestern BC to facilitate large-scale oil and gas development there, for example, or whether to build a large (900 MW) dam on the Peace River. Likewise the decision to change BC's own energy policy priority from one of cost-effective self-sufficiency to being a 'clean energy powerhouse' suggests a maximization of energy production in the province, something that may in fact be deeply problematic in terms of mitigating and adapting to climate change.

The point I wish to emphasize here concerns less the substance of the decisions being made, however, than the implications of, on the one hand, failing to robustly integrate climate and energy policy, and, on the other, of excluding the public from engagement with these policy decisions. If we accept the framing of climate change as an energy problem presented above, these decisions are some of the most vital when it comes to choosing how to respond to climate change. Further, they are decisions with direct and very long-term implications for society. Given the nature of climate change as an energy problem, the energy system could provide a powerful tool to assist society in responding to climate change. Establishing feedback loops around energy use and impact, for example, could encourage individual, social and technological innovation to increase the sustainability of society. Creating the possibility that the energy system should be developed in accordance with wider social values and commitments could in this way provide a robust focus for the kind of social transformation necessary to respond effectively to climate change. Perhaps many of the decisions reached collectively would mirror or echo those being made on behalf of the public now, but if so they would proceed with social license – and understanding and appreciation of what is at stake in the decisions – rather than the resistance they face today.

As this suggests, perhaps the most important issue raised when we reframe climate change as an energy problem is the issue of politics. When we understand how central energy systems are both to climate mitigation and to social, economic, and ecological futures, it poses the question of how to respond to this politically. It causes us to confront the considerable momentum around an emissions reduction policy focus that might indeed achieve part of its goal, but whose goal is insufficient to the potential we face. At the very least, a primary focus on emissions reduction is a risky strategy – the possibilities for climate change mitigation that arise from an energy systems focus are much more diverse and robust. But more, such a focus excludes the social, ecological and political benefits that could arise from a serious engagement with energy systems. What such an engagement might look like is beyond the scope of this paper, but we can see potential roots of it emerging in the struggle of environmental groups in BC to situate energy policy within an ecological, social and political context. To put it perhaps most bluntly: the challenges of putting energy systems at the center of environmental politics are myriad, but in a world seeking to respond to climate change there is no more salient political focus.

Acknowledgements

The author owes thanks to many people for their help with this work, in particular Jamie Biggar, Naomi Devine, Nathaniel Gosman, Lawrence Pitt, and two anonymous reviewers.

Notes

1. The most obvious example of this is the focus within international negotiations on achieving binding targets for emissions reduction, at times to the marginalization of other considerations (and consequent failure of negotiations). Many environmental organizations have sought to broaden this focus: my argument here seeks to support and help focus such efforts.
2. My use of 'we' is not intended to assume an undifferentiated social subject: as I emphasize below, our use of energy, and our access to and participation in collective decision-making around energy use (such as infrastructure planning), is highly differentiated. It is, however, intended to emphasize the concrete ways in which each and all of us are embedded in energetic systems. Such awareness is a key element of activating an energy systems approach to climate mitigation.
3. Those who rank high, however, vary significantly in their per-capita energy use, suggesting important space for potential action.
4. Energy intensity is the amount of energy used to produce each unit of economic productivity.

5. There is ample evidence of this in the worldwide government anxiety produced by recessionary growth trends. For one explanation of the dynamics of this, see Booth (2004).
6. This is evident, for example, in the case study developed below, in which the policy approach focuses on emissions targets supported by carbon pricing and expansion of renewable energy, but absent any focus on ecological or social sustainability, equity, or justice.
7. By this I mean hydroelectric with a storage reservoir, as opposed to run of a river, discussed below.
8. Energy density is the amount of energy stored in a given system or region of space per unit volume.
9. Space prevents me from elaborating on social impacts, but these are potentially diverse. They range from how energy system design and governance distribute risk and benefit across society, to which parts of society are engaged in and empowered by decision-making about energy system design, to how energy system design encourages or discourages social change itself.
10. Although substantial, Campbell's climate initiatives have important limits. See, for example, Hoberg (2010) and Beers (2009).
11. The only explicit endorsement of the Liberals came from Tzeporah Berman (then of ForestEthics, but soon to become Executive Director of PowerUp), an environmentalist with a long history of activism in BC. Other organizations associated with this position included the David Suzuki Foundation and the Pembina Institute. Both were strongly critical of the New Democratic Party's opposition to the carbon tax, but neither explicitly endorsed the Liberal Party.
12. There is some debate about this. For an account of this debate and the shifting context of energy policy in BC, see Hoberg and Sopinka (2011).
13. Run of river hydroelectric power is generated by building a small dam to divert water into penstock pipes leading to turbine(s) at lower elevation. It thus avoids a large storage reservoir, which minimizes some kinds of environmental impact. However, the lack of storage also makes the energy less dispatchable: it can only produce energy when the river flow is high enough for diversion.
14. Importantly, not all of these licenses will be developed; the license only grants the right to apply for permission to develop a generating facility. For details on water license applications, see IPP Watch (http://www.ippwatch.info/w/). The site contains a useful map showing the location and details of all water license applications in the province.
15. As articulated, for example, by Tzeporah Berman (PowerUp Canada) on the Bill Good Show (22 January 2009), a prominent public affairs radio show in BC: 'I will say that I think the opposition that we're seeing in British Columbia by some environmental groups and others to the move towards green power, the whole kind of save our rivers piece, needs to be rethought ... We need to reduce carbon emissions, as a priority. And yes, we need to do it smart; we need to be careful about our rivers. But the fact is we need to support the move to green power.'
16. A variety of concerns were raised on the latter point, particularly about the timing and character of the runoff that would allow the run of river plants to produce energy (that it would coincide with Spring runoff when some of the large heritage dams in the province might be spilling, thus their power would be excess to need); the impact of the developments themselves on forest habitat and thus carbon emissions; the long-term viability of the plants under conditions of climate change (where reduced snowpack is one predicted impact in the region), and the general approach of adding new capacity rather than encouraging greater conservation and efficiency measures.
17. That said, it is worth noting that two ends of the spectrum, PowerUp and Western Canada Wilderness Committee, did not endorse the Recommendations.

18. There are actually several twists and turns to the story that space prevents me from detailing.
19. There are many absolutely vital issues embedded in these conflicts that I have not had the space to touch on. Just to highlight three examples: the unique situation of First Nations in the province, and the importance and complexity of their involvement in energy resource development; the unique situation of BC as a biodiversity hotspot in North America, refuge for the last remaining large multi-species predator–prey systems, and the way this is threatened by the habitat fragmentation that will accompany renewable energy development; and the rapid rise – with Liberal government encouragement – of the oil and gas sector in the province, with its implications for both GHG emissions and energy demand. There are also many more issues, highlighting the importance of sustained and wide-ranging public engagement with decision-making on these issues.
20. For a useful analysis of a parallel to the case and issues around the framing of climate solutions discussed here, see Pralle and Boscarino (2011).
21. A robust planning and assessment process is the minimal precondition for the former, although much more ambitious approaches could also be imagined. The latter could be facilitated by supporting rural communities in developing their regional energy sources, with the benefits flowing back to them, for example. It could also be facilitated with a range of other policy tools.
22. On the challenges of developing such a framework, see Hoberg and Sopinka (2011).
23. As BC Hydro negotiates long-term contracts for purchasing energy at the time of the plant development and then sells it on for export, the risks and possible benefits of volatile energy prices are spread between private investors and the public of BC.

References

Beers, D., 2009. Think Gordon Campbell is a climate guru? Read on. *Globe and Mail*, 22 January. Available from: http://www.theglobeandmail.com/servlet/story/RTGAM.20090121.wcocampbell22/BNStory/specialComment/home

Booth, D.E., 2004. *Hooked on growth: economic addictions and the environment*. Lanham, MD: Rowman & Littlefield Publishers.

Boyle, G., ed. 2007. *Renewable energy and the grid: the challenge of variability*. London: Earthscan.

Burrows, J., 2009. Tzeporah Berman responds to critics in BC environmental movement. *In: The Georgia Straight*. Vancouver, BC, 17 April. Available from: http://www.straight.com/article-215030/tzeporah-berman-responds-critics-bc-environmental-movement

Caldicott, A., 2007. Rivers of riches. *Watershed Sentinel*, January–February. Available from: http://www.watershedsentinel.ca/

Calvert, J., 2007. *Liquid gold: energy privatization in British Columbia*. Black Point, NS: Fernwood Publishing.

Cuddihy, J., Kennedy, C. and Byer, P., 2005. Energy use in Canada: environmental impacts and opportunities in relationship to infrastructure systems. *Canadian Journal of Civil Engineering*, 32 (1), 1–15.

David Suzuki Foundation, Pembina Institute, Watershed Watch Society, and West Coast Environmental Law, 2009. *Recommendations for responsible clean energy development in British Columbia*. Available from: http://pubs.pembina.org/reports/clean-electricity-recommendations.pdf

ESB National Grid, 2004. *Impact of wind power generation in Ireland on the operation of conventional plant and the economic implications*. Dublin: ESB National Grid.

Green, C., Baski, S. and Dilmaghani, M., 2007. Challenges to a climate stabilizing energy future. *Energy Policy*, 35 (1), 616–626.

Haberl, H., 2006. The global socioeconomic energetic metabolism as a sustainability problem. *Energy*, 31, 87–99.
Hoberg, G., 2010. Bringing the market back in: BC natural resource policies during the Campbell years. *In*: M. Howlett, D. Pilon and T. Summerville, eds. *British Columbia politics and government*. Toronto: Emond Montgomery Publications, 331–352.
Hoberg, G. and Sopinka, A., 2011. *The export question: designing policy for British Columbia electricity trade*. Victoria, BC: Pacific Institute for Climate Solutions. Available from: http://www.pics.uvic.ca/white_papers.php
Hoffert, M.I., *et al.*, 2002. Advanced technology paths for climate stability: energy for a greenhouse planet. *Science*, 298, 981–987.
Hunter, J., 2006. Environmentalists vow to punish NDP for plan to dismantle B.C.'s carbon tax. *Globe & Mail* (Toronto, Canada), 14 April, p. A4.
International Energy Agency, 2010. *Key world energy statistics 2010*. Paris: IEA.
International Energy Agency, 2011. *Harnessing variable renewables: a guide to the balancing challenge*. Paris: IEA.
Kimmett, C., 2008. Private river power draws diverse foes. *The Tyee*, 19 February. Available from: http://thetyee.ca/News/2008/02/19/RunOfRiver/
Kimmett. C., 2009. BC's clashing shades of green: how 'run of river' and global warming are splitting enviros this election. *The Tyee*, 7 April. Available from: http://thetyee.ca/News/2009/04/07/ShadesOfGreen/
Littlemore, R., 2009. Cannibalizing environmentalism: Tzeporah Berman under attack. *DeSmogBlog.com*, 5 May. Available from: http://www.desmogblog.com/canabalizing-environmentalism-tzeporah-berman-under-attack
Pacala, S. and Socolow, R., 2004. Stabilization wedges: solving the climate problem for the next 50 years with current technologies. *Science*, 35 (13 August), 968–972.
Pitt, L., *et al.*, 2005. Utility-scale wind power: impact of increased penetration. Paper presented at *International Green Energy Conference*, 12–16 June, Waterloo, Ontario, Canada.
Pralle, S. and Boscarino, J., 2011. Framing tradeoffs: the politics of nuclear power and wind energy in an age of global climate change. *Review of Policy Research*, 28 (4), 323–346.
Rockström, J., *et al.*, 2009. A safe operating space for humanity. *Nature*, 461 (24 September), 472–475.
Smil, V., 2003. *Energy at the crossroads: global perspectives and uncertainties* Cambridge, MA: MIT Press.
Smil, V., 2006. *Energy: a beginner's guide*. Oxford: Oneworld Publications.
Tieleman, B., 2009. Furious rebuke to Suzuki, Berman. *The Tyee*, 21 April. Available from: http://thetyee.ca/Views/2009/04/21/SuzukiRebuke/
World Commission on Dams, 2000. *Dams and development*. London: Earthscan Publishers.

Government publications

Environment Canada, 2008. Canada's 2008 Greenhouse gas inventory: a summary of trends. Available from: http://www.ec.gc.ca/ges-ghg/default.asp?lang=En&n=0590640B-1
Green Energy Advisory Task Force, 2010. Green energy advisory task force report. Available from: http://www.empr.gov.bc.ca/EAED/Documents/GreenEnergyAdvisoryTaskForce.pdf
Province of British Columbia, 2007. Premier outlines new steps to combat climate change. Press release, 28 September. Available from: http://www2.news.gov.bc.ca/news_releases_2005-2009/2007OTP0141-001209.htm

Province of British Columbia, 2010. Bill 17 – 2010: Clean Energy Bill. Available from: http://www.leg.bc.ca/39th2nd/1st_read/gov17-1.htm (Introduction to the legislation and background issues available from: http://www.mediaroom.gov.bc.ca/DisplayEventDetails.aspx?eventId=490).

Squamish-Lillooet Regional District, 2003. Independent Power Project development in the SLRD, July. Available from: http://www.slrd.bc.ca/siteengine/ActivePage.asp?PageID=19

Squamish-Lillooet Regional District, 2006. Report on Ashlu IPP rezoning application, 19 January. Squamish-Lillooet Regional District, Squamish, BC, Canada.

Union of BC Municipalities, 2006. *2006 UBCM Resolutions: excerpted from minutes of the one hundred and third annual convention of the Union of BC Municipalities*, 24–27 October, Victoria, BC, p. 3. Union of BC Municipalities, Victoria, BC, Canada.

Index

Page numbers in *Italics* represent tables.
Page numbers followed by n represent endnotes.

60 Minutes 90

Aberystwyth approach 32
Advanced Boiling Water Reactor (ABWR) 70, 73
Advisory Council on the Environment (SRU) Germany 123
Africa 9, 13, 24; North 123–34; sub-Saharan 11, 19–22
agriculture 38, 87, 139
Albers, D. 93
Alberta's tar sands 30–1
Aleklett, K. 29
Algeria 124, 130–2
Alliance for Responsible Energy Policy 95
Alps 127
Altham, J. 57
American Council for an Energy-Efficient Economy (ACEEE) 113–16
analytic decision theories 57–8
Angola 19–22; civil war 20–2
Angolan government 20–1
anti-nuclear activists 50, *see also* environmentalists
Areva 74
Argandoña, M. 91, 93–4
Ashlu River 147
assimilados 20
Association of Home Appliance Manufacturers (AHAM) 113, 116
Aswan dam 124
Atomic Energy Commission 66
Australia 4
Austria 121
authoritarianism 39–40
autonomy 32, 52, 110
Azzarraga, E. 17

banks 73, 129–30

Bavaria 122
Bayart, J. 24–5
Bayesian decision rule 51, 53, 57
BC Hydro 146, 150, 155n
Beck, J. 86
Beck, U. 44, 46, 48–50, 59
benefit-cost analysis 92
Berlin Conference (1884) 20
Bill 30: The Miscellaneous Statues Amendment Act (Canada) 147, 151
biomass 123, 140
Bolivarian Revolution 18–19
boom-bust cycles 14, 16, 24
Booth, K. 32–3
Boston 114
Botswana 22
Brand, S. 47
Brazil 19
Britain 19
British Columbia (BC) 9, 137–57
British Columbia Utilities Commission (BCUC) 147, 150–1
British Columbian government 150
Brown, L. 36
Bureau of Land Management (BLM) 84, 93
Bush Global Climate Change Policy Book (2002) 118
Bush, President George H. 84, 113
Buttel, F. 102–3

Cabinda province (Angola) 20–2
California 8, 81–98, 107, 114, 145; large-scale solar projects 84–6; Renewables Portfolio Standard Program 83
California Department of Fish and Game 90
California Desert Protection Act (CDPA) 95–6

INDEX

California Energy Commission 84–5
California Environmental Quality Act (CEQA) 85
California Wilderness Coalition 94
Cambridge Energy Research Associates 74
Campbell, G. 145–6, 151
Canada 9, 137–57; Western Canada Wilderness Committee 147
Canadian government 146–8, 151–2; Energy Plan (2002) 146; Liberal government 145–6, 149, 151–2, 155n
cap and trade system 64, 145
Cape Cod 96
capitalism 86, 96, 100–3, 108, 117
Caracazo 18
carbon capture 4, 122
carbon dioxide 4, 83, 121
carbon pricing schemes 4
carbon tax 4, 9, 64, 75–7, 145
Carson, R. 38
Carter, President J. 109–10, 117
Catton, W. 38
Center for Energy Efficiency and Renewable Technology 94
Chávez, President Hugo 18–19
Chernobyl 49, 71
Chicago 50–2
China 1, 19, 21, 39
Chu, S. 66, 95
Cipra, M. 94
citizen behavioral changes 99, 117
citizen participation 67–8
civilization 36–9, 44
Clarkson, Jim 73
Clean Energy Act (BC, Canada) 150–2
clientalism 23
climate change 2, 4, 8–9, 12, 45–7, 49, 53, 56–9, 64–5, 83, 88–90, 94, 117; discourse 99–100; mitigation 137–57; nuclear power renaissance 62–80; reframing 138–41
Climate Change Action Plan 113–14
climate policy 7, 45, 49
climate-nuclear dilemma 57–9
Clinton, President 'Bill' 9, 113, 116
coal 2–5, 28–30, 47–8, 65, 74–5, 77, 113, 117, 129–30; power plants 47–8, 142
Cohen, B. 47
Cold War 25, 109
colonialism 5, 13, 19–22, 24–5, 87
combined operating license (COL) 66–8
concentrating solar power (CSP) 83–5, 89, 126–30

Congressional Budget Office (CBO) USA 73, 75, 77
conservation 45, 82, 88, 90–6, 110–11
Consortium for Energy Efficiency 114
Constellation Energy Group 73, 77n
consumer consumption 99–100, 117
Consumers Union 110
Copenhagen 47
Copenhagen School 32
Critical Security Studies 5, 27–8, 32
Cuba 22
Czech Republic 122

Dawkins, Richard 38
debt 16–18
decarbonization 9–10, 48, 57–9, 122, 124
decision rule 50–3
decision theory 6, 57
decision-making 57, 102–3, 141–2, 144, 154n
Defenders of Wildlife 92–3
Deffeyes, K. 37
Delucchi, M.: and Jacobsen, M. 3
demand smoothing 124–5
democracy 5, 18, 23, 35, 46, 57–8
Democratic Party (USA) 109, 113
Denmark 121
Department of Energy (US DOE) 36, 66, 69, 72–4, 77n, 89, 109–13, 115–16; Nuclear Power 2010 program 66
Department of the Interior (USA) 84
dependency theory 13, 24
Desert Protective Council 95
Desert Report (Sierra Club) 85
Desertec 130, 132–3
deserts 81–98; communities 96; ecology 89; land grab 94; rhetorical tropes 86
developing countries 11–26, 53, 140
discourse analysis 88
distributive justice 46
Dubos, R.: and Ward, B. 34
Duffy, R. 2, 7, 62–80
Dutch Disease 11

ecological economics 30
ecological modernization 4, 8–9, 59, 89, 99–120; from (1992–2001) 113–16
Economic Benefits Provided by Natural Lands (Defenders of Wildlife) 92
ecosystems 1–8, 85, 91–2, 94, 101, 103, 138–40, 142–4
Egypt 124, 133
elites 11–19, 21–5, 34

160

INDEX

Ellenbeck, S.: and Lilliestam, J. 132
embedded energy 138–40
Emissions Trading Scheme 122
endangered species 90
energy crisis 23, 108–10
energy descent 5, 27–43
energy efficient appliances 99–120
Energy Information Administration (USA) 2, 31, 63–4
energy infrastructure 58
Energy Policy Acts 49, 75; (1975) 110; (1992) 67, 113; (2005) 65–6, 70, 72–3, 77
energy prices 106, 140
energy security 7, 27–43, 130–3; death 33, 38–9; energy descent 28–31; freedom 34–6; government secrecy 39–40; securitization 31–4, 39–40; uncertainty 33–4, 36–8
energy slaves 35
energy sources 3–4; decline 27; low-carbon 6, 48, 59
energy systems 3, 81, 100, 106, 116; environmental politics 137–57
energy utilities 106, 114–15
energy weapon 131
environmental governance 44–61
environmental impacts 12, 85, 89–90, 101–4, 107, 111, 143–4, 148
environmental politics 137–57; energy and sustainability 141–5; green politics 145–51; reframing climate change 138–41
Environmental Protection Agency (EPA) 114
environmental security 28
environmental social movement organizations (ESMOs) 103, 113–14
environmentalists 9, 81–98, 104–6, 109, 115, 137–57
European Climate Foundation (ECF) 124–6
European Commission 122
European renewable power deployment 121–36
European Solar Thermal Electricity Association (ESTELA) 128
European Union (EU) 9, 64; Climate and Energy Package 122; renewable energy 121–36
European-North African Supergrid 123–7; attracting investors 129–30; political issues 127–33; site access 126–7; supply security 130–3

Evolutionary Power Reactor (EPR) 73
exceptionalism 39–40
Eximbank 21
external risks 44
extraversion 13, 24–5

Federal Land Policy and Management Act (1976) 84
Federal Register 109
Federal Reserve 16–17
Feinstein, Senator D. 95
financial risk 55
Finland 74
First Nations communities 150–1, 155n
Florida 74–5
Florida Power and Light 74–5
food 38
Ford, President G. 109
foreign exchange revenue 11
fossil fuels 2–5, 7–8, 45–6, 48, 58–9, 62–5, 75, 107, 117, 140–3; energy descent 27–43; price volatility 65; regulation 4–5
France 121, 130
free market philosophy 109
freedom 32–3, 34–6
Front for the Liberation of the Enclave of Cabinda (FLEC) 21
Fukushima Daiichi nuclear plant 1–2, 7, 45, 48–9, 62–4, 69–73, 76–7

Gaia theory 47
game theory 57
GE-Hitachi 70–1
Georgescu-Roegen, N. 30, 37
Georgia 70, 73, 74
Georgia Power 74
Germany 1, 7, 64, 121–3, 126
Ghaddaffi, H. 131
Gingrich, N. 115
Glen Canyon Dam 87
global capital 14
global financial crisis 21, 31
global horizontal irradiance 126
globalization 103–4
Gomez, J. 17
Gould, K.: et al 100, 104
Gowan, P. 17
Grand Solar Plan 8
Grant, S. 75
Green Energy Advisory Task Force (Canada) 149–51
green products 99–120

greenhouse gases 2–3, 45, 56, 58, 64, 76, 81, 83, 88, 100, 107, 117–18, 122, 138, 141–5, 148, 152
Guarantee of Origin (GO) trading scheme 122
The Guardian 37
Gulf Oil 20

Haber, S.: and Menaldo, V. 23
habitat destruction 84
Hall, C.: *et al* 29
Hannigan, J. 103
Harsanyi, J. 50–2, 54
Harvey, J. 94
Hay, L. 74
Herrington, J. 111–12
Hirsch, R. 36
Hobbes, T. 33
Hokkaido (Japan) 75
Hooks, G. 100
Hoover dam 87
House of Representatives 64, 116
Hubbert, M. 29
Human Development Index (HDI) 138–9
human ecology 27–43
human population 30–1, 34, 37–8, 46
human rights 32, 39
human-nature relationships 138–9
Hunold, C.: and Leitner, S. 8–10, 81–98
Huysman, J. 32–3
hydroelectric power 10, 124, 143–6, 154n

identity 34
ideology 35, 86
Independent Power Projects (IPPs) 147, 151
Indonesia 22
industrialization 16, 28, 102–3, 140, 147
inequality 14, 19
inflation 18
inspections tests analyses and acceptance criteria (ITAAC) 68
institutional conditions 13, 15, 17, 23, 25, 100–3
Intergovernmental Panel on Climate Change (IPCC) 47, 122
Interior and Related Agencies Appropriations Act 116
International Energy Agency 64
International Institute for Applied Systems Analysis (IIASA) 128

International Monetary Fund (IMF) 17–18, 21
International Nuclear Events Scale 1
International Scientific Congress on Climate Change 47
Iraq War 113
irrigation systems 87
Italy 1

Jacobsen, M.: and Delucchi, M. 3, 7
Japan 62–4, 70–1, 73, 75–6; Fukushima disaster (11th March 2011) 1, 7, 45, 48–9, 62–4, 69–73, 76–7
Japan Steel Works Lt Facility 75
Jazcko, G. 70
Josefsson, L. 130
Joshua Tree National Park 94–5

Karl, T. 15, 17–18, 23
Kassel University 124–5
Kempton, W.: *et al* 125
Keystone Center 64, 74
Klare, M. 37
Klein, D. 70
Kuletz, V. 87
Kumetat, D.: and Lacher, W. 131–2

labor 34–5, 128
Lacher, W.: and Kumetat, D. 131–2
Latin America 11, 13
Leitner, S.: and Hunold, C. 8–10, 81–98
Liberal Party (Canada) 145, 147–8, 154n
liberalism 35
Libya 130–1, 133
Libyan-Swiss political conflict 131
life quality 33–4, 139
Lilliestam, J.: and Ellenbeck, S. 132
Limits to Growth debates 27–8
Lindblom, C. 3
Lisbon 20
Los Angeles 96
Los Angeles Times 91
Lovelock, J. 47
Lovins, A. 108
low-carbon economy 4, 8
Luanda (Angola) 20
Lusinchi, J. 18

majority rule 57
Malthus, T. 38
market production 100–1, 107; failures 106–7; pre-regulation 108–13; regulation 106, 113–18

INDEX

market transformation 113–16
Massachusetts Institute of Technology (MIT) 74, 75
maximin decision rule 50–3
Mayan civilization 39
media 88, 99, 129, 131, 133
Mediterranean Solar Plan 128
Menaldo, V.: and Haber, S. 23
Merton, R. 100
mestiços 20
Mexican government 16, 22–3; Salinas administration 17
Mexico 15–18, 22–3; economy 15–17; peso 16, 22
Middle East 109, 124
middle range theorization 99–120; ecological modernization (1992–2001) 113–16; EMT and TOP middle-range adaptation 104–5; energy-efficient appliances 105–6; green energy politics 101–4; treadmill of production (TOP) 108–13; US political economy 106–8
Miller, A. 113
Minns, J. 16
modernization 4, 8–9, 29, 46, 59, 86, 89, 102
Mojave desert solar plants 8, 81–98
Monbiot, G. 37
Montefiore, H. 47
Moore, P. 47
Morocco 124–5
Mulligan, S. 5–6

National Appliance Energy Conservation Act (NAECA) 112–13, 115
National Energy Conservation and Policy Act (ECPA) 109–11
National Environmental Protection Act 84
National Liberation Front of Angola (FNLA) 20
National Parks Conservation Association 91–2, 94
National Renewable Energy Laboratory (USA) 89, 128
National Union for the Total Independence of Angola (UNITA) 20
natural capital 30
natural gas 28–30, 38–9, 40n, 48, 65, 74–5, 117, 130–2
natural resource exports 11–26

Natural Resources Defense Council (NRDC) 82, 110–14, 116
nature 87, 89, 96
neoliberalism 13, 19, 21, 103, 145
net energy 29–30
net primary productivity 140
Nevada 94
New Democratic Party (Canada) 145
New York 50–1, 107, 114
New York Times 108, 110
North American Free Trade Agreement (NAFTA) 17
North Sea oil discoveries 29
northern Europe 125–6
NRDC v. Herrington 112
NRG Energy 63, 73
nuclear energy 1–3, 6–7, 62–80, 106; nuclear option 47–50, 55–6, 58; regulatory responsibility 44–51
Nuclear Energy Institute 64, 65, 69
nuclear plants 63–4, 106; economics 65–6, 72–6; licensing 66–8, 70–2; opposition 67–8; reactor designs 65, 70–1; safety 1–2, 6, 48–50, 53–7, 65, 67, 69–72, 76; waste disposal 69–70, 76
nuclear power renaissance 7, 62–80; commercial nuclear power's status 63–4; obstacles 69–76; renewed nuclear power interest 64–8
Nuclear Regulatory Commission (US NRC) 63, 66–8, 70–1, 75
Nuclear Waste Fund 69
Nuclear Waste Policy Act (1982) 69

Obama, President Barack 1–2, 19, 66, 69–70, 73, 76; State of Union address 66
oil 2–6, 15, 106, 113, 117, 130–2; dependence 6; imported 6; prices 14, 16, 18, 21, 30–1, 65, 108, 110, 130; resources 11–26
oil production 12–13; Angola 21; peak oil 5, 27–43, 65
oil shock (1973) 15, 105
oil states 13
Ophuls, W. 35
Organization of the Petroleum Exporting Countries (OPEC) 15, 108

Pacific Gas & Electric (PG&E) 114
Patt, A.: *et al* 9, 121–36
Peace River 152
Peet, J. 35

INDEX

Pemex 16
Perez, C. 18
petro-dollars 15–16, 18, 22
photovoltaic (PV) technology 83, 85, 122–3, 126
plutonium: weapons grade 6
political economy 24, 101–4, 106–8, 142
politics 39–40, 88, 137–57
pollution 4, 28, 141
popular culture 24
Portugal 19–20; colonialism 19–21
Portuguese Colonial Act (1930) 20
Portuguese government 20
Potsdam Institute for Climate Impact Research (PIK) 128–9
poverty 18–19, 21
power mix smoothing 125–6
Progress Energy 74, 75
Prugh, T.: *et al* 30
Public Utility Regulatory Policies Act 113

race 20
Rajan, S. 5, 11–26
Rawlsian difference principle 50, 52
Reagan, President Ronald 9, 17, 108–13, 116–17
recession (1981) 110, 112
regional integration 121–36
regulatory responsibility 44–61; commensurable risk 56–8; nuclear option 47–50; weighing risks and uncertainties 50–5
renewable energy 2–4, 7–10, 58–9; power plants 81–98, 125; regional deployment 121–36
Renewable Energy Directive (EU) 122
renewable energy portfolio standards (RPS) 83
rent-seeking 13–14, 16, 23, 25
repression 32–3
Republican Party (USA) 64, 70, 75–6, 109, 111, 113, 116
resource booms 15
resource curse 5, 11–26; cases 15–22; causes 22–5; characterizing 14–15
resource extraction 14–15
resource wars 36, 39
resource wealth 5, 11–26
resource-poor countries 14
resource-rich countries 11–26; economies 14–15; regimes 12–13, 15, 17, 22, 25

risk assessment 46, *50*, 51, *53*, 54, 56–7, *56*
risk displacement 55
risk distribution 44–61
risk imposition 52–5, 58
risk society 44–6, 50, 59
risk-taking 52, 54
risks: manufactured 44–6
Robinson, J: *et al* 15
Roman Empire 39
Rosa, E.: and York, R. 102
Russia 19, 39, 132

Sachs, J.: and Warner, A. 12
Sall, A. 94
San Diego 96
Scandinavia 127
Schellekens, G.: *et al* 133
Schnaiberg, A. 103, 108
Schuyler, G. 18
Schwarzenegger, governor A. 83, 90, 145
Scientific American Magazine 89
security concerns *see* energy security
Shaw, K. 9–10, 137–57
Shrader-Frechette, K. 46, 51–3, 55, 58
Shwom, R. 8–9, 99–120
Sierra Club 82, 85, 93–4
slavery 19, 24, 35
social cost 4
social justice 6, 149
social license 149–50
societal risk 52–5
Socolow, R. 100
soft energy path 108
Solar Energy Industries Association (SEIA) 95
Solar Grand Plan 81–98; conservationist counter-narratives 91–5; defining 88–91; deserts and technological projects 86–8; Solar Renaissance 83–6
solar industry 81–98; photovoltaic (PV) technology 83, 85, 122–3, 126
solar plants 3, 8, 81–98, 125–6; Application for Certification 85; land-use considerations 84; opposition 81–98; technological progress 83
solar power 38, 81–98
South California Electric and Gas 73
Southern Company 70, 73
Southern Europe 126–7
Spain 121, 126
Squamish (Canada) 147
state security 27–43
stochastic supply smoothing 125

INDEX

Stockman, D. 109
Suharto, President 22
Super Efficient Refrigerator Program (SERP) 114
Supergrid 9, *see also* European-North African Supergrid
sustainability 3, 6–9, 8, 10, 30, 88, 141–52
Svinicki, K. 63, 71
Switzerland 1, 7, 64, 131

Taiwan 70
Taylor, J.: and Van Doren, P. 132
technology 2–4, 8, 29–31, 36, 58–9, 65, 75, 95, 122–3, 129, 141–2; energy efficient 99–120; grand technological projects 85; nuclear 71; solar plants 81–98
terrorism 131–2
Texas 63, 74
Three Mile Island 49, 53, 71
Toft, P.: *et al* 132
transnational corporations 104
transportation 38
treadmill of production (TOP) theory 8–9, 99–120; (1981–1986) 108–13
Tunisia 133

Ullman, R. 32
Union of BC Municipalities 147
United Nations (UN) 130, 138–9; Development Programme 130; Framework Convention on Climate Change (1992) 47
United States of America (USA) 1–2, 7–8, 16, 19–22, 29–31, 34, 47–9, 53, 56, 118, 125, 131, 134n; economy 110; energy efficiency policy 99–120; energy production 48–9, 63–4, 82, 106; nuclear power use 62–80; Southwestern deserts 81–98
Ural Mountains 125
US Army 36
US Congress 66–7, 109, 112, 115
US government 49, 62, 64, 69, 72, 107–10, 116–17; Bush administration 84, 113; Carter administration 109–10, 117; Clinton administration 113; Ford administration 109; Obama administration 69–70, 76; Reagan administration 17, 109–10, 112
US Government Accountability Office 71
US Senate 116
US Treasury 17

valuing discourses 92
Van Doren, P.: and Taylor, J. 132
Vanderheiden, S. 1–10, 44–61
Venezuela 17–19, 22–3; economy 18–19; February 1989 protests 18; oil embargo (1973/4) 18
Venezuelan government 18–19, 22–3
Vogtle reactors 70, 73
Volcker, P. 17–18

Wæver, O. 39
Ward, B.: and Dubos, R. 34
Warner, A.: and Sachs, J. 12
Washington 67, 115
Wehr, K. 87
welfare 33, 44
Western Canada Wilderness Committee 147
Westinghouse 65; AP 1000 reactors 70
Whirlpool Corporation 16
White House 2, 70, 113
Whiteside, K. 49
wilderness preservation 89
Wildlands Conservancy 94
Williams, M. 31
Williges, K.: *et al* 129
wind power 3, 96, 122–3, 125–6, 143; smoothing 125
world energy consumption 1, 3, 140

York, R. 85; and Rosa, E. 102
Yucca Mountain nuclear waste facility 69–70, 76

Zichella, C. 94

www.routledge.com/9780415668545

Related titles from Routledge

Green Activism in Post-Socialist Europe and the Former Soviet Union
Edited by Adam Fagan and JoAnn Carmin

Green activism played a critical role in the downfall of Soviet-style communism in Eastern Europe at the end of the 1980s. After the revolutions, environmentalists were expected to exert influence within the new democracies and to form the bedrock of the new civil societies that were predicted to flourish across the region; the prospect of EU membership provided activist networks with even greater optimism about their political opportunities.

Through country case-studies and comparative analysis of national movements, this edited volume addresses each of these questions and provides a different perspective of green politics in the region.

This book was previously published as a special issue of *Environmental Politics*.

Adam Fagan is based at Queen Mary, University of London, UK.

JoAnn Carmin is based at the Massachusetts Institute of Technology, USA.

March 2011: 234 x 156: 176pp
Hb: 978-0-415-66854-5
£90 / $133

For more information and to order a copy visit
www.routledge.com/9780415668545

Available from all good bookshops

www.routledge.com/9780415613200

Related titles from Routledge

The Politics of Biofuels, Land and Agrarian Change
Edited by Saturnino M. Borras Jr., Philip McMichael and Ian Scoones

The book analyses the institutional structures, and cultures of energy consumption on which a biofuels complex depends, and the alternative political and ecological visions emerging that call the biofuels complex into question. Across sixteen chapters presenting material from five regions across the North-South divide and focusing on fourteen countries including Brazil, Indonesia, India, USA and Germany, these topics are addressed within the following themes: global (re)configurations; agro-ecological visions; conflicts, resistances and diverse outcomes; state, capital and society relations; mobilising opposition, creating alternatives; and change and continuity.

This book was published as a special issue of the *Journal of Peasant Studies*.

Saturnino M. Borras Jr. Is based at the International Institute of Social Studies (ISS) in The Hague, Netherlands in January 2011.

Philip McMichael is a Professor of Development Sociology at Cornell University.

Ian Scoones is a Professorial Fellow at the Institute of Development Studies, University of Sussex, UK.

March 2011: 246 x 174: 408pp
Hb: 978-0-415-61320-0
£95 / $158

For more information and to order a copy visit
www.routledge.com/9780415613200

Available from all good bookshops